The Civil War

THE CIVIL WAR

*Primary Documents on Events
from 1860 to 1865*

Ford Risley

Debating Historical Issues in the Media of the Time
David A. Copeland, Series Editor

GREENWOOD PRESS
Westport, Connecticut • London

Library of Congress Cataloging-in-Publication Data

The Civil War : primary documents on events from 1860 to 1865 / Ford Risley.
    p. cm. — (Debating historical issues in the media of the time)
  Includes bibliographical references and index.
  ISBN 0–313–32126–4
  1. United States—History—Civil War, 1861–1865—Sources. I. Risley, Ford. II. Series.
  E464.C54   2004
  973.7—dc22   2004014048

British Library Cataloguing in Publication Data is available.

Library of Congress Catalog Card Number: 2004014048
ISBN: 0–313–32126–4
ISSN: 1542–8079

First published in 2004

Greenwood Press, 88 Post Road West, Westport, CT 06881
An imprint of Greenwood Publishing Group, Inc.
www.greenwood.com

Printed in the United States of America

The paper used in this book complies with the
Permanent Paper Standard issued by the National
Information Standards Organization (Z39.48–1984).

10 9 8 7 6 5 4 3 2 1

Contents

Contents

Series Foreword

As the eighteenth century was giving way to the nineteenth, the January 1, 1799, issue of the *Boston Columbian Centinel* quoted a wise judge who said, "Give to any set men the command of the press, and you give them the command of the country, for you give them the command of public opinion, which commands everything." One month later, Thomas Jefferson wrote to James Madison with a similar insight. "We are sensible," Jefferson said of the efforts it would take to put their party—the Republicans—in power, "The engine is the press."

Both writers were correct in their assessment of the role the press would play in American life in the years ahead. The press was already helping shape the opinions and direction of America. It had been doing so for decades, but its influence erupted following the Revolutionary War and continued into the 1920s and further. From less than 40 newspapers in 1783—each with circulations of about 500—the number of papers erupted in the United States. By 1860, newspaper circulation exceeded 1 million, and in 1898, Joseph Pulitzer's *World* alone had a daily circulation of 1.3 million. By the beginning of World War I, about 16,600 daily and weekly newspapers were published, and circulation figures passed 22.5 million copies per day with no slowdown in sight. Magazines grew even more impressively. From about five at the end of the Revolution, journalism historian Frank Luther Mott counted 600 in 1860 and a phenomenal 3,300 by 1885. Some circulations surpassed 1 million, and the number of magazines continued to grow into the twentieth century.

The amazing growth of the press happened because the printed page of periodicals assumed a critical role in the United States. Newspapers and magazines became the place where Americans discussed and debated the issues that affected them. Newspapers, editors, and citizens took sides, and they used the press as the conduit for discussion. The Debating the Issues series offers a glimpse into how the press was used by Americans to shape and influence the major events and issues facing the nation during different periods of its development. Each volume is based on the documents, that is, the writings that appeared in the press of the time. Each volume presents articles, essays, and editorials that support opposing interests on the events and issues, and each provides readers with background and explanation of the events, issues, and, if possible, the people who wrote the articles that have been selected. Each volume also includes a chronology of events and a selected bibliography. The series is based on the Greenwood Press publication, *Debating the Issues in Colonial Newspapers*. Books in the Debating the Issues series cover the following periods: the Revolution and the young republic, the Federalist era, the antebellum period, the Civil War, Reconstruction, the progressive era, and World War I.

This volume on the Civil War focuses on the issues and events that affected the nation in its most volatile time. The very nature of secession created highly partisan newspapers and newspaper editors. One should not assume, however, that all newspapers in the North and the South supported their respective governments; they did not. In the North, especially, many editors sympathized with the South. Here, you can read how newspapers editorialized about the major battles and events of the war, as well as how they debated the issues that led to war and those that arose as a result of the conflict that divided a nation.

Chronology of Events

1860

November 6   Abraham Lincoln elected president of the United States

December 20   South Carolina becomes the first state to secede from the Union

December 26   Federal garrison in Charleston moves to Fort Sumter

1861

January 9   *Star of the West* fails to relieve Fort Sumter

February 4   Convention of seceded states meets in Montgomery, Alabama.

February 18   Jefferson Davis inaugurated president of the Confederacy

March 4   Lincoln inaugurated president of the United States

April 12   Fort Sumter fired upon, beginning Civil War

April 15   President Lincoln calls for federal troops

April 19   Soldiers and civilians clash in Baltimore

May 20   North Carolina becomes eleventh state to leave Union

July 21   Battle of First Bull Run

October 24   Pro-Unionist *Knoxville Whig* forced to cease publishing

November 8	*Trent* affair begins with seizure of Confederate commissioners
December 26	United States surrenders commissioners, ending *Trent* affair

1862

February 16	Surrender of Fort Donelson, Tenn.
March 7–8	Battle of Pea Ridge
March 9	USS *Monitor* and CSS *Merrimack* battle
April 6–7	Battle of Shiloh
April 25	Federal fleet arrives in New Orleans
June 5	*Memphis Appeal* flees before Union forces capture city
June 25–July 1	Seven Days Campaign
August 20	*New-York Tribune* publishes "The Prayer of Twenty Millions"
August 29–30	Battle of Second Bull Run
September 17	Battle of Antietam
September 22	Preliminary Emancipation Proclamation announced
November 7	Major General George McClellan removed from command
December 13	Battle of Fredericksburg

1863

January 1	Emancipation Proclamation announced
April 2	Bread riot breaks out in Richmond
May 1–4	Battle of Chancellorsville
May 5	Peace leader Clement Vallandigham arrested
May 10	"Stonewall" Jackson dies from wounds received at Battle of Chancellorsville
May 18	Siege of Vicksburg begins
June 1	*Chicago Times* shut down by General Ambrose E. Burnside
June 9	Battle of Brandy Station
June 20	West Virginia joins Union as 35th state
July 1–3	Battle of Gettysburg
July 4	Vicksburg surrenders
July 10	Siege of Battery Wagner, Charleston Harbor, begins
July 13	Draft riots in New York
August 21	Sacking of Lawrence, Kansas
September 19–20	Battle of Chickamauga
November 19	Lincoln issues Gettysburg Address
November 23–25	Battle of Chattanooga

1864

March 10	Grant given command of Federal armies
April 12	Massacre at Fort Pillow
May 5–6	Battle of Wilderness
May 7	Union Army begins Atlanta Campaign
May 8–21	Spotsylvania Campaign
June 1–3	Battle of Cold Harbor
June 18	Siege of Petersburg begins
June 19	CSS *Alabama* sunk by USS *Kearsarge*
June 27	Battle of Kennesaw Mountain
September 2	Federal Army occupies Atlanta
November 8	President Lincoln reelected
November 16	"March to the Sea" begins
December 15–16	Battle of Nashville
December 21	Union Army occupies Savannah

1865

January 15	Union troops capture Fort Fisher
January 31	House of Representatives passes Thirteenth Amendment
February 3	Hampton Roads Peace Conference
March 4	President Lincoln gives second inaugural address
March 13	Confederacy approves use of black soldiers
April 3	Union troops occupy Richmond
April 9	Gen. Lee surrenders to Gen. Grant
April 14	President Lincoln mortally wounded
April 15	Vice President Andrew Johnson sworn in as president
May 10	President Davis captured
May 26	Confederate Army of Trans-Mississippi surrenders

Introduction: Newspapers in Civil War America

By the summer of 1862, *New-York Tribune* editor Horace Greeley had become convinced that the United States could not wait any longer to free the country's slaves. Greeley, a brilliant writer who was one of the founders of the antislavery Republican Party, published a series of editorials in his newspaper calling attention to the problems of slavery. But the editorials, which called on Union leaders to enforce the confiscation bills recently passed by Congress, seemingly had made little impact. An exasperated Greeley then used the editorial page of his newspaper on August 20 to write an open letter to President Abraham Lincoln demanding ungrudging execution of the confiscation laws granting freedom to the slaves of those resisting the Union. Titled "The Prayer of Twenty Millions," it was a bold editorial and considered intemperate by many readers, even those who admired the feisty editor.[1]

Greeley's editorial stature was such, however, that the savvy president knew he must respond. The *Tribune* had become one of the most popular newspapers by the time the Civil War began, and Greeley was widely respected for his views, including his opposition to slavery. Significantly, Lincoln chose another newspaper to publish his reply, the *National Intelligencer* in Washington, D.C. In one of his most memorable public statements, the president responded to Greeley simply and directly. Lincoln wrote, "My paramount object in this struggle *is* to save the Union, and is *not* either to save or to destroy slavery. If I could save the Union without freeing *any* slave I would do it, and if I could save it by freeing *all* the slaves, I would do it; and if I could save it by freeing some and leaving others alone, I would also do that."[2]

The president's response in summarizing the contentious issue defused Greeley's criticism. A month later, after the Union victory at the battle of

Antietam, Lincoln issued the Preliminary Emancipation Proclamation. It decreed freedom for slaves in the Confederate states on January 1, 1863, and it cited sections of the Confiscation Act dealing with slavery and ordered military service to enforce the provisions. Greeley was ecstatic over the announcement, and the next day the *Tribune* proclaimed, "It is the beginning of the end of the rebellion; the beginning of the new life of the nation. GOD BLESS ABRAHAM LINCOLN!"[3]

The remarkable exchange between Greeley and Lincoln is an indication of the important role that newspaper editorials played during the Civil War. When the war began, newspapers were the most popular reading material available to most Americans. The director of the Census of 1860 wrote that newspapers and periodicals "furnish nearly the whole of the reading which the greater number, whether from inclination or necessity, permit themselves to enjoy."[4] Americans learned of almost everything taking place outside their own communities from newspapers. This gave editors tremendous influence and responsibility, a fact recognized by observers of the period. In 1860, statesman and political philosopher Edward Everett said, "The newspaper press of the U.S. is, for good or evil, the most powerful influence that acts on the public mind—the most powerful in itself and as the channel through which most other influence act."[5] The influence of newspaper editorials continued to increase after the war began and as the demand for newspapers soared. The interest in newspapers was probably best expressed by Oliver Wendell Holmes, a Union officer who would go on to become chief justice of the U.S. Supreme Court. Toward the end of the war, Holmes remarked, "We must have something to eat, and the papers to read. Everything else we can give up."[6]

Newspapers played a pivotal role in events leading up to the Civil War. Beginning in the 1830s, abolitionists made great use of papers to spread opposition to slavery. For example, the *Liberator,* published by William Lloyd Garrison, called for an immediate end to slavery, which made it the most controversial and influential abolitionist publication. Garrison was physically threatened for his radical views but always managed to escape unharmed. Elijah Lovejoy, a former Presbyterian minister turned abolitionist editor, met a worse fate. Local mobs destroyed the press of his newspaper, the *St. Louis Observer,* three times. Lovejoy vowed to protect his paper and in 1837, when an armed mob arrived to seize the press, shooting broke out. Lovejoy was killed, making him a martyr for the abolitionist movement.

White abolitionists such as Garrison and Lovejoy were joined by African American publishers who also fought to end slavery. The best known of these was Frederick Douglass, whose *North Star* was first published in 1847. Douglass, a former slave, used his publication on behalf of various causes for black Americans. It later was renamed *Douglass' Monthly* and published

Newspapers in Camp. *This drawing by artist Edwin Forbes captures the interest of Civil War soldiers in getting the latest news. Newspapers were one of the most popular reading materials among soldiers in both the Union and Confederate armies. (Division of Prints and Photographs, Library of Congress Collection)*

during the Civil War when it took up various causes, including the enlistment of black troops.

At the same time that abolitionist publications agitated for an end to slavery, a new group of newspapers emerged in big cities such as New York. Dubbed the penny press, these low-priced papers were aimed at attracting a large audience through their news coverage. Although the penny papers emphasized news, they remained advocates for political parties. Greeley's *New-York Tribune* helped found the Republican Party and supported Abraham Lincoln's bid for president in 1860. The *Tribune* was joined by other newspapers in supporting the Republicans, most notably the *Chicago Tribune, New-York Times,* and *Springfield (Mass.) Republican.*

Many Southern newspapers used their editorial pages to fight the growing opposition to slavery. These papers were devoted supporters of the South's way of life and were sharply critical of any threats to it. Even the South's handful of penny papers, which declared themselves independent of political parties, could not stay out of the debate over slavery. Particularly outspoken were the so-called fire-eaters, who defended slavery and attacked abolitionists at every opportunity. The dean of Southern fire-eaters was

Robert Barnwell Rhett, Sr., editor of the *Charleston Mercury*, who was often called the "father of secession." As the debate over slavery grew increasingly intense, the *Mercury* was joined by papers such as the *Richmond Examiner*, Jackson *Mississippian*, and Atlanta *Daily Intelligencer* (Atlanta, Ga.), in calling for the South to declare its independence and secede from the United States.

The newspaper debate over slavery did not just pit the North against the South. Plenty of Northern papers, including the *New York Herald* and *Chicago Times*, sided with the South in its defense of slavery. Likewise, some Southern papers, including the *Richmond Whig* and New Orleans *Daily Picayune*, opposed the idea of the South seceding.

The number of newspapers in the United States grew steadily in the decades leading up to the war, thanks to the increasing population and declining illiteracy rate. In 1840, America's population was 17,069,000 and 1,404 newspapers were being published. By 1860, the population had jumped 84 percent to 31,443,000 and the number of papers had grown by 265 percent to 3,725. Weeklies still constituted the greatest number of newspapers, but the percentage of dailies rose from 138 in 1840 to 387 in 1860, a growth rate of 276 percent. Many towns and cities in the North and South—even those with only a few thousand residents—had two papers or more.[7]

Daily newspapers of the era typically ran four pages, although some in big cities were larger. The first page carried news and a considerable amount of advertising. Page two generally contained editorials, letters from readers, and other news items, although these sometimes were found on page three or four. The rest of the paper contained news, official notices, serialized fiction, and more advertising.

Many newspapers, especially in the South, still used hand presses at the beginning of the Civil War. But a growing number of newspapers in large cities were using steam-powered cylinder presses. Far faster than their older counterparts, the steam-powered presses required printers to place separate sheets of paper into revolving cylinders that printed two pages side by side. Once dry, the printed pages were fed in again to print two pages on the other side. The sheets then were inserted into machines that folded them to make four pages. Soon after the war began, the *New-York Tribune* introduced the process of stereotyping, which made it possible to produce type onto a solid plate, curved to fit a cylinder. This made printing even faster, and both the *New-York Times* and *New York Herald* soon adopted the process.

The public's growing appetite for news led to widespread use of Sunday editions and afternoon editions. Changes in newspaper makeup also were introduced. Although use of woodcut images still was not widespread, a growing number of papers published maps of major battles or campaigns. Most papers preferred one-column headlines for most stories, but many used multiple decks when important news events warranted it.

The circulation of newspapers varied greatly. Metropolitan penny papers such as the *New York Herald* and *New-York Tribune* had circulations ranging from 150,000 to 200,000. But far more daily papers sold between 5,000 and 10,000 issues. And many papers that published only once, twice, or three times a week had circulations in the hundreds rather than thousands. With a largely rural population and fewer large cities, the South had far fewer newspapers than the North. Moreover, no Southern papers could claim the big circulations that some in the North enjoyed. The publisher of the Augusta *Chronicle & Sentinel* bragged that he was selling 6,500 papers daily, more than any other paper in the state. No other paper disputed that figure. The Richmond *Daily Dispatch,* which had a circulation of 30,000 during the war, probably had the largest readership in the South.

The advent of the penny press in the 1830s had changed the way newspapers were sold in big cities. Newsboys hawked papers on the street that sold from one to three cents. Still, the great majority of readers subscribed to papers and had them delivered by carriers or the postal service. Subscription rates averaged about five dollars annually when the war began. That price stayed generally the same in the North during the war. However, subscription rates rose dramatically in the South because of shortages and a steep climb in prices for ink, paper, and other supplies. The *Macon (Ga.) Telegraph* had an annual subscription rate of 5 dollars when the war began. By May 1863, the rate had climbed to 12 dollars a year. Later that year, the paper was only available by quarterly subscription, and that rate jumped to 9 dollars early in 1864. The skyrocketing cost of living in the South also led many editors to begin allowing readers to pay for their papers with produce and livestock.

Advertising was the other major revenue source for Civil War newspapers. As the circulation of newspapers grew in the 1800s, advertising became an attractive way for businesses to sell their products and services. Many publishers also put more emphasis on selling advertising, and because of this, newspaper advertising became more sophisticated by the time the war began. Not only had the size of ads grown, but many ads also featured illustrations, catchy slogans, and varied type sizes to attract the attention of readers. During this time, it was not unusual for advertising to constitute more than half of a newspaper. Ads were found throughout the paper, including the front page. Although the amount of advertising grew in the North during the war, it declined in the South because of the steadily worsening economy. By the end of the war, every single Southern newspaper had seen the amount of advertising fall to half or less of what it had been when the fighting began.

By the time fighting began, New York was the newspaper center of America. The city had 17 daily newspapers in 1861, but the leaders were a trio of publications known throughout the country. Each was closely identified with its editor: James Gordon Bennett of the *New York Herald*, Greeley of the *New-York Tribune*, and Henry Raymond of the *New-York Times*. Bennett, one of the pioneers of the penny press, was a journalistic innovator who sided with the South on many issues. Greeley was an irascible, eccentric editor who nonetheless made his editorial page perhaps the most influential in the country. Raymond was a far more moderate editor who attracted readers interested in a stable editorial policy.

Other major cities in the North, including Philadelphia; Chicago; Washington, D.C.; Boston; and Cleveland, were lively newspaper centers. All had three or more daily newspapers that took different sides in the various debates of the war. Often these papers spent as much time attacking one another as they did their political opponents. This was certainly the case in Chicago where the *Tribune* was one of the biggest supporters of the Lincoln administration and the *Times* was one of the president's most critical opponents.

Although less well known than their big-city counterparts, the newspapers of smaller towns were no less passionate in their views on the war's issues. Most sided with one political party or the other. The Republicans could count on support from such papers as the *Providence (R.I.) Daily Journal*, *Illinois State Journal* (Springfield), and *Harrisburg (Pa.) Telegraph*. At the same time, the Democrats could count on support from such papers as the *Dubuque (Iowa) Herald*, *Crisis* (Columbus, Ohio), and *Fort Wayne (Ind.) Sentinel*.

Richmond was the center of the Southern press. Richmond was not the largest city in the South; that honor went to New Orleans. But New Orleans was captured in 1862, and its newspapers fell into Union hands. Richmond was the capital of the Confederacy, and it had some of the most influential newspapers in the South. When the war began, four major dailies were published in the city: the *Daily Dispatch, Enquirer, Examiner,* and *Whig.* (A fifth paper, the *Sentinel,* relocated to Richmond from Alexandria in 1863 after that city was captured.) The *Daily Dispatch* maintained a neutral policy on most governmental matters, directing its criticism at the North. Likewise, the *Enquirer* generally supported the Davis administration and avoided subjects that might threaten the Confederate cause. In stark contrast, the *Examiner* could be brutal in its criticism of the Confederate government, often singling out the president himself for condemnation. The *Whig* had opposed secession, and although the paper initially supported the Confederate government, it became increasingly hostile toward the Davis administration.

Charleston had lively newspaper competition between the *Mercury* and the *Courier*. The *Mercury* had been a champion of secession, but once the war began, the paper criticized the Davis administration at virtually every turn. The *Courier*, on the other hand, was a faithful supporter of Davis and condemned its rival for undermining the Confederate government. Most of the South's other cities of real size, including Augusta, Jackson, Memphis,

Mobile, Montgomery, Nashville, Raleigh, and Savannah, had two or more newspapers. Editorially, most tended to support the Confederate government until late in the war.

Although some Southern newspapers such as the *Richmond Examiner* and *Charleston Mercury* could be stinging critics of the Davis administration, only a few openly supported the North or advocated early peace in the same way that the Copperhead journals of the North did. William G. "Parson" Brownlow published the *Knoxville Whig*, which opposed secession and led the Union movement in East Tennessee. Confederate authorities arrested Brownlow in December 1861; he was later freed and allowed to move to the North. William W. Holden, publisher of the *North Carolina Standard*, was a bitter critic of the Confederate government and in 1863 began openly advocating peace with the Union. His peace position angered many, including a group of Georgia troops who wrecked the newspaper office while passing through Raleigh. About the same time, Nathan B. Morse acquired the Augusta *Chronicle & Sentinel* and turned it into a vicious critic of the Davis administration. When the editor began openly advocating peace, John Forsyth of the *Mobile Register & Advertiser* became so angry that he challenged Morse to a duel.

Newspapers on both sides weighed in with editorials on all aspects of the war, from military and social to political and economic. Editors of New York's largest papers gave so much military advice early in the war that they became known derisively as the newspaper generals. The *New-York Tribune*'s editorial cry, "Forward to Richmond," put pressure on the Lincoln administration to march on Richmond. When the Union army was routed at the battle of First Bull Run, Greeley and the other newspaper generals received withering criticism. Issues such as the Emancipation Proclamation and the enlistment of black troops sparked widespread editorial debate. Although Republican newspapers generally applauded Lincoln's move to free the slaves, his Democratic opponents in the press often resorted to abusive language when they criticized the president. From the outset of the war, the Lincoln administration took an aggressive policy against its most bitter newspaper critics. Newspapers such as the *Chicago Times* and *New York World* were suspended for brief periods on various charges, including interfering with the war effort. And several editors, including Samuel Medary of the *Crisis* and Dennis Mahoney of the *Dubuque Herald*, were jailed briefly.

The right of newspapers to comment on all aspects of the war perhaps was best expressed by the *New-York Times*, which said, "While we emphatically disclaim and deny any right as inhering in journalist or others to incite, advocate, abet, uphold or justify treason or rebellion; we respectfully but firmly affirm and maintain the right of the press to criticize freely and fearlessly the acts of those charged with the administration of the Government;

also those of their civil and military subordinates...."[8] Moreover, the editorial page remained the great love of many editors. A friend of John M. Daniel, editor of the *Richmond Examiner*, once remarked, "He was the only newspaper proprietor I ever heard of who would throw out, without hesitation, paying advertisements, in order to make room for editorials, or for contributions which particularly pleased him."[9]

Certainly, the writing style of newspaper editorials was far different in the mid-1800s than that found in newspapers today. Many editors used the flowery, purple prose popular with many writers. Consider the editorial that appeared in the *St. Paul (Minn.) Pioneer-Press* following the news of President Lincoln's assassination:

> The saddest word that ever fell on the ears of living mortals sobbed through the wires yesterday and died brokenhearted in its flight. A huge eclipse has struck the nation down from its high noon of joy to a chaos of thick darkness. Weep, orphaned people of America, bereaved of your deliverer! Weep, Liberty, widowed in your bridal hour; for Abraham Lincoln, the wise, the good, the great of heart, the Savior of the Republic, the type and pillar of its cause, the man in whom was centered all the hopes and affections of the nation—is DEAD—yes, God help us, dead....[10]

Concise writing was not valued as it is today. A typical editorial ran more than 1,000 words, and it was not unusual for them to run even longer. Many newspapers chose to carry only one long editorial rather than several shorter in length. In their editorials, many writers frequently resorted to abusive language to describe political opponents or policies they did not like. President Lincoln, for one, was called everything from the Baboon to Abraham the First. Editors also frequently invoked God or the Almighty to help their side.

The topics of editorials, both in the North and South, varied greatly. Issues relating to the war and polices were the most popular subjects, but editors also addressed racial, social, economic, and diplomatic matters on a regular basis. Editors on both sides had no shortage of advice for the political and military leaders who were directing the war effort. They also endorsed candidates at all levels of government. Issues of national and state interest received the most attention from editors. But they also turned their pens on local subjects, including farm crops, schools, and public safety.

It is difficult to determine who wrote the editorials that appeared in Civil War newspapers because few newspaper editors attached their names to the editorials. The best-known exception was Greeley of the *New-York Tribune*, who occasionally addressed his editorials as letters to an individual and put his name at the end. As a rule, editors or assistant editors wrote most of the editorials that appeared in their papers. Some papers that had close connections with a political party or officeholder would allow a party leader or elected official to pen an editorial. The most famous example of this was the *National Intelligencer,* a Democratic paper in Washington, D.C., with close ties to the president. As already noted, when Greeley wrote his editorial, "The Prayer of Twenty Millions," the *Intelligencer* allowed Lincoln to respond on its editorial page.

The ability of the South's newspapers to comment editorially was limited as the war went on by the toll that the fighting took on the Confederacy. The skyrocketing cost of paper led virtually all papers in the South to reduce the physical size of their publications at one time or another. By July 1862, all of the Richmond dailies were publishing only two pages per issue, and many papers soon followed suit. Beginning in September 1861, the *Charleston Courier* reduced its size several times, until by early 1865, the two-page paper was only 10 by 15 inches in size. The paper shortage forced some publishers to use whatever paper was available, including colored paper. During the siege of Vicksburg in 1863, the *Vicksburg (Miss.) Whig* even published on the back of wallpaper. A scarcity of ink also was a problem and led some papers to use homemade substitutes. The *Memphis Appeal* even used shoeblacking for a time.

Southern newspapers also were hurt by the large number of employees who enlisted in the Confederate army. Hundreds of reporters, printers, and mailing clerks fought for the South, placing a heavy burden on those who remained behind. Even though they could claim a military exemption, dozens of editors enlisted to fight and left their papers in the hands of their staff. By September 1864, the small staff of the *Savannah Republican* included two disabled war veterans, two soldiers assigned to work in the office because of their printing skills, and two women.

An additional pressure was the fact that most of the fighting took place in the South, and as the war dragged on, the Union army captured increasing numbers of towns and cities. Most editors who found themselves in the path of Federal troops did one of two things: closed their offices and fled or packed up their papers and published elsewhere. During the first year of the war, 40 newspapers in Virginia alone suspended publishing. The *Memphis Appeal* was one of several papers that moved to stay ahead of the advancing Union army. The *Appeal* moved so many times, in fact, that it became known as the Moving Appeal. By January 1865, as a result of military occupation and other difficulties, there were fewer newspapers in the entire Confederacy than there were in the state of Virginia before the war.[11]

From the start of the fighting, the editors of Civil War newspapers recognized that it was the greatest event of their lives. Indeed, the war proved to be one of the central events in American history. The Civil War settled two fundamental issues that had plagued America since the country's founding: whether the United States was to be a nation with a strong central government or a loose confederation of states, and whether or not the nation was to continue as the largest slaveholding country in the world. Settling the issues took four years—from the shelling of Fort Sumter on April 12, 1861, to the surrender at Appomattox Courthouse on April 9, 1865. In all, more than 10,000 military actions took place across 18 states. They ranged from dozens of major battles to thousands of smaller skirmishes. More than 2.5 million men served in the armies of the Union and the Confederacy, and more than 620,000 died during the fighting. That figure is almost equal to the number of American deaths in the rest of the nation's wars combined.[12]

This book presents editorial debates on significant issues during the Civil War. Each chapter focuses on an event or issue during the period between the presidential election of 1860 and the end of the war in 1865. The book presents editorials on both sides of the issues, not only from the perspective of the North and South but also from the perspective of newspapers in each region that took opposing sides. The editorials are taken from approximately 75 newspapers in the two regions. The largest share comes from papers in major cities in the North and South, including New York, Philadelphia, Washington, D.C., Chicago, Richmond, and Charleston. With larger staffs, these papers could provide far more editorial commentary on the war. Whereas a rural newspaper like the *Macon Telegraph* might have carried only three editorials a week, a metropolitan paper like the *New York Tribune* often published three or more editorials a day. The selection of editorials also was limited to the availability of newspapers in the South. When Southern cities, such as New Orleans, Nashville, and Savannah, fell to Union forces, their newspapers often were taken over by the occupiers. Although the newspapers began publishing again, they no longer reflected a Southern viewpoint and thus were not used in this book. As a result, readers will find relatively few editorials from New Orleans newspapers, even though New Orleans was the largest city in the South.

Although most editorials in the book were published in American newspapers, a few come from magazines of the period. More than one hundred magazines were published in the North and South during the war, but they were not as influential editorially because they generally had smaller circulations and most came out monthly. Many also were specialty publications that did not publish editorials of general interest. Among the exceptions were *Harper's Weekly*, one of the few weekly magazines published in America, and *Douglass' Monthly*, the influential abolitionist periodical.

The events and issues used in the book were selected for their historical significance and because newspapers of the period engaged in lively debate on the particular subject of the Civil War. In some cases, major events of the war, particularly major battles, are not included because there was insufficient editorial debate. In general, the book is organized chronologically by event or issue. Some issues that spanned the entire war, such as emancipation, diplomacy, and prisoners of war, also are included.

Readers may be uncomfortable with the racial language found in a few of the editorials, particularly the words *nigger* and *sambo*. It is important to keep in mind that racial attitudes were far different than today and that many people in both the North and South during the nineteenth century used the words in everyday language to refer to African Americans. Any work that attempts to capture the editorial flavor of the period must necessarily have writing with such language, even though it is considered offensive today.

In transcribing the original documents, the original spelling and punctuation have been used. To enhance readability, the use of *sic* has been kept to a minimum. Titles or headlines appeared in many of the editorials used but not in all. In the case of editorials that had headlines, the headlines were not changed and are printed with quotation marks. In the case of editorials published without headlines, headlines were made up and quotation marks are not used. Careful readers will note that some of the New York newspapers, such as the *New-York Times* and *New-York Tribune*, used a hyphen in their name. That practice continued through the war, although the hyphen eventually was dropped.

Notes

1. *New-York Tribune,* 20 August 1862.

2. *National Intelligencer* (Washington, D.C.), 23 August 1862.

3. *New-York Tribune,* 23 September 1862.

4. Joseph C.G. Kennedy, *Preliminary Report on the Eighth Census, 1860* (Washington, D.C.: Government Printing Office, 1862), 101–2.

5. As quoted in Lambert Wilmer, *Our Press Gang* (Philadelphia: J.T. Lloyd, 1860), 63.

6. "Bread and the Newspaper," *Atlantic Monthly,* 8 September 1861, 346–48.

7. Allan Pred, *Urban Growth and City-Systems in the United States, 1840–1860* (Cambridge: Harvard University Press, 1980), 222.

8. *New-York Times,* 9 June 1863.

9. As quoted in Carl R. Osthaus, *Partisans of the Southern Press: Editorial Spokesmen of the Nineteenth Century* (Lexington: University Press of Kentucky, 1994), 104.

10. *St. Paul (Minn.) Pioneer-Press,* 16 April 1865.

11. J. Cutler Andrews, *The South Reports the Civil War* (Princeton, N.J.: Princeton University Press, 1970), 44.

12. James M. McPherson, *Battle Cry of Freedom: The Civil War Era* (New York: Oxford University Press, 1988).

CHAPTER I

Lincoln Elected President, 1860

By the 1850s, political issues had sectionalized the United States. Passage of the Kansas-Nebraska Act in 1854 sparked the emergence of the Republican Party, which declared ending slavery as its primary issue. During the election of 1858, Republicans warned that Southern slave power was trying to convert the country into a slave empire. National attention focused on the race for Illinois's open Senate seat, pitting Republican Abraham Lincoln against Democrat Stephen Douglas. Lincoln was an outspoken critic of slavery, whereas Douglas championed popular sovereignty, which allowed the citizens of western territories to make their own decision on slavery. The highlight of the Lincoln-Douglas race was a series of seven debates on slavery. Douglas defeated Lincoln, but the debates clarified the issues between Democrats and Republicans. Lincoln also emerged from the debate as a national spokesman for the Republican Party.

The Democratic Party, which had lost the White House only twice since 1832, had become divided on the future of slavery. In the hopes of achieving party unity, Democrats agreed to hold the 1860 national convention in Charleston, South Carolina, starting on April 23. Douglas was the Democratic front-runner for the presidential nomination, but a Southern rights faction proposed replacing the popular sovereignty platform with the assurance that slavery would be protected everywhere under U.S. jurisdiction. Douglas's nomination became stalled, and the split party was forced to adjourn before meeting six weeks later in Baltimore. Democrats faced the same problem when they met again on June 18. Southern rights supporters walked out of the convention, leaving the remaining delegates to nominate Douglas for president and Herschel V. Johnson of Georgia for vice president. Southern rights leaders organized an impromptu convention a few days later in Baltimore and nominated John C. Breckenridge of Kentucky for president and Joseph Lane of Oregon for vice president. The Democratic Party had split.

The Republicans, bolstered by Congressional victories in 1858, met in Chicago beginning on May 16. William H. Seward of New York was the front-runner going into the convention. Waiting in the wings were four other favorite-son candidates: Salmon P. Chase of Ohio, Simon Cameron of Pennsylvania, Edward Bates of Missouri, and Lincoln. But delegates in critical swing states viewed Seward as too radical on the subject of slavery. He did not win victory on the first ballot, and delegates turned to Lincoln. Known as Honest Abe, Lincoln had a reputation for integrity. Born in a log cabin, his success story made him an appealing symbol of the party. He also was viewed as a moderate who could win critical states in the Midwest. Lincoln secured the Republican nomination on the third ballot. The convention selected Hannibal Hamlin of Maine, a friend of Seward, as Lincoln's running mate.

Members of the old Whig Party also met as the re-formed Constitutional Union Party and nominated John Bell of Tennessee and Edward Everett of Massachusetts. The aging group of conservatives, sometimes known as the Old Gentleman's Party, took no stand on the issue of slavery. They adopted a resolution pledging, "to recognize no political principle other than *the Constitution…the Union…and the Enforcement of the Laws.*"[1] Recognizing that they likely could not win the election, their goal was to deny all four candidates a majority of electoral votes so that the election would be thrown into the House of Representatives. There they hoped the crisis over slavery could reach a compromise.

The presidential campaign reflected how sectionalized the country had become. The race in the North largely pitted Douglas against Lincoln. Neither man could expect to win in the South, where the race was between Breckenridge and Bell. Political tradition dictated the presidential candidates remain silent and leave the campaigning to their spokesmen, who stumped the country arguing over issues such tariffs, internal improvements, and immigration policy. However, the overriding issue of the campaign was race. Douglas Democrats and the Constitutional Unionists branded Republicans as racial egalitarians who wanted to give blacks the same status of whites, including the right to vote.

During the campaign, Southern rights leaders threatened to secede from the union if the Republicans were victorious. Unionists in the South urged the North to heed the threats. But Northerners had heard such warnings for years from Southern leaders and believed they were merely a bluff. Lincoln refused to make any overtures that might mollify the South, claiming there was nothing he could say that would satisfy the leaders. Breaking with tradition, Douglas campaigned for himself by touring the country. He claimed to be the only national candidate and the only leader who could prevent the country from splitting. In visits to the South, he warned against secession, even threatening to hang any man who would attempt to break up the Union.

On the eve of the election, with a Republican victory seemingly assured, there were last-minute attempts to forge a unified anti-Republican coalition. None of them had any real success. Lincoln won only 40 percent of the popular vote, but garnered 180 electoral votes. Breckenridge won 72 electoral votes, Bell 39, and Douglas 12. The nation's 16th president won every Northern state except New Jersey. He did not win a single state in the South.[2] Southerners saw the magnitude of Lincoln's victory in the North as an ominous sign. The future of slavery, they believed, was in jeopardy. More than ever before, there was serious talk of states leaving the Union.

This chapter follows editorial debate on the pivotal presidential election of 1860. In the months leading up to the election, Northern newspapers were divided on the four presidential candidates. Southern papers were split mainly among Bell, Breckenridge, and Douglas. Lincoln had virtually no support in the South. Newspapers reacted variously to Lincoln's victory. In the North, the *New-York Times* argued that Lincoln's election would check the power of slave interests, while the *Democratic Standard* (Concord, N.H.) said the North risked warfare by its attack on slavery. In the South, the *Chronicle & Sentinel* (Augusta, Ga.) urged the South to carefully deliberate any future moves, but the *Charleston Mercury* said the time had come to form a Southern Confederacy.

ELECTION CAMPAIGN

The Chicago Times, *a Douglas backer, argued that the Southern states had the constitutional right to practice slavery and said the Republican Party was waging war on the region.*

Chicago Times, 6 November 1860

An Anonymous Writer: "Do It With Your Eyes Open"

The course of the Republican leaders has been to blind the people of the North to the true feelings and position of the Southern States. The efforts to blind them, and keep them blinded, have been unceasing and determined.

It is not only due to the South, but it is a matter of sheer justice to ourselves, that we should act with our eyes wide open in this perilous crisis. He who would suppress the truth, and elude the people in this dangerous hour, is a moral traitor to the country and the enemy of American civilization and liberty.

The *people* of the South have never wronged the North nor felt like doing so. Fire-eating disunionists have insulted us, and committed personal indignity upon some individuals; but the Southern people have never sought nor desired to force their institution upon us, nor to attack those which we already possess. Under these circumstances, then, the South had a right to expect that her rights under the Constitution would be maintained in good faith and her peace respected. Has this been done so far as the Republican party is concerned? Have the South just reason to believe that it *will* be done, if they win the election? Let facts speak.

For thirty years and more, there has been a continuous war waged upon the institutions, property and constitutional rights of the people of the South. They have the undoubted right to a return of their fugitive slaves. This right is directly overridden by State legislation by more than half of the Northern States, and its practical benefits utterly denied in nearly all of them. They have the undoubted moral and constitutional right to judge of their own institutions, and to the peaceable enjoyment of such as they may adopt. And yet the Northern agitators have, for thirty years, kept them in hot water by their incendiary efforts against their most vital institution; have organized a system of robbery of their property; have already robbed them of millions' worth of that property, and as time progresses have only increased their efforts to render it more insecure and worthless. The people of the South have an undoubted right to peace and repose in the Union, with whatever domestic institutions they may have. And yet these anti-slavery agitators have rendered insecure every home south of the Mason & Dixon's line, and by their machinations have induced armed bands of fanatics to invade the peaceful homes of the South; have stirred up servile insurrections, and have caused bloodshed and crimes of the most atrocious character. These acts of hatred and aggression have grown in number and atrocity, as time has advanced, until the Southern people feel that there is to be no end to them, and that there is no hope of safety for life or property in the present condition of things. Should matters even grow no worse than they have been in the last five years, *they regard* such a state of insecurity and excitement as utterly intolerable and subversive of the very ends for which governments a[re] formed.

The Illinois State Register, *a Democratic journal and Douglas supporter, said the presidential race came down to the issue of what to do with the nation's blacks. The* Register *argued that blacks were not entitled to the same rights as whites and that the Southern states should be permitted to retain slavery.*

Illinois State Register (Springfield), 28 September 1860

An Anonymous Writer: "The Difference between the Two Parties"

The great point upon which the political parties of the country are at variance, is that of slavery. Who shall decide whether slavery shall continue to exist in the states where it is now tolerated? Who shall decide whether it shall be tolerated in the territories of the Union? Upon these two questions the policy of the democratic party differs widely from that of the republican party, and to the people of the United States is submitted the choice.

The republican party assert [*sic*] that slavery is an evil of the greatest magnitude; that it is a curse to the state where it is permitted, a curse to the society which tolerates it, and a curse to all men who participate in it as masters and owners. In his letter to the Boston committee, Mr. Lincoln declares that the man who will not emancipate his slaves in this life, must undergo an eternity of bondage and slavery in the life to come; that he must in the great hereafter, expiate in eternal punishment the crime of holding slaves in this world. This evil of slavery is so odious that Lincoln has placed on record, in his famous Chicago speech, that he "hates" it worse than any abolitionist hates it. He says that it is such an offence against laws of right and justice that this Union cannot stand, cannot survive unless the nation take immediate steps to appease divine wrath by legislation for its rapid and ultimate extinction. He proposes remedies for the evil. He lays down as cardinal principles that the negro is entitled to all the rights of white men: that any law which deprives him of his liberty is void: that the negro is entitled to all the products of his own labor, and that the man who, under the pretence of ownership, deprives the negro of his own labor, is a tyrant and oppressor, whose authority may be lawfully overthrown by the slaves if they have the physical power to do so. He proposes as the policy of the republican party, the immediate recognition by the federal government of the rights of the oppressed African; he proposes to legislate so that slavery must soon be extinguished. As a part of this policy, he insists that the negroes as long as they are slaves must remain within the borders of the present slave states, there to increase until they shall outnumber the white population. He proposes the remodel the supreme court of the United States by adding to it a number of republican judges, who shall be pledged to decide against slavery and slave owners. Having thus possession of the executive, legislative and judicial departments of the government, he proposes to carry out his policy by freeing the negroes and thus ultimately extinguishing slavery. The plan is an effectual one if practicable. It would be practicable if he could only induce the white people of the United States to submit to it. If he could overturn the constitution, extinguish state rights and obliterate private rights he might succeed, but to carry out his policy he must do all these things....

The democratic party however has a much shorter and more direct policy. It has for its cardinal principle that this nation is a nation of white men, in which negroes have no voice whatever in the regulation of its political affairs. Negroes who are here, are entitled to be treated with all the kindness that humanity and christianity can suggest, but they are not entitled to any of the prerogatives of the government. They are the inferior race, and must remain so, politically, forever. The regulation and government of this negro race, whether as free or as slave, has been wisely left by the constitution to the people of each state within their respective jurisdictions. The democratic party propose to leave that question where the constitution has left it, and where it has been regulated with great satisfaction for over seventy years. They propose that the white people of Illinois shall have exclusive control over the question of negro rights in Illinois; and that the people of the other states shall have the same exclusive control over the matter in their respective states. They insist that as the people of Illinois have excluded free negroes and slave negroes, that each other state shall have the same privilege. They propose that the entire question of slavery and negroism shall be left to the people of each state to be decided by themselves in their own good time, in such manner as their interests may dictate. They are opposed to overturning the whole policy of the past, overturning the whole theory of American government, and are opposed to prostituting the government and destroying the peace and harmony of the Union to gratify the wild, extravagant ambition of abolition demagogues.

The democratic party propose [*sic*] that the great constitutional doctrine of leaving to each people the exclusive privilege of regulating their domestic institutions for themselves, and of having or rejecting African slavery as they may deem best, shall be recognized to the fullest extent in the people of each territory of the United States. Under that policy we will have no nationalization of slavery. We will have the entire subject committed to the exclusive control of the people of each state and territory, to be decided by them for their own weal or woe. The nation will not then be responsible if slavery shall be admitted into new territories, nor if it be excluded, but the people of those territories, who are alone to be affected by the absence or presence of the institution, alone will bear the burden or enjoy the profit of their own choice.

Under this policy there will be no pretext for disunion or strife between states or sections. The negro race will continue as at present. The country will not be overrun with millions of free negroes, but the United States will continue to be a nation of free white people.

That is popular sovereignty, and that is democracy.

The New York Herald, *a Breckenridge supporter, claimed that Lincoln's election would spark a war of the races.*

New York Herald, 19 September 1860

An Anonymous Writer: "Our Historic Development—Shall It Be Superseded by a War of Races?"

Party divisions among us have hitherto been based on questions of policy in government, but without departing from the great principle of the rightful preponderance of the white race. Thus, in the first division of parties after the establishment of the constitution, the lines of the federal and republican organizations were drawn on the great question of a stronger or weaker form of federal government, involving the right of controlling personal liberty, the freedom of the press, and other questions of a similar character, which marked our legislation and political agitation during the closing years of the last century. This was succeeded by party divisions on the question of a second war with England in defence of our rights on the ocean, and the patriotic sacrifices the war party then led the country to make in the face of the bitter opposition of "the Massachusetts school" were the foundations of our present commercial glory. After this came the great division under Jackson, on the questions of bank, tariff and internal improvements by the general government. All of these questions were discussed with partisan bitterness, but in them the doubt of the right of the white man to rule never entered.

The only party division that exists to-day, aside from the bickerings of selfish and unscrupulous leaders, who are each endeavoring, with their petty cockle boats, to gather the fragments that are floating upon the tide of party revolution, involves a far deeper and older question than any that has previously been discussed among us during our national career. The issue that is presented by the black republican party involves the whole question of our social and national existence. Black republicanism, founded on and animated by the anti-slavery idea, and pursuing an exaggerated notion of individual rights, involves not only an attempt to equalize dissimilar and discordant races in their social and immunities, but also the most destructive theories in regard to the organization of society....

This anti-slavery idea aims to establish a new social policy in this country—the policy of an equalization of the white and black races—which has never produced anything but bloodshed in other parts of the world, and which can only result in the subjugation or destruction of the numerically weaker race. There is no possibility of the black and the white existing harmoniously together in social and political equality....It is then the question of a revolution in our social organization that the black republicans present to the people—a revolution that brings with it a perpetual war of races, which must endure, when once inaugurated, until the blacks now on this continent have been swept from the face of the earth. With the abolition of slavery in the Northern States, the negroes that once existed among us in family servitude have been almost exterminated. The paucity of their numbers prevented their presenting any resistance to this social extermination, and the same reason applies to the fact that the loss of their labor was not felt to any great degree by the material interests of the community.

But this does not and cannot apply to the Southern States, where four millions of blacks are now held in a position of social subjection, which contributes to their own moral and material welfare, and to that of the whole community in which they exist. The triumph of the antislavery sentiment, through the election of Lincoln to the Presidency, will initiate a social revolution among us which will require generations, and perhaps centuries, for its consummation, if we exist through it so long. Such a war of races will absorb all the powers of our society, diverting them from the prosecution of domestic industry and foreign trade. Above all, it will produce division and conflict among ourselves, as it has divided the whites everywhere that it has prevailed, while the blacks, without other policy or impulses, will be united by the bond of color....

The real question, therefore, now presented to the people of the United States is the question of our social development for generations yet to come, and involving our very existence as a nation. If we once begin the war of races, which will inevitably follow from the triumph of the abolition idea and its control of our government, it cannot cease until the black race has been exterminated or driven from among us. Such a war will involve the cessation of the prosecution of many of the industrial pursuits that now constitute our prosperity and national greatness. It will bring civil and servile war to our now peaceful land. It will consume all the elements that now contribute to our intellectual and material development. With such certainties before us, involving our posterity for centuries in conflict and ruin, it becomes every man to take heart and do his utmost to defeat the fanatical and revolutionary black republicans, who, blinded by their own zeal, following a fallacy that elsewhere has conducted only to destruction, and obstinately refusing to learn wisdom from the experience and disasters of other lands and nations, are bent on establishing here the most destructive conflict of races that the world has ever witnessed.

The North Carolina Standard, *another Breckenridge supporter, argued that talk of leaving the union was premature.*

North Carolina Standard (Raleigh), 11 July 1860

An Anonymous Writer: "A Constitutional Union"

[N]o reason exists why North Carolina should contemplate at this time a dissolution of the Union. While we would surrender no right of our State, and while we would preserve her honor untarnished among her sisters, yet disunion is one of the last things to be thought of. Disunion would be fraternal strife, civil and servile war, murder, arson, pillage, robbery, and fire and blood through long and cruel years. It would unsettle all business, diminish the value of all property, put the lives of both sexes and all ages in peril, and launch the States on a sea of scenes which no eye has scanned and no navigator sounded. It would bring debt, and misrule, and oppressive taxes, to be followed, perhaps, by the military rule of titled tyrants. It would wrench apart the tenderly entwined affections of millions of hearts, making it a crime in the North to have been born in the South, and a crime in the South to have been born in the North. It would convert the great body of the conservative men of the North, who are now our friends, into either deadly enemies or indifferent spectators of our intestine struggles, which would increase in intensity until law, order, justice, and civil rule would be forgotten and unknown. We repeat, there is no good cause now for dissolving the Union. The cause may arise, but let us not hasten to make or meet it. Who desires it now? Who would cause it? Who would "precipitate the States" into bloodshed and revolution? Who would darken the stars that now flash in the flag of the Union? Who, without cause and for no sufficient reason, would have war instead of peace, discord in the place of concord, and all the calamities which must result from the dissolution of a government such as ours? If such a man exists, let him stand forth to be blasted by the indignant maledictions of patriotic millions. Voices from the past, voices innumerable in the present, appeal to us not to peril rashly our Constitutional Union. From all battle-fields where Southern blood has mingled with Northern blood beneath one common and glorious banner; from the shores of Delaware, over whose breaking ice, on that stormy night, pressed the wary and bleeding feet of those two thousand soldiers, the only, the forlorn, the last hope of great Washington himself; from the kingdoms of the earth, in which the down-trodden millions struggle beneath the iron hoof of despotism, casting long-ing and hopeful glances towards this, the first, as it may be the last great experiment of self-government among men; from the whole civilized world, interested in our material prosperity and in the progress and happiness of man, there comes up to us with thundering sound—and over all of it, and ringing through all of it as with the blast of a trumpet, the spirit-voice of the immortal Jackson, speaking from his record and from his whole military and civil life—"The Federal Union—it must and shall be preserved!" Preserved, not consolidated, aggressive, usurping Union but as a *Constitutional* Union, protecting all equally, and dispensing its benefits and blessings as much to one section as another. Let us cling to such a Union as "the mariner clings to his last plank when night and the tempest close around him." As long as the Constitution is preserved inviolate we shall have nothing to fear. It will be time enough when that instrument, which is the bond of the Union, shall have been broken, or its spirit disregarded, to dissolve existing relations and provide new guards for future security.

The Cincinnati Daily Times *supported the Constitutional Union Party's goal of compromise on the issue of slavery. The editorial repeatedly asked the question, "Why should we quarrel?"*

Cincinnati Daily Times, **22 September 1860**

An Anonymous Writer: "Why Should We Quarrel?"

Why should we quarrel? Are we not the bond-slaves of reason? Has not the Great Infinite, in his wisdom, implanted in man the duty to obey "inex-orable logic," and to discard that which in his heart he believes to be untrue? "Let us reason together," should be the inspiration of every mind, and to the only bias of judgment should we lean; taught by the lesson of experience which the Past has brought, and indulging hopes of the Future which ra-tionality inspires. We are all of one family—we are all of one nation. The wis-dom of our fathers, inspired from Heaven, gave us a government, unequaled in the annals of the world for the exquisiteness of its machinery and the sound[ness] of philosophy on which it was based. For two-thirds of a century, nearly, we have thriven under it, and, from a few weak and oppressed colonies, have become a mighty and a prosperous nation, composed of an industrious, enterprising, fast and—would we could say—a happy and contented people.

Why should we quarrel? The written Constitution was broad enough to cover the whole situation, as with a blanket; and for years, although we had our individual imaginary and petty grievances, we still were happy, and grew up in friendship and harmony. We were National, then. Ambition had been busy in moving the springs of action in men's minds, but in the only instance that secession of any part of the Confederacy was contemplated with the view of forming a great Southern empire, it was regarded as treason, and the eminent person whose eloquence and plausible pretext had fomented the so-called conspiracy was regarded as a traitor, narrowly escaped condign punishment, and his odious and rank in the scale of infamy. We were national then, and patriotic. It was all our country over which the Constitution spread its aegis. The Government was the palladium of liberty, and one State, and the people of one State, thought no more of interfering with the rights of another, than they had of severing the great compact that united them under one banner. And for long years this harmony existed and flourished, and all things went well. As a nation, we were content, we were honest, we were virtuous, we were prosperous, we were happy. Why cannot we be so now? Why should we quarrel?...

Patriotism no more rules the American heart. The love of country that was the theme of every tongue in the morning of our lives, no more thrills the pulses of the sons of freedom, as we were proud to call ourselves. It is now, with one-half of this great nation, the pursuit of an abstract notion—a phantom, an ignis fatuus that traitorous demagogues flash in the faces of a bewildered and infatuated people, to misguide them to become entangled in difficult mazes and discover their error too late. And now they quarrel, and grow angry in their disputations, challenging the vocabulary for names of reproach with which to assail each other. The *cordiale entente* no more prevails. Brothers cease to be brothers—friends no longer friends. A wide gap is opening and growing wider, wider every day. Why should it be so? Why should we quarrel? Why not emulate each other in our devotion to our country and in attachment to the Union, the sole arbiter of America's great destiny? Why not permit each State, as by original compact, and it was thought was secured by the great instrument under which we have grown great and prospered, to hew out its own destiny in its own way, and with its own institutions, without interference from its sister States? Why seek to meddle with that which concerns us not? Why not return to the happy days, when we were homogenous, and undivided in sentiment from Maine to Georgia? Why should we quarrel?

The Nashville Patriot *also supported the Constitutional Union candidate, claiming that Bell was the only candidate who had consistently promoted peace.*

Nashville Patriot, 25 July 1860

An Anonymous Writer: "The Country Wants Peace, and the Country Must Have Peace"

Unlike all three of the others, each of whom is directly mixed up, in his political history and personal schemes, with this agitation, Mr. Bell has let no opportunity pass, in an active public career covering the entire period of strife to within something over a year past, without doing all in his power, consistent with the constitution and the principles of State equality, to discountenance and quiet agitation on this subject. His course has been marked from the outset by a desire to promote peace and concord. He has never proved untrue to any section, but all his antecedents are elevated, national and conservative. By the circumstances of his nomination he is placed before the people in opposition to the extremists of the South and to the sectionalists of the North. His election would be not only the nominal defeat of both, but it would be an emphatic declaration on the part of the people, that on an issue between the North and the South, involving the fate of the Union, they were prepared to stand by, uphold and defend the Union on the basis of the Constitution and the Laws of the land. On what other ground can the Union continue? On what other can we have peace? On what other can the dangers which threaten to engulf us in ruin be averted? Cannot the friends of the Union, on the basis named, forget, for a time, party feeling and lay aside party prejudice? Cannot the conservative people of all parties and sections sacrifice, for the time being, something of past party recollections and love, to the impulses of a noble and generous patriotism and to the obligations it imposes? We do not ask the support of the disunionists, nor of the fanatical abolitionists; but we appeal to the true-hearted lovers of the Union everywhere to unite with us in crushing both....

The Pittsburgh Gazette, *a Republican journal, said voters should not be swayed by Southern threats to leave the Union if Lincoln should be elected. The South must submit to the decision of the majority, the paper declared.*

Pittsburgh (Pa.) Gazette, **2 November 1860**

An Anonymous Writer: "Who Shall Rule"

The great question to be settled by the approaching Presidential election is, Shall the majority rule?...

A large party—*how* large we cannot say, but we know it is very noisy—contends that the South should not submit to a President constitutionally chosen by a majority of the people. Nay, more, they contend that the mere choice of a particular man, no matter what he may profess, nor how carefully the constitutional forms may be observed in his election, will of itself be sufficient cause for rebellion against the government. They declare that they will not submit to a President chosen by a party other than their own....We live, nominally, under a Constitutional government. The Constitution guarantees to us certain rights, among which is the right of the majority to choose a President in the way pointed out in that instrument. If that right has any value it consists in the enjoyment of it without hindrance or extraneous restriction. An attempt is now making to cripple the exercise of it; to say that it shall be used only for the elevation of certain men; and that if the majority choose to exercise it in any other way the government shall be rent in twain.

The grand, overshadowing issue of the campaign, therefore is, Will the people submit to this dictation? Will they assert their rights or yield to those who menace them? Will they maintain, intact, the privilege secured to them by the Fathers of the Republic, or will they basely yield them at the bidding of the southern oligarchy—a pitiful minority which has insinuated itself into the control of the government?

These are the questions to be answered on Tuesday next. It is no longer a mere contest between four men, but a struggle for the maintenance of the great majority principle in this Government. Shall the people rule?...

The time has come for a firm and resolute assertion of the majority principle. Our government can be maintained upon no other. The majority has the right to rule only within Constitutional limits; but within those limits it *must* rule or yield up the government to a usurping minority. The North has always acted upon this principle. When beaten it has uniformly submitted, although always the sufferer by submission. It has stood firm by the Union under Embargo Acts and low tariffs. It has seen its commerce swept from the ocean by the former; and when it turned its active energies to manufactures it has seen them also swept away by the free trade theories of the southern dictatorship. Beggary and starvation have been endured. Merchants have seen their ships rot at the wharves. Manufacturers have seen their spindles lying idle and their workmen gaunt and famished for food;

and yet the North has always been true to the Union of the States, seeking no remedy except within the Union and beneath the Constitution. And now when the hour of the remedy has come, when the twenty millions of the North are reaching out their hands to right themselves in the way provided by the Constitution, seeking only their own rights and not the wrong of any man, they are met with the cry of Secession and Disunion!

If it has come to this; if we have reached that degraded state of serfdom that we dare not vote without the consenting nod of Southern dictation, then let us assign our share in the government to South Carolina, and humbly request that chivalric State to do our thinking for us, and assume the charge of our federal interests. But until it has come to that, let us do our own thinking and acting, and stand prepared to back up our acts with a resolution adequate to the occasion. We have always yielded, when the fate of war was against us, and the South must be taught to follow our example and learn that she does not possess a monopoly of the government.

The Chicago Daily Democrat, *a Lincoln supporter, said the election would decide the future of slavery in the United States. The paper quoted from one of Lincoln's most memorable remarks during the debate with Douglas: "The Union cannot endure permanently half slave and half free."*

Chicago Daily Democrat, 5 November 1860

An Anonymous Writer: "The Great Battle"

The greatest political battle which has been fought in America since the formation of this Government, is to be decided to-morrow. Issues the most momentous hang upon the result. Let us enumerate them, briefly and simply:

In the first place, if the pro-slavery party triumph to-morrow throughout the Union, one of two things will be inevitable, to wit:

Either the slave power will go on from conquering to conquer, driving every vestige of freedom before it, planting the institution of slavery on every foot of our land, degrading free labor, and erecting an oligarchy of capital and an aristocracy of wealth, the way for all which is already marked out by the decisions of the Supreme Court and the construction of existing laws; or else, driven to desperation, and deprived of the hope of obtaining redress through the ballot-box, the people of the North will rise against the oppressors and sweep them away forever. True, the defeat of Mr. Lincoln to-morrow may not prevent the election of an anti-slavery President four years hence, or eight years hence; but it will be easier and safer to elect one now. Nothing but embarrassment and dangers can arise from any further delays.

The irrepressible conflict must be decided sooner or later, and the sooner the better. The Union cannot endure permanently half slave and half free. We do not expect the Union to be dissolved—if a Republican President is elected it cannot be dissolved—but we do expect it will cease to be divided. If Mr. Lincoln is elected, the Administration of which he will be the head, will arrest the further spread of slavery, and place it where the public mind shall rest in the belief of its ultimate extinction. If he is defeated, its advocates will push it forward until it reigns over all the land.

Secondly, If Mr. Lincoln be elected to-morrow we may consider the question of the suppression of the slave trade fully settled. During Mr. Buchanan's Administration the slave trade has flourished to an almost unprecedented extent. Thousands of negroes have been stolen from Africa and landed on our shores. Some of them have been reclaimed and sent back; a far larger number have died; still more are now toiling in the cotton fields and rice swamps of the far South. All this will be put to a sudden and complete stop, under Mr. Lincoln's government.

Thirdly, The pro-slavery interpretations of the Constitution of the United States which have been so freely and continually disseminated and enforced will be reversed and that glorious instrument will be construed, as its framers intended it should, as a charter of freedom, and not as a bulwark of slavery.

Fourthly, The present infamous Fugitive Slave Law will be repealed, and a law substituted in its place which will give the slave owners only what the Constitution provides, not a jot more. Their pound of flesh they may have, but not a drop of blood.

In a word, the whole policy of the government will be a policy of freedom. The spirit that will actuate all its departments will be a spirit of liberty. The patronage and the influence of the government, at home and abroad, will be exerted on the side of freedom. The rights of all the citizens of the United States will be made as secure in South Carolina as it is in Massachusetts. The sanctity of the mails will not be invaded, and the postmasters of the southern States will no longer be allowed to decide what newspapers their neighbors may read. Liberty shall be proclaimed through all the land and to all the inhabitants thereof. The slave States will be surrounded by a cordon of free States, and slavery, confined to its present limits—limits, too, speedily to be still further circumscribed by Delaware and Missouri becoming free—will become unprofitable, and a pecuniary, as well as a moral curse. Then emancipation societies will spring up in all the slave States, and the blessed work will go on, until the last slave is free, and America is redeemed from the foul stain that now degrades her in the eyes of all mankind.

Such are the issues depending on the result of the great battle to be fought to-morrow. In view of these, who that loves his country, his race, the rights of man, and the blessings of a free government, will hesitate to do his duty at the polls? The weather to-morrow may be unpleasant; it may be rainy and cold, and very disagreeable. But we had better endure every privation and make every sacrifice, rather than by our failure to do our duty, lose the inestimable blessings which the election of Abraham Lincoln will confer upon us and our posterity.

LINCOLN ELECTED

The New-York Times, *an outspoken Republican supporter, said Lincoln's election would check the power of slave interests.*

New-York Times, 7 November 1860

An Anonymous Writer: "The Election—Lincoln Triumphant"

We have no disposition to exult over this victory, signal and important as it is. The contest, on the part of the Republicans, has been throughout one of principle; on the part of their opponents it has been waged almost exclusively on the basis of fear. There has been no union of principle among them, nor have they been able to concentrate their strength upon a single candidate. The result is what might have been expected—disorganization, demoralization and defeat.

This election will inaugurate a marked and most important change in the administration of the Government. The policy of extending Slavery, and increasing its political power, will now be checked. The Slave interest will no longer impose its claims and its law upon the Federal Government. The Constitution will no longer be regarded as a mere instrument for fortifying and increasing Slavery. The African Slave-trade will not be reopened, and more vigorous and effective measure will be taken for its suppression.

But above all, we shall have established at Washington a rule of honesty and patriotism, in place of the corruption, imbecility and intrigue which have controlled our public councils for the last few years. It is quite time we had a change in these respects. The Republicans now have it in their power to lay the basis for the most useful, popular and permanent admisistration [*sic*] the country has seen for a long time. But they must not conceal from themselves the obstacles which they will be compelled to encounter.

The Democratic Standard *in Concord, N.H., a Southern sympathizer, said the North must cease its warfare on slavery or risk breaking up the Union.*

Democratic Standard (Concord, N.H.), 24 November 1860

An Anonymous Writer: "The Union—Its Danger—How Shall It Be Preserved?"

Whatever some men may talk, or whatever they may pretend to believe, no one can shut his eyes to the fact, that the great American Union, at this moment, is in imminent danger of dissolution.... Men may talk doubtingly; those, in some measure, responsible for the great evil that impends over us, may talk sneeringly; but no intelligent man can deny that now there is danger of the disruption of this mighty Confederacy of sovereign States—the pride and the hope of mankind.

What has brought this appalling danger upon our country? It requires no prophet nor philosopher to tell. The second-boy of ordinary intelligence knows the cause, and can give the reply. *It is the war which has been waged by the fanatics and demagogues of the North upon the domestic institutions of the South, culminating at last in the election of a President upon the avowed principle of hostility to the South.* It is the fruits of the crusade of Northern Abolitionism against Southern Slavery, carried on in violation of both the letter and spirit of the Constitutional compact under which both sections have agreed to live: That war has been waged in all forms insulting to the South, and subversive of her rights—by gross misrepresentation; by insulting invective; by invasions of her rights of property; by a violation of the express provisions of the Constitution in the form of State nullification of the Fugitive Slave Law; by refusing to the South an equal enjoyment of the common domain of the Republic; by actual invasion of the territory of a sovereign State and the murderer of its citizens. Of all this has the North been guilty. Without any right so to do, the people of the North, now constituting an actual majority, speaking through the fanatical priest and the political demagogue, have proclaimed their determination to extirpate, ultimately, an institution of the South—her system of organized labor, on which her prosperity depends—and, of course, to change her social system and her present form of civilization—to effect, indeed, in her institutions a more radical change than was effected between these States and the mother country by the American Revolution....

These are the causes of the crisis that has come upon us. Now what is the remedy? Within a few days we have heard that remedy suggested by the authors of the evil, which they think will be adequate, sufficient, and the rightful remedy. The thoughtless and guilty Black Republican imagines that coercion is the true remedy. Nothing but war and bloodshed suggests [*sic*] themselves to the brood of unthinking religious and political fanatics whose heedless and reckless conduct has brought this impending calamity upon their country. Send down an army and fight the South back into subjection. That is the remedy which they would apply to the portentous and appalling evil which they have brought upon their country....

In conclusion, we repeat, that the time has come when the conduct of the North, with respect to the institutions of the South, has got to be changed, totally and radically. The North must now cease her warfare upon the institutions of the South; acknowledge the equality of the South under our common constitution; acknowledge her claim to the equal protection of her property, of whatever nature it may be, in the common domain of the Union; recognize her constitution of society and her forms of civilization, whatever they may be, and respect them; or prepare for a disruption of the Republic. Forbearance and Justice alone can preserve the Union; not force and coercion.

Frederick Douglass, a former slave, well-known abolitionist, and editor of his own newspaper, did not express confidence that the new president would end slavery. But Douglass claimed the election was significant because it signaled the end of the South's domination in national affairs.

Douglass' Monthly, December 1860

Frederick Douglass: "The Late Election"

With the single exception of the question of slavery extension, Mr. Lincoln proposes no measure which can bring him into antagonistic collision with the traffickers in human flesh, either in the States or in the District of Columbia. The Union will, therefore, be saved simply because there is no cause in the election of Mr. Lincoln for its dissolution. Slavery will be safe, and safer, in the Union under such a President, than it can be under any President of a Southern Confederacy. This is our impression, and we deeply regret our facts from which it is derived.

The Northern people have elected against the opposition of the slaveholding South, a man for President who declared his opposition to the further extension of slavery over the soil belonging to the United States. Such is the head and front, and the full extent of the offense, for which "minute men" are forming, drums are beating, flags are flying, people are arming, "banks are closing," "stocks are falling," and the South generally taking on dreadfully.

What, then, has been gained to the anti-slavery cause by the election of Mr. Lincoln? Not much, in itself considered, but very much when viewed in the light of its relations and hearings. For fifty years the country has taken the law from the lips of an exacting, haughty and imperious slave oligarchy. The masters of slaves have been the masters of the Republic. Their authority was almost undisputed, and their power irresistible. They were the President makers of the Republic, and no aspirant dared to hope for success against their frown. Lincoln's election has vitiated their authority, and broken their power. It has taught the North its strength, and shown the South its weakness.

The Augusta Chronicle & Sentinel *acknowledged that Lincoln's election was a serious blow to the future of slavery. But the paper urged the South to carefully deliberate its future or risk igniting a civil war.*

Chronicle & Sentinel (Augusta, Ga.), 8 November 1860

An Anonymous Writer: "The Result"

We have met the enemy, and they have conquered. We do not yet know much of the details, nor have we much stomach for them. It is sufficient to know that Lincoln has carried nearly if not altogether the entire North, while the South is divided. And what does this election show? A triumph of sectionalism certainly, but is it a triumph also of antislavery fanaticism? It looks very much so, but still we must all know that besides anti-slavery there was another powerful element that came in to the aid of the Republican party. And that was undying hatred to Democracy, and it may be that hatred of Democracy had as much to do with it as hatred of slavery....

But now the question is, what shall be done? No one can doubt that there is a demoniac, fanatic, anti-slavery sentiment in the North which would, if it dared, put the heel of a numerical majority upon the necks of a Constitutional, law-abiding minority. No one can doubt that this spirit is manifest in the Republican party, is its life and soul and ruling power, but still it may be doubted, first whether this fanaticism is the thing uppermost in this election, and secondly whether this hell's own child can accomplish what it may desire, or even seriously jeopardy [*sic*] the interests, the security, the peace, of the eight millions of people inhabiting the fifteen slave States....

What shall be done? Well, in the first place, the times require that we should be perfectly cool, or as cool as we can be, and that we proceed in this business with due deliberation, putting aside rashness and passion as far as possible....Precipitate action now, or attempts at precipitate action, threaten to defeat the very end aimed at, to arouse our own selves against domestic tyranny and intolerance, to fire our own hearts with all manner of bitterness, and, instead of accomplishing a peaceable separation from the North, and the inauguration of a Southern Confederacy, to light the fire of civil and perhaps servile war around our own homes. Let men then be prudent and thoughtful—not rash and turbulent.

The Richmond Enquirer *said the North had declared war on the South by electing Lincoln president.*

Richmond Enquirer, 19 November 1860

An Anonymous Writer: "A Declaration of War"

The significant fact which menaces the South is not that Abraham Lincoln is elected President, but that the Northern people, by a sectional vote, have elected a President of the avowed purpose of aggression on Southern rights. The purpose of aggression has been declared. This is a *declaration of war.*

In light of Lincoln's election, the Charleston Mercury, *one of the most outspoken proponents of secession, said the time had come for South Carolina to leave the Union and form a Southern Confederacy.*

Charleston Mercury, 19 November 1860

An Anonymous Writer: Henceforth We Are Two People

[We] want no conference but in the Convention which will assemble to frame the Constitution, and complete the organization of a Southern Confederacy...The day for new guarantees is gone. Henceforth we are two peoples.

QUESTIONS

1. Do you think the *Pittsburgh Gazette* made a persuasive argument that the South must submit to the will of the majority? Explain.
2. Do you find the way *Cincinnati Times* repeatedly asked the question

"Why should we quarrel?" to be an effective editorial technique? Why or why not?

3. Do you think it was possible, as the *Chronicle & Sentinel* suggested, that the South could peacefully leave the Union? Explain.

4. Why would the *Richmond Enquirer* argue that Lincoln's election was a "declaration of war" against the South?

Notes

1. James M. McPherson, *Battle Cry of Freedom: The Civil War Era* (New York: Oxford University Press, 1988), 224.

2. J.G. Randall and David Donald, *The Civil War and Reconstruction*, 2nd ed. (Boston: Heath, 1961), 133.

CHAPTER 2

Southern States Secede, 1860–61

The idea of states being able to leave or secede from the Union rested on the constitutional doctrine of state sovereignty. Those who held the states' rights position maintained that the United States Constitution created a confederation of sovereign states. They believed individual states could leave the union by calling a special state convention and putting the matter to a vote. Opponents of this position believed the states had no legal right to leave the Union. They argued that the states had surrendered their sovereignty when they joined the Union. In their view, secession was an act of revolution against the United States.

The South had used the doctrine of states' rights to defend slavery since the Missouri crisis of 1819–20. Opponents of slavery attached a resolution to the bill granting statehood for Missouri, banning the future introduction of slaves. However, Southern leaders threatened to leave the Union if the bill passed. They forced a compromise in which Missouri was admitted as a slave state with no restrictions on the institution, and Maine was admitted as a free state. Slavery was prohibited in the remainder of the Louisiana Purchase territory north of latitude 36°30′, the Southern boundary of Missouri. During the 1830s, abolitionists burst onto the national scene determined to end the institution of slavery. Supporters of states' rights threatened secession again if slavery was not protected. Congress hammered out a compromise in 1850 that admitted California as a free state but strengthened the Fugitive Slave Act, designed to help slaveholders recover their escaped slaves.

The sectional crisis was renewed with passage of the Kansas-Nebraska Act passed by Congress in 1854. The act created two new territories—Kansas and Nebraska—while repealing the Missouri Compromise line. The question of whether the territories would be slave or free would be left to settlers to decide. Repealing the Missouri Compromise outraged many in the North who believed that the slave power in the South was trampling over constitutional rights and monopolizing the new territories for slavery. During this time, the Republican Party emerged, committed to preventing the spread of slavery in the territories.

South Carolina had long been one of the leaders of the secession movement. Despite vast inequalities in wealth between plantation owners and plain folk, South Carolina was more united on secession than was any other Southern state. The secession movement gained steam in 1860 with the Republican Party's nomination of Abraham Lincoln, an outspoken opponent of slavery. Following Lincoln's nomination, a group of Charleston secessionists formed the 1860 Association, which became a leading publisher of pamphlets calling for secession. After Lincoln's election in November, the South Carolina state legislature called a convention to consider secession. The 169 delegates gathered in Charleston amid scenes of fireworks, marching bands, and street rallies. On December 20, the delegates unanimously approved an ordinance making South Carolina the first state to leave the Union. By the end of the month, South Carolina troops seized the Federal Arsenal in Charleston and occupied all federal property in the area except Fort Sumter.

When South Carolina elected to secede, it was not clear what the other Southern states would do. A large group opposed to immediate secession argued that the South had to be united. Known as cooperationists, they believed the states should leave as a bloc. To thwart the cooperationists, supporters of immediate secession called for a convention to launch a provisional government for the Confederate States of America. The convention was scheduled to begin February 4, 1861, in Montgomery, Alabama. To meet the deadline, Mississippi, Florida, Alabama, Georgia, Louisiana, and Texas held conventions and approved ordinances of secession. In each state, cooperationists argued against any hasty moves and said the South should make last-ditch appeals to the Republican leadership. But the secessionists had momentum on their side as the vote of one state made it easier for the next to follow.

President James Buchanan and Congress did nothing to stem the tide of states leaving the Union. Buchanan, a lame-duck president who remained in office until Lincoln was sworn in on March 4, blamed Republicans for the crisis and decided to leave the problem for the new administration to settle. The House and Senate appointed committees to consider compromise measures to guarantee Southern rights and keep other states from leaving the Union.

The Crittenden Compromise, proposed by Senator John J. Crittenden of Kentucky, offered a series of six amendments to the Constitution. The plan would have protected slavery in states against future interference, prohibited slavery in states north of 36°30', and protected it south of the line in all territories "now held or hereafter acquired." Republicans opposed what they saw as a blank check for the future expansion of slavery, so on January 16, the Senate rejected the Crittenden Compromise by a vote of 25–23. Re-

CHARLESTON

MERCURY

EXTRA:

Passed unanimously at 1.15 o'clock, P. M. December 20th, 1860.

AN ORDINANCE

To dissolve the Union between the State of South Carolina and other States united with her under the compact entitled " The Constitution of the United States of America."

We, the People of the State of South Carolina, in Convention assembled, do declare and ordain, and it is hereby declared and ordained,

That the Ordinance adopted by us in Convention, on the twenty-third day of May, in the year of our Lord one thousand seven hundred and eighty-eight, whereby the Constitution of the United States of America was ratified, and also, all Acts and parts of Acts of the General Assembly of this State, ratifying amendments of the said Constitution, are hereby repealed; and that the union now subsisting between South Carolina and other States, under the name of " The United States of America," is hereby dissolved.

THE

UNION

IS

DISSOLVED!

Union Dissolved. *On December 20, 1860, South Carolina became the first state to leave the Union when the legislature approved an ordinance of secession. After the vote, the* Charleston Mercury *rushed out a one-page extra edition proclaiming the news. The* Mercury *had been a major supporter of the South seceding.*

publicans cast all 25 votes against the compromise. Fourteen senators from states that had left the Union or were about to secede did not vote.[1]

Although seven states had quickly left the Union, other Southern states labored over the question of what to do. The upper South, which did not depend on slavery in the same way as the so-called cotton states did, had blocs of Unionist voters who did not support secession. The legislatures in five states issued calls for secession conventions. But voters in Arkansas, Virginia, and Missouri elected a majority of delegates who favored staying in the Union. The electorate in North Carolina and Tennessee voted against holding a convention. When delegates to the Confederate convention met in Montgomery, they had high hopes for the new Confederate States of America. However, they also recognized that they needed the states of the upper South, especially Virginia, if the Confederacy was to have a real chance for survival.

This chapter begins with editorials on the constitutional question of whether or not states could legally secede from the Union. Editors on both sides disagreed on the question. South Carolina's decision to secede provoked a variety of reactions. Not surprisingly, the *Charleston Mercury*, one of the most outspoken advocates of a Southern Confederacy, hailed the decision. The *Daily Palladium* reacted angrily and said the North must quell the rebellion. South Carolina's decision forced other Southern states to confront the question of leaving the Union. In Tennessee, the *Memphis Avalanche* and the *Republican Banner* took different sides on the question. Newspapers also reacted variously to attempts at compromise, including the Crittenden Compromise.

CAN STATES SECEDE?

The Illinois State Journal *in Springfield said South Carolina's secession would not dissolve the Union.*

Illinois State Journal (Springfield), 20 December 1860

An Anonymous Writer: "The Union, It Must Be Preserved"

There are not a few who seem to think that the Union will be dissolved whenever the South Carolina Secession Convention passes a resolution to that effect. The Union cannot be dissolved by the passage of resolutions. South Carolina may resolve that she is no longer a part of this Union. She may hold secession meetings, mount disunion cockades, plant palmetto trees, make palmetto flags, trample under foot the glorious flag of our country, and proclaim from the housetops her treason and her shame, but all this will not dissolve the Union. She may compel her citizens to resign the official place held under the Federal Government—she may close her courts and post offices, and put her own people to a great deal of inconvenience and trouble, but she will be collected at her ports, and any resistance on her part will lead to war. At the close of that war we can tell with certainty whether she [is] in or out of the Union. While this Government endures there can be no disunion. If South Carolina does not obstruct the collection of the revenue at her ports nor violate any other Federal law, there will be no trouble, and she will not be out of the Union. If she violates the laws, then comes the tug of war. The President of the United States, in such an emergency, has a plain duty to perform. Buchanan may shirk it, or the emergency may not exist during his administration. If the overt act, on the part of South Carolina takes place on, or after the 1st of March, 1861, then the duty of executing the laws will devolve upon Mr. Lincoln. The laws of the United States must be executed—the President has no discretionary power on the subject—his duty is emphatically pronounced in the Constitution. Mr. Lincoln will perform that duty. Disunion, by armed force, is TREASON, and treason must and will be put down at all hazards. This Union is not, will not, and cannot be dissolved until this Government is overthrown by the traitors who have raised the disunion flag. Can they overthrow it? We think not. "They may disturb its peace—they may interrupt the course of its prosperity—they may cloud its reputation for stability—but its tranquility will be restored, its prosperity will return, and the stain upon its National character will be transferred and remain an eternal blot on the memory of those who caused the disorder." Let the secessionists understand—let the press proclaim it—let it fly on the wings of the lightning, and fall like a thunder bolt among those now plotting treason in Convention, that the Republican party, that the great North, aided by hundreds of thousands of patriotic men in the slave States, have determined to preserve the Union—peaceably if they can, forcibly if they must.

The South had support among some members of the Northern press. The Dubuque Herald *argued that states had a right to secede if the federal government failed to meets its needs.*

Dubuque (Iowa) Herald, 11 November 1860

An Anonymous Writer: "Can a State Constitutionally Secede?"

This is one of the questions of the day, and it appears to be no longer a mere abstract or theoretical question. The constitution makes no provision for secession. A Government is not a corporation whose existence is limited by a fixed period of time, nor does it provide a means for its own dissolution. The constitution of the United States provides that it may be amended, and prescribes how this may be done, but it does not, as it exists now, contemplate its own destruction, nor a dissolution of the Government of which it is the living evidence. Constitutionally, there can be no such thing as secession of a State from the Union.

But it does not follow that because a State cannot secede constitutionally, it is obliged under all circumstances to remain in the Union. There is a natural right, which is reserved by all men, and which cannot be given to any Government, and no Government can take it away. It is the natural right of a people to form a Government for their mutual protection, for the promotion of their mutual welfare, and for such other purposes as they may deem most conducive to their mutual happiness and prosperity; but if for any cause the Government so formed should become inimical to the rights and interests of the people, instead of affording protection to their persons and property, and securing the happiness and prosperity, to attain which it was established, it is the natural right of the people to change the Government regardless of Constitutions. For be it borne in mind, the Constitution is an agreement made among the people that the Government formed by it is to be just such a Government as it prescribes; that when it recognizes a right to exist, it must protect the person in the enjoyment of that right, and when it imposes a reciprocal duty upon a portion of the people, the performance of that duty it will have enforced. When a Government fails in any of these essential respects, it is not the Government the people intended it to be, and it is their right to modify or abolish it.

So, if the rights of the people of the United States, as recognized by the Constitution, are not secured to them by the Government, and the people of any State have no other means to redress their grievances except by separating themselves from their oppressors, it is their undoubted natural right to do so....

The New Orleans Bee *argued that the Union could not be saved "as long as slavery is looked upon by the North with abhorrence." The South must declare its independence, the paper argued.*

New Orleans Bee, 14 December 1860

An Anonymous Writer: "Vain Hopes"

The political charlatans of the North and the patriotic but mistaken public men of the border slave States appear to outvie each other in efforts to discover a remedy for existing evils. They do not perceive that the wound inflicted by the North upon the South is essentially incurable. They think, on the contrary, it may be plastered, and bandaged, and dressed in some sort of fashion and will do very well. The Union is broken in two, but the political doctors fancy that the ruptured extremities can be readily brought together, and that by the aid of the world-renowned "compromise" machine, the integrity of the fractured parts may be completely restored. Without further figure of speech, let us say that we hardly know whether to smile or sigh over the innumerable devices resorted to by members of Congress to save the Union. With just about as much hope of success might they expect to breathe life into a corpse, or look for green leaves, bright flowers, and savory fruit from the blackened and withered trunk of a blasted tree, as imagine that the Union may yet be preserved....

But the grand, overwhelming objection to these feeble and fruitless projects is the absolute impossibility of revolutionizing Northern opinion in relation to slavery. Without a change of heart, radical and thorough, all guarantees which might be offered are not worth the paper on which they would be inscribed. As long as slavery is looked upon by the North with abhorrence; as long as the South is regarded as a mere slave-breeding and slave-driving community; as long as false and pernicious theories are cherished respecting the inherent equality and rights of every human being, there can be no satisfactory political union between the two sections. If one-half the people believe the other half to be deeply dyed in iniquity; to be daily and hourly in the perpetration of the most atrocious moral offense, and at the same time knowing them to be their countrymen and fellow-citizens, conceive themselves authorized and in some sort constrained to lecture them, to abuse them, to employ all possible means to break up their institutions, and to take from them what the Northern half consider property unrighteously held, or no property at all, how can two such antagonistic nationalities dwell together in fraternal concord under the same government? Is not the thing clearly impossible? Has not the experiment been tried for more than seventy years, and have not the final results demonstrated its failure? The feelings, customs, mode of thought and education of the two sections, are discrepant and often antagonistic. The North and South are heterogeneous and are better apart. Were we foreign to the North, that section would treat us as our Government now treats Mexico or England—abstaining from interference in the internal policy of a country with which we have nothing to do, and with which we are at peace. As it is, we are persuaded that while the South continues a part of the American confederacy, there is no power which can prevent her progressive degradation, humiliation and spoliation by the victorious North. We are doomed if we proclaim not our political independence.

The Wilmington Herald *warned that South Carolina was trying to drag other Southern states into leaving the Union. It said the United States enjoyed many blessings as a nation.*

Wilmington (N.C) Herald, 9 November 1860

An Anonymous Writer: "A Few Reflections on Secession"

It is thought by some persons that a dismemberment of our government is imminent, and almost inevitable; others are more sanguine as to the result of our present difficulties, but all agree that there is some cause for apprehension....

We do not propose to argue the *right* of secession. The ablest statesmen of the country have differed about that, although the weight of authority is greatly against it; but, admitting the right, there are other considerations which a good man, an honest man and a true patriot cannot disregard. There are a great many so-called *rights,* incident both to the nations and to individuals, which it would be very unwise and impolitic to exercise. There is, too, a vast difference, sometimes, between a legal and a moral right. And it is to the moral and the economical aspect of secession we wish to look. Peaceable secession is an impossibility. The State that secedes must pass through a baptism of blood, in which the garments of her surrounding sisters will be freely dipped, although against their will. Self-defense, which is nature's first law, can alone justify such a course on the part of any State, and the necessity for self-defense does not exist. Any State that exercises the so called right of secession, *under any circumstances,* does it at the expense of her neighbors, and to that extent, inflicts upon them an injury; and this, when not done in self-defense, nothing can justify. This principle underlies all law human, and divine. And we are not begging the question in asserting that the necessity does not exist. The ostensible reason for secession, and indeed, the only reason given, is the election of Lincoln, and it is admitted that he is powerless to do harm to the South if he desired, inasmuch as he has neither judicial nor legislative power to aid him. To confess this, and attempt to avoid it by anticipating his *future* ability to do harm, is yielding the position entirely. And in involving other States in the consequences of secession, the injury is not confined to the loss of some blood. The foundations of government are broken up, nationality is destroyed, trade is ruined, the industrial pursuits of the country are stopped, and universal distress, and bankruptcy follow. Is there anything, even in Lincoln's election, to justify all this? It does seem as if our people are tempting the vengeance of God by the madness of their conduct, and their total disregard of the untold blessings he has poured upon us beyond all other people.

As a nation, we possess all the elements of greatness and power.

Peace smiles upon us from all quarters of the globe; a material prosperity, unparalleled in the annals of the world, surrounds us; our territory embraces almost the entire continent; we enjoy wide-spread intelligence, and universal plenty; we are happy, WE ARE FREE, and yet—degrading thought—there are those among us, who, regardless of all, would have us exchange these blessings for the expected benefits of a Southern Confederacy!

Are the enlightened and conservative people of North Carolina desirous of the change? Do they wish, will they *submit*, to be dragged into revolution and anarchy, and all to please the State of South Carolina, who, by her insufferable arrogance, and conceited self-importance, has been a constant source of annoyance and disquietude to the whole county, North and South, for the last thirty years? Will our people so far forget their independence, and their manhood, as blindly to follow the lead of that State into civil war? Where is the fraternal bond between us? Is it to be seen in the self-sufficiency and offensive air of superiority, which the people of that State have ever exhibited towards the people of this, in all their intercourse, of every kind, with us? We say unhesitatingly, that there are no two adjoining States in the Union, whose people have so little community of feeling as North and South Carolina; and no one State that owes less to another than the former to the latter—but our people are charitable and generous to a fault, and in this is our danger, and against this *we* intend to struggle.

SOUTH CAROLINA SECEDES

The Charleston Mercury *hailed the news of South Carolina's secession, saying the state would "establish for herself and for her posterity, her rights, her liberties and her institutions."*

Charleston Mercury, 21 December 1860

An Anonymous Writer: "The 20th Day of December in the Year of Our Lord, 1860"

Inscribed among the calends of the world—memorable in time to come—the 20th day of December, in the year of our Lord 1860, has become an epoch in the history of the human race. A great Confederated Republic, overwrought with arrogant and tyrannous oppressions, has fallen from its high estate amongst the nations of the earth. Conservative liberty has been vindicated. Mobocratic license has been stricken down. Order has conquered, yet liberty has survived. *Right* has raised his banner aloft, and bidden defiance to *Might*. The problem of self-government under the check-balance of slavery, has secured itself from threatened destruction.

South Carolina has resumed her entire sovereign powers, and, unshackled, has become one of the nations of the earth....

The State of South Carolina has recorded herself before the universe. In reverence before God, fearless of man, unawed by power, unterrified by clamor, she has cut the Gordian knot of colonial dependence and her dignity before the world. Prescribing to none, she will be dictated to by none; willing for peace, she is ready for war. Deprecating blood, she is willing to shed it. Valuing her liberties, she will maintain them. Neither swerved by frowns of foes, nor swayed by timorous solicitations of friends, she will pursue her direct path, and establish for herself and for her posterity, her rights, her liberties and her institutions. Though friends may fail her in her need, though the cannon of her enemies may belch destruction among her people, South Carolina, unawed, unconquerable, will still hold aloft her flag, "ANIMIS OPTBUSQUE PARATI."

The Review in Charlottesville, Virginia, argued that the South had no right to secede. South Carolina had initiated "revolution and anarchy" by leaving the Union. But the paper said Virginia probably would be forced to join South Carolina or risk humiliation.

The Review (Charlottesville, Va.), 4 January 1861

An Anonymous Writer: "Coercion"

We are among those who believe that the United States is a government, and not a league. We regard the Constitution as a fundamental national law, and not as a treaty. We consider that we are citizens of the United States, and owe an allegiance to the Federal Government. Any resistance to the Federal authority we regard as rebellion.

We moreover love the United States. We revere that magnificent government which, formed with so much difficulty, and by so many compromises, has thrown over us its shield for seventy years, and raised us to our present dominion and greatness. It is to us the palladium of civil liberty at home, and in the world. We do not regard the Union as having been oppressive to one section or the other. We do not regard the South or the North as having dominated over the other section, or taken to itself the main benefits of the Confederation. The influence of the National Government seems to us in nearly all things to have been beneficent and enabling to all the States of the Union. So far from considering that an irreconcilable conflict exists between the sections of the country, we esteem the welfare of each to be bound up with that of the other, and the interests to be co-ordinate and conjunctive....

So important do we regard the Union, so much do we cherish it, that the pulling down of its splendid columns is to us like the fall of the paternal walls and roof, and the demolition of all the most endearing emblems of home. We know that we shall never find any other such country. We know that we shall never see any other such flag. We know we shall never stand up as proudly and as exultant under any other nationality....

Even as the matter stands, we entertain towards South Carolina the most bitter resentment. We feel that she has not only precipitately thrown down the bulwarks of the Union, and inaugurated on her own responsibility revolution and anarchy; but she has done so with the full knowledge—aye the intention—to hold Virginia and the border States between her and the Storm, and to carry out her caprices, regardless of these border States, while relying on them.

But—however it has been done—an issue has been made. The subjection of South Carolina or any seceding State, in consequence of their determination not to submit to the policy of the Republicans, is a blow at the entire South—subjection to all. We are, thenceforth, humiliated. We are conquered. We could not hold up our heads in that Union any more. We would meet a Northern man as the Saxon met the Norman....

For the Pittsburgh Daily Post, *South Carolina's secession was "a dark day," but the paper maintained that bloodshed could still be avoided.*

Daily Post (Pittsburgh, Pa.), 20 December 1860

An Anonymous Writer: "South Carolina Has Seceded"

We are no longer one people. The black day in the history of our country has come when a partner in the compact has broken it in sunder.

We regret this action on the part of South Carolina. We regard it as hasty and inconsiderate....

It is a dark day for the country—but in any event we say: "Put away the sword." States may be saved without it.

The New Haven Daily Palladium *said South Carolina and other Southern states had declared war on the United States through their seizure of various forts and arsenals. The country was "on trial" for its life, the paper argued, and government must take swift action to quell the rebellion.*

Daily Palladium (New Haven, Conn.), 11 January 1861

An Anonymous Writer: "Law or No Law"

The cotton States have drawn the sword against the Union, the Constitution and the Law. They cut short all consultation; they strike the first blow; they seize the property of the Union, garrison its forts against the officers of law, take possession of its revenue-cutters, rifle its arsenals to arm their forces against its authority, gather armies to seize the Federal capitol its public buildings add its archives, and fire upon the national troops while peacefully obeying orders. This is not secession; it is not dissolution; *it is rebellion and aggressive war!* ...

One issue confronts us: Shall the majority of Law and the authority of government be vindicated, or have we mob-law and anarchy? Compromise with treason is treason itself. Nothing can be done until the sword of treason is sheathed and the sanctity of law acknowledged. Are rebels to seize the United States arsenals and forts with impunity? Then what protects the country against a rebellion every month? Is there no power in all the land to enforce the laws and quell treason? Then what power is there to carry into execution any scheme of conciliation. If any faction or State or section may remedy a defeat at the ballot-box by an appeal to force, and beat down the authority of law by arms, any other may do the same....

With rebel armies making war upon the United States it is no time to be talking about fugitive slave laws or personal liberty bills, party platforms or constitutional amendments. The very government is on trial for life. The new issue is not our making. The people of the North, of whatever party, were anxious to settle all differences in a peaceful and law-abiding way, and were willing to submit quietly to the lawful decision. The traitors of the cotton States have precipitated the new issue upon us. So long as they presented requests, however intemperately, and passed resolutions, however passionately, so long as they talked of peaceable secession and sent commissioners to arrange and arbitrate, we could consult with calmness and offer the olive branch with dignity. But when they take arms to inaugurate in this country a Mexican revolution, when they make war upon the United States, and organize forces to seize upon the Federal Capital, they leave us no alternative, and every honest man of the North will answer: The Constitution shall be obeyed! [T]he flag of our country shall be respected! [T]he laws shall be enforced!

SECESSION DEBATED ELSEWHERE

As the debate over whether or not Tennessee would secede dragged on, the Memphis Avalanche *became impatient. It said the state's leaders should act immediately to pass an ordinance of secession.*

Memphis Avalanche, 1 May 1861

An Anonymous Writer: "People Are Getting Impatient"

How long will Tennessee remain in Abe Lincoln's Union? Our people are getting impatient. The legislature has been in session nearly a week, and the Ordinance of Secession has not passed!...To see Tennessee out of the Union is now the acme of our ambition. For these long many years, amid abuse and slander, we have labored and toiled for this great object; and when it shall have been attained, we expect to experience emotions akin to those which filled the bosom of Columbus when he discovered the land for which his weary being had so long yearned.

Tennessee was one of the states that labored over the question of whether or not to leave the Union. The conservative Republican Banner *argued that staying in the Union was the only way to ensure that slavery would survive.*

Republican Banner (Nashville, Tenn.), 26 January 1861

An Anonymous Writer: "Disunion the Doom of Slavery"

Those who are plotting the disruption of this Government and the establishment of a Southern Confederacy, claim to be the only true friends of the South and its institutions. Those who are for maintaining the Government are denounced as Republicans, abolitionists, &c. Any man with half a man's reasoning power can see that the friends of the existing Government are the only true friends of slavery. The prosperity of the South—its wealth and refinement—has resulted from the existence of the institution of slavery—and that institution has depended mainly for its existence upon the protection afforded it by the Constitution, which has bound the free States of the Confederacy as well as the slave to its maintenance. No other government in the world has been able to sustain slavery so successfully as this—none, indeed, to sustain it at all. The constitutional supports of seventeen free States, united with fifteen slave states, and forming one of the first powers of the earth, has extended over this institution a protection which has kept the anti-slavery sentiment of the whole world at bay, as far as any practical interference jeopardizing our safety is concerned. But how will it be after the present government is dissolved, and the Northern States are absolved from their Constitutional obligations, and instead of being parties to the maintenance of slavery, as they are under the Constitution, become its open and avowed enemies, not in the abstract, but practically, and as a republic? It is clear to be seen that the South will be greatly and fatally weakened, and the doom of slavery irrevocably fixed.

THE CRITTENDEN COMPROMISE

The New-York Tribune *argued against the Crittenden Compromise, saying the Union should "stand by" the Constitution. As he often did, editor Horace Greeley wrote his editorial in the form of a letter to Senator Crittenden.*

New-York Tribune, 7 January 1861

Horace Greeley: "The Attitude of the North"

To the Hon. John J. Crittenden, *U.S. Senate:*

Dear Sir: The People of the Free States observe and appreciate your efforts to reconcile what are improperly termed "sectional" differences and maintain the integrity of the Union. They do not doubt your sincerity nor your patriotism. They realize that, even when you most wronged yourself in upholding the policy embodied in Nebraska bill and the consequent dragooning of the free settlers of Kansas with intent to bend their necks to the yoke of Slavery, you yielded to a local ignorance and prejudice which you could not control, and which, because you would not minister unreservedly to its wild exactions, has consigned you to private life after the 4th of March next. They make due allowance for the ferocity of the Pro-Slavery fanaticism which has thus ostracized you, and leniently judge that, though a bolder man might have done better, an average man would have done worse, and they are not ungrateful for your honest and earnest efforts to save the Union from disruption and the country from the horrors of civil war. They feel sure that, were the People of the Slave States in the average, as enlightened and as just as you are, the dangers now impeding might be dispelled or averted. Nevertheless, they do not and will not assent to the Compromise proposed by you—that is a fixed fact. Here and there one who never shared their convictions, but only some high office, or who owns real estate in Washington City and feels that it is likely to be ruined by the Disunion, or who has a great Railroad contract in Missouri or some other Slave State, and may be broken by the depreciation of that State's bonds, or who is a lame duck in the Stock Market and hopes to win back all he has lost and more with it if a Compromise can be fixed up, may accede to your project or to something equivalent; but ninety-nine of every hundred Republicans are opposed to any such bargain, and will not be concluded by it if made. Moreover, thousands of Democrats and of Conservatives who stood with you on the platform of "The Union, the Constitution, and the enforcement of the Laws," are also opposed to any such arrangement while the Federal authority is defied and the Union threatened with subversion....

Mr. Crittenden! the People of the Free States, with every respect for you, propose to stand by the Constitution as it is; to respect the rightful authorities, State and Federal; to let Congress enact such laws as to the majority shall seem good; and to back the Executive in enforcing those laws and maintaining the integrity of the Union. For whatever troubles may impend or arise, those who conspire and rebel are justly responsible; if they would submit when beaten, as we do, there would be unbroken peace and prosperity.... In any case, allow me with deference to suggest that your proper place is with those who, whether in or out of power, defer to rightfully constituted Government and uphold the majesty of Law.

Yours,
Horace Greeley
New-York, Jan. 7, 1861.

The New Orleans Bee *supported the Crittenden Compromise, arguing that it offered something to both the South and North. The paper maintained that despite the claims of Republicans, many people in the North supported the compromise.*

New Orleans Bee (reprinted in **Republican Banner** [Nashville, Tenn.]), 25 January 1861

An Anonymous Writer: Crittenden Compromise

Of the various plans of adjustment called forth by the crisis, that of Mr. Crittenden is the only one that seems fully inspired by a sense of justice. It offers something tangible—something which the South could and probably would agree to take into consideration, and which the North, or that portion of it which boasts its nationality, might accept without the smallest sacrifice of dignity or right. Mr. Crittenden himself entertains such entire confidence in the validity or his scheme of settlement that he is anxious to submit it to the ordeal of popular suffrage. Now, the Black Republicans boast that the people of the North are with them. We believe that with the possible exception of a few of the New England States, there is not a non-slaveholding Commonwealth of which the people would not accept the Crittenden amendments by an overwhelming majority. Give them but a chance to do so, and our firm conviction is that they would record a sentence of condemnation against Black Republicanism such as it has never yet received.

QUESTIONS

1. Do you agree with the argument of Southern states that they had a right to leave the Union? Support your answer.
2. How would you describe the writing style of the *Charleston Mercury* in its editorial after South Carolina voted to secede from the Union?
3. Do you find Horace Greeley's practice of writing editorials in the form of a letter, as he did to Senator John Crittenden, to be effective? Why or why not?

NOTE

1. Kenneth M. Stampp, *And the War Came: The North and the Secession Crisis: 1860–1861* (Baton Rouge: Louisiana State University Press, 1950).

CHAPTER 3

Confederacy Takes Shape, 1861

D elegates from the first seven states to secede from the Union gathered in Montgomery, Alabama, on February 4 to launch the Confederate States of America. Montgomery was chosen as the first capital of the Confederacy because of its central location among the seceded states as well as its excellent transportation facilities. A prosperous town of about 9,000 residents, Montgomery had served as the capital of Alabama since 1849 and so had experience being the seat of government.

The seven states represented (South Carolina, Georgia, Florida, Alabama, Mississippi, Louisiana, and Texas) were allowed the same number of representatives as their delegation in the United States Congress. Selected by the secession conventions in their respective states, the 37 men who served in Montgomery constituted a cross-section of the South's political leadership. They included both Democrats and Whigs, and about half were Unionists who had opposed secession. The delegates held their deliberations in secret. Despite protests from the press, the delegates wanted to present a unified front and minimize reports of disagreement. After electing former Georgia Governor Howell Cobb as president of the convention, the delegates quickly drafted a provisional constitution and turned themselves into a provisional congress for the new government.

One of the first tasks of the Congress was to write a constitution for the Confederate States of America. Wanting to reassure their friends of the essential conservatism of the Confederacy, members chose to copy most of the constitution verbatim from the United States Constitution. Delegates believed that the framers had written a worthy constitution but that the North had since made a mockery of the revered document. The Confederate Constitution had significant differences, however. The preamble omitted the phrase "a more perfect Union" and added a clause after "We, the people": "each state acting in its sovereign and independent character." The confederate constitution called a slave a slave, avoiding the roundabout language on the subject found in the U.S. Constitution. It also protected slavery in the states and any territories that might be acquired. But the constitution prohibited importing slaves from abroad. This was done largely to avoid alienating the upper South, which had a major economic stake in the interstate slave trade.

The constitution allowed the president a single-item veto of appropriation bills. It limited the Confederate president to a single six-year term in office. The Confederate Constitution established the departments of State, Treasury, Justice, War, Navy, and Post Office. Their functions generally mirrored those of the U.S. department they were patterned after. In fact, the new postal service simply succeeded the old service without a break, as employees of the U.S. Post Office became employees of the Confederate government overnight.[1]

After approving the provisional constitution, the convention turned to the task of electing the president and vice-president of the Confederacy. Although there were several qualified candidates, including radical secessionists such as William Lowndes Yancey and Robert Barnwell Rhett, Sr., the name most often mentioned by the members was Jefferson Davis of Mississippi. Davis seemed ideally qualified for the presidency. A graduate of West Point, he had military experience, having served with distinction in the Mexican War. He was a Democrat who had served as a United States congressman and senator, as well as in the cabinet as secretary of war. He was a moderate Southerner and, as such, was acceptable to the pro-secession states in the upper South that the convention was trying to convince to join the Confederacy. To appease Georgia, which was the most populous state in the Deep South, convention delegates elected Alexander H. Stephens as vice president. A conservative congressman from Georgia, Stephens had initially opposed secession, but delegates believed he could attract his fellow Unionists in states still considering secession.

Davis arrived in Montgomery on February 16. The outspoken fire-eater, Yancey, introduced the new president to a cheering crowd, declaring, "The man and the hour have met." Two days later, an estimated 10,000 people watched as Davis was inaugurated provisional president of the Confederacy. In his address, Davis drew parallels between the South's rebellion against the North with the American revolt against England. Seeking to allay fears, he spent much of his speech arguing that little had changed in the South after secession. "We have changed the constituent parts, but not the system of our Government," he declared.[2]

After the inauguration, the convention drafted a permanent constitution. Many of the basic changes delegates made to the U.S. Constitution remained in the permanent Confederate Constitution. Ironically, the Confederate Constitution was not the radical document that might have been expected from states in rebellion. The permanent constitution called for much the same kind of government Southerners had left.[3] In its remaining days in Montgomery, the provisional Congress also selected the Stars and Bars as the national flag for the Confederacy; dispatched commissioners to foreign countries to seek recognition of the new government; created an army, authorizing the recruitment of 100,000 troops to serve either six-month or one-year enlistments; and authorized issuing $15 million worth of Treasury bonds to finance the Confederate government.

One of the final acts of the Montgomery convention was debating whether to move the Confederate capital. Delegates had not been happy about Montgomery's limited hotel accommodations and lack of office space. As a larger city, Richmond, Virginia, also could offer many of the amenities that Montgomery could not. So before adjourning on May 21, Congress elected to make Richmond the new capital of the Confederacy.

The organization of the Confederate government produced a great deal of editorial debate. The *Memphis Appeal* sought to contrast the harmony of Confederate leaders with the divisions evident in the North. At the same time, the *Chicago Tribune* argued, Davis faced a host of difficulties in organizing the new government. The election of Davis as Confederate president sparked many editorials in the North and South. The *Montgomery Advertiser* hailed the selection of Davis, but the *Evening Post* disputed the president's comparison of Southerners to American revolutionaries. Discussions over moving the Confederate capital led many editors to chime in, some suggesting their hometowns. Not surprisingly, the *Richmond Examiner* said the Virginia capital would make an ideal seat of government.

CONFEDERATE GOVERNMENT ORGANIZED

The Memphis Appeal *contrasted the first days of the convention, which proceeded harmoniously, with the divisiveness that seemed to be plaguing the Union.*

Memphis Appeal, 17 February 1861

An Anonymous Writer: "The Contrast"

While such hostile hearing and deadly feuds mark the legislative assembly of the Northern Confederacy, it is cheering to the lovers of free and liberal government throughout the world and more especially to American pa-triots, to turn to the Congress of the Confederate States of America at Mont-gomery. No discordant elements of character; no diversities inculcated by education; no prejudices instilled by religious fanaticism....

The Chicago Tribune *maintained that Jefferson Davis faced a host of dif-ficulties in organizing a new government.*

Chicago Tribune, 14 February 1861

An Anonymous Writer: "Jeff. Davis and His Chances"

Now that a Southern Confederacy has been established on paper, we may reasonably look for some "regular business" on the part of the guerrilla bands which have been hitherto snarling at Fort Sumter, running away from Fort Pickens...seizing unarmed vessels, pilfering the mails and erecting bat-teries on the Mississippi. Mr. Jefferson Davis, the principal Tycoon of the new government, is a man who understands the value of *order*. It will occur to him as chief magistrate of the moot confederacy, that this random bush-whacking will not answer the purpose of "forming a more perfect union, es-tablishing justice, ensuring domestic tranquility, providing the general welfare," etc. Mr. Davis understands perfectly that a strong government is the prime necessity in his new establishment, and that without discipline, system, obedience and the et ceteras of a strong government, his fabric will go to pieces after the Mexican fashion, in less than six months, it its own rot-tenness. But there are many difficulties in the way of restoring order in so complete a chaos as that now pervading the seceding States. We refer not to those outside difficulties which may prove insurmountable, but to the inter-nal and inherent difficulties of his situation....

An immediate and unfavorable difficulty is to be found in the state of af-fairs around Fort Sumter. If, as reported, the constitution of the United States has been adopted by the Montgomery Convention, Mr. Davis is a commander-in-chief of the army and navy (?), and the war-making power is lodged in the hands of the Congress. South Carolina can no longer declare war, nor can Gov. Pickens direct any attacks to be made upon Major Ander-son, nor can Gov. Brown seize any more vessels in the harbor of Savannah, nor can the Mobile militia any longer garrison Fort Morgan, nor can Louisiana keep possessions of the $870,000 which she has recently stolen, nor can Florida retain the Navy Yard at Pensacola. In short, all these mad-caps must put their fingers in their mouths and go about their own decent and indecent avocations. Will they do so? We shall watch the several steps in this interesting process with satisfaction. After Mr. Davis shall have "ensured domestic tranquility," he will have a small bill to settle with the United States of America.

JEFFERSON DAVIS ELECTED PRESIDENT

The Montgomery Advertiser *thrilled at the sight of the city decked out for the inauguration of President Davis.*

Montgomery Advertiser, 19 February 1861

An Anonymous Writer: "The Inauguration"

Never did Montgomery present such an appearance as on yesterday.... [T]he streets, dwellings, and Capitol hill were literally thronged with visitors....[T]he assemblage could not have numbered less than ten thousand persons all animated by a common desire to maintain the dignity, honor, and independence of the Confederate States. If the people of the North could only have witnessed the high resolve which animated every heart in Montgomery on yesterday, we would fain believe they would be struck with amazement and indignation at the monstrous delusion which has been practiced upon their credulity by Northern presses and politicians, who have told them that this flood tide of secession is the movement of sectional aspirants, and not of the people....

No man, not even Gen. Washington, was ever called to preside over a people with more general acclamation and confidence than Gen. Davis. His past service and spotless private and public character are the surest guarantees that he will not disappoint the just expectations of the country.

Virginia was debating whether or not to secede when Jefferson Davis was inaugurated president of the Confederacy. The Richmond Enquirer *laid out the daunting tasks facing the new chief executive.*

Richmond Enquirer, 19 February 1861

An Anonymous Writer: "The Confederated States of America"

[T]he first great weight of responsibility now rests upon one man—the man who wields the whole Executive power of the new Confederate Government, and whose urgent recommendation on matters of immediate and serious necessity may be presumed to command a controlling influence, almost imperative, over the deliberations of the Confederate Congress. Jefferson Davis is now called upon to exercise the highest and broadest reach of those varied qualifications which he is reputed to possess. As a legislator, his is not the ordinary task of merely regulating the machinery of Government. He finds that machinery yet incomplete. He must complete it. He finds that machinery at a stand still. He must put it in motion. As Chief Executive, he must not only direct Administration, but must first organize and appoint an entire body of Executive and Administrative officials. As Commander-in-chief of the military and naval forces, he must organize an army and navy with the shortest possible delay, and at once dispose every arm of defence in the manner to protect a large Territory already invaded, and every foot of whose borders is already menaced with further invasion.

The Burlington Free Press *said the Confederate president defied logic in his inaugural address by claiming the states were within their constitutional rights to secede from the Union.*

Burlington (Vt.) Free Press, 20 February 1861

An Anonymous Writer: Marvel of Impudence

Jefferson Davis' inaugural speech at Montgomery, Ala., Feb. 18, is a marvel of impudence. He says the action of the Convention which declared the seceding States free of the U.S. Government, was in every respect regular and constitutional, and that "it is by the abuse of language that their act has been denominated revolution." They are anxious to cultivate peaceful relations with all, he says, but are ready to maintain their position of a new Confederacy with the sword, if need be....He says, "we have changed the constituent parts but not the system of our Government. The Constitution formed by our fathers is that of the confederated States"—from which the inference is plain, that if they, the *minority*, could only have been allowed to rule over the *majority* of the Nation, there would have been no call for the new Confederacy.

The Evening Post *was outraged that Davis would compare the secession of Southern states to the American Revolution. The South's goal, the newspa-*

per claimed, was "not to unloose any chains from anybody's limbs, but to rivet them the firmer on a poor, helpless and despised race."

Evening Post (New York), 18 February 1861

An Anonymous Writer: "The Two Presidents"

It is a libel upon the whole character and conduct of the men of '76 to compare their proceedings with those of the seceders. They rejected the supremacy of Great Britain, but they did so because that supremacy was exerted illegally for their oppression. They revolted in order to establish the rights of man. The motives which actuated them, and the principles they established, were the motives and principles of universal liberty. Their deed resounded throughout the world as one of the grand deeds of history. All men of noble hearts and generous impulses all over the globe, hailed it not only as the emancipation of a few struggling colonies, or of a race, but as the death note of despotism everywhere. Time has confirmed that verdict, and mankind rejoices to acknowledge the American patriots as benefactors of all their kind.

The government they established, as the result of the revolution they won, was a liberal government in every feature. It secured on the eternal basis of order the eternal principles of human freedom. Ever since it went into operation its effects have been beneficent. No citizen under it has ever had reason to complain of it; no foreign nation has ever been plundered or wronged by it; and the friends of liberty have always made it their model in the formation of new and free communities.

But it is against this wise, this upright, this inoffensive, this beneficent government that the southern rebels have taken their stand. They have done it, not in the interest of general humanity, but of a domestic despotism. Their end is not to unloose any chains from anybody's limbs, but to rivet them the firmer on a poor, helpless and despised race. Their motto is not liberty, but slavery. Their scheme is, not to extend the principles of popular government, but to build up a vast slaveholding military tyranny. Throughout the world, their conduct excites no approval, but provokes rather odium and disgrace. No nation will ever hail them as benefactors, no individual of a long posterity ever rise up to call them blessed.

When Mr. Davis, then, compares his position with that of the fathers of the republic, he either wilfully falsifies history, or is made insane by a rotten conceit. He and his confederates are no more like Washington and his compeers than a Chimpanzee stealing an African baby is like Columbus discovering a new continent. We wonder, while he spoke, that the ghosts of those illustrious men did not cry shame from their graves.

CONFEDERATE CAPITAL MOVES

When word got out that the Confederate government was considering moving the capital, many editors suggested their towns would make excellent seats of government. Among these was the editor of the Upson County Pilot *in Thomaston, Georgia, who emphasized his small town's virtues.*

*Upson County (Ga.) Pilot***, 16 February 1861**

An Anonymous Writer: "New Seat of Government"

We have a fine climate, a productive country, and a virtuous and intelligent population....[W]e can supply all of the officers of the government with old bacon and fresh greens and a cigar and a bottle of old Bourbon or Trice's Best on Saturday nights.

During the debate over moving the Confederate capital, the Richmond Examiner *said there were many reasons why the city made sense, chief among these that the president could direct the military better from Virginia.*

Richmond Examiner, **18 May 1861**

An Anonymous Writer: "The President Should Be in Virginia"

When the permanent location of the Southern capital comes to be determined upon, there are many reasons to be urged why Richmond, or some point near the Atlantic seaboard, should be preferred to the remotely inland town of Montgomery. But that question is not now before the public. The question is, where ought the President of the South to be at this juncture of affairs; for where he is there must be the Government. It is obvious that he ought to be in Virginia, and ought not to be in Alabama; not merely because he, an accomplished and able military chieftain, can direct affairs with more efficiency here than from so remote a distance, but because his presence here would speak a language to friend and foe more potential than many brigades.

QUESTIONS

1. Did you think the *Memphis Appeal* made a convincing argument in contrasting the harmonious start of the Confederate government with the divisions plaguing the Union? Explain.
2. Why would Jefferson Davis seek to draw parallels between what the Southerners were doing and what their revolutionary forefathers had done?
3. Do you think the *Evening Post* effectively rebutted Davis's claims in its editorial? What were its main points against his claims?

NOTES

1. Charles Robert Lee, Jr., *The Confederate Constitutions* (Chapel Hill: University of North Carolina Press, 1963).

2. Ibid., 66.

3. Emory M. Thomas, *The Confederate Nation, 1861–1865* (New York: Harper & Row, 1979), 62–65.

CHAPTER 4

Attack on Fort Sumter, 1861

The Southern states that left the Union seized most of the United States government property within their borders soon after they seceded. However, a few coastal forts in the South remained under Federal control. The most conspicuous of these was Fort Sumter, which guarded the harbor of Charleston, South Carolina. Fort Sumter stood on a man-made island at the entrance to the harbor. A pentagon, with brick walls 40 feet high and 8 to 12 feet thick, the fort still was under construction in 1860. The U.S. Army garrison assigned to Charleston Harbor was headquartered at nearby Fort Moultrie and had been threatened by South Carolinians repeatedly since the state left the Union in December. Having declared their independence, South Carolinians resented the presence of what they considered a foreign flag.

Major Robert Anderson, a native of Kentucky who had owned slaves, commanded the garrison. Although he sympathized with the South, Anderson remained loyal to the country he had served for 35 years as a member of the U.S. Army. With his garrison increasingly threatened by South Carolina, Anderson began quietly making plans to abandon Fort Moultrie, which was virtually indefensible by land, and move to Fort Sumter. On the evening of December 26, Anderson assembled his men without notice, loaded them onto boats, and they rowed to Fort Sumter. There they joined the construction workers, and together the 128 men began fortifying their position.

Anderson's move outraged authorities in South Carolina who viewed it as an act of aggression by the U.S. government. Governor Francis Pickens, who had moved the state government to Charleston, immediately demanded the fort's surrender. The major refused and requested help. The administration of President James Buchanan, in its last days in office, wanted to avoid fighting at all costs and dispatched an unarmed merchant ship, the *Star of the West,* with reinforcements and supplies for the garrison. But when the *Star of the West* arrived in Charleston Harbor on January 9 prominently flying the U.S. flag, South Carolina shore batteries fired on the ship, forcing it to turn around. Anderson's men wanted to return fire, but the major, under orders to remain on the defensive, refused.[1]

Both sides wanted to avoid a war, but the situation at Fort Sumter was rapidly reaching an impasse. The provisional Confederate Congress meeting in Montgomery resolved that immediate steps must be taken to gain posses- sion of the Southern forts either by negotiation or force. Confederate Presi- dent Jefferson Davis tried to negotiate the transfer of Fort Sumter to the new government, but at the same time he ordered General Pierre G.T. Beaure- gard to take command of the forces at Charleston. Ironically, Beauregard had been one of Anderson's artillery students at West Point. Beauregard set about strengthening the harbor's defenses and the guns facing Fort Sumter.

By early March, the garrison at Fort Sumter was running dangerously short on supplies. The new administration of President Abraham Lincoln faced a political dilemma. It could use force to resupply the fort and risk starting a war. Such a move would likely divide the North and unite the South, including pivotal states in the upper South that had not yet seceded. Or, the administration could surrender the fort and prolong peace. But that would be an implicit acknowledgement of Confederate independence and anger many in the Republican Party.[2]

Most of the president's advisers recommended abandoning the fort. But after deliberating for several weeks, Lincoln decided on another plan. He publicly announced that he would resupply the garrison in Fort Sumter but not reinforce it. The supply ships would enter Charleston Harbor peace- fully. If Confederate forces fired upon the unarmed ships, they would be the aggressors, and the president reasoned that the North would unite behind his administration. Davis also was under pressure to take action. Unwilling to allow the symbol of Federal authority in Charleston any longer, the Con- federate president ordered Beauregard to prevent the fort from being sup- plied.

On April 11, Beauregard sent three men to Fort Sumter to demand its surrender. After polling his officers, who unanimously opposed surrender, Anderson refused. Soon after midnight, Beauregard sent Anderson an ulti- matum: surrender or be attacked. When the major refused again, Confeder- ate cannons opened fire at 4:30 A.M. on April 12. This time the Fort Sumter garrison fired back, and for almost 40 hours the two sides battled while res- idents of Charleston watched the progress of the fighting from rooftops and the city's battery. Anderson and his men received no help from U.S. ships, which stood helplessly offshore. The superior Confederate firepower bat- tered the fort's walls and set the barracks on fire. At seven o'clock on the evening of April 13, Anderson sent word that he was surrendering the fort. The next morning, the U.S. garrison paraded around the fort and lowered the United States flag. When cannons fired a salute, a gun burst, killing one Union soldier and mortally wounding another, the first casualties of the fighting. Later, with the governor of South Carolina looking on, Southern troops proudly raised the new Confederate flag over Fort Sumter. The Civil War had begun.[3]

This chapter follows editorial debate during the period between Major Anderson moving the U.S. garrison to Fort Sumter and the Confederate attack on the fort. It begins with editorials about the dilemma of what the Union and Confederacy should do about Fort Sumter now that U.S. troops occupied it. The *Star of the West* incident prompted a new round of editorials from newspapers in the North and South.

When the dilemma of what to do about Fort Sumter was being discussed by the Lincoln and Davis administrations, editors expressed their varied opinions. Of course, the Confederacy's attack on Fort Sumter prompted a flood of editorials in newspapers, North and South. Editors generally supported their governments, although those who had been critical in the past tempered their support. The *Knoxville Whig*, for one, blamed both sides for the fighting.

WHAT TO DO ABOUT FORT SUMTER

When news of the garrison's move to Fort Sumter became known, Anderson was hailed as a hero in the North. The Chicago Tribune *said Anderson deserved the nation's gratitude for his patriotism.*

Chicago Tribune, 14 January 1861

An Anonymous Writer: "Major Anderson"

The march of events since the 26th of December, when Major Anderson eloped with his little command from Forth Moultrie to Fort Sumter, has brought with it not merely a nation's gratitude for the patriotism of the man, but a nation's admiration for the genius which conceived and the decision which executed the act. While the public fortress, ungarrisoned and fenceless, are falling into the hands of the enemies of the United States from North Carolina to Texas, the strongest of them all still bears aloft the national colors and frowns destruction upon the very head and front of the general Treason.

The Charleston Mercury *blamed Anderson for opening war by transferring the garrison to Fort Sumter.*

Charleston Mercury, 28 December 1860

An Anonymous Writer: "Major Anderson"

Maj. Robert Anderson, U.S.A., has achieved the unenviable distinction of opening civil war between American citizens by an act of gross breach of faith. He has, under counsels of a panic, deserted his post at Fort Moultrie, and under false pretexts, has transferred his garrison and military stores and supplies to Fort Sumter....

The excitement which the promulgation of this news created in Charleston cannot be described and we cannot compose ourselves to attempt the details. The bulletin boards and all places of public concourse were thronged with eager inquirers, and settled determination was marked on every face....

He has virtually and grossly violated a solemn pledge given by his Chief and accepted by South Carolina; and he had all possible assurance from South Carolina that his honor, and position, and duty would be respected until a proper and open declaration of war. While the enemies of South Carolina have been falsely accusing her of violence and precipitation, and have been endeavoring, by exciting rumors, to urge her or her sons to such premature demonstrations, South Carolina took her position honorably and fairly.

Major Anderson has clandestinely taken refuge in an unfinished fortress, and has thus violated the solemn pledges that assured us that Fort Sumter would not be garrisoned.

STAR OF THE WEST

Unionist newspapers in the South such as the Richmond Whig *claimed that the attack on the* Star of the West *was proof that South Carolina wanted to draw the entire South into war.*

Richmond Whig, 1 January 1861

An Anonymous Writer: "South Carolina Dragging Out Other States"

We have never had a doubt that it was the deliberate purpose of South Carolina, by some rash, illegal steps, to involve all her sister Southern States in the calamity of civil war. She is not content to be allowed to go out of the Union peaceably. Her object is to "drag" other States with her, and involve them all in a common and terrible conflict with the General Government. Her self-conceit and her selfishness know no bounds. But will Virginia become "hitched on," a miserable dependant [*sic*], to her tail? We shall see.

The Charleston Mercury *argued that South Carolina had no choice but to prevent the* Star of the West *from resupplying Fort Sumter.*

Charleston Mercury, 20 January 1861

An Anonymous Writer: "The War Begun"

When Major Anderson spiked the guns of Fort Moultrie, and transferred his command to Fort Sumter, he perpetrated hostile acts against this State. They clearly looked to a bitter instrumentality to coerce South Carolina by military power. The President of the United States understood this when he agreed with the South Carolina members of Congress not to change the *military status* in the bay of Charleston, upon the condition that we would not attack the forts. He knew perfectly well that if South Carolina had a right to secede from the Union, she had a right to have the forts in our harbor delivered up to her. These forts were built on her soil, for her defence against foreign nations. The obligation on the part of the Government of the United States to defend the State of South Carolina by these forts, fell with secession of the State....

Not content, however, with holding the fort, the Government of the United States determines to make actively efficient the military command of our waters, and sends additional troops to work its guns against the State. Whether coming by land or water, there was but one course left for the State to pursue, consistent with her sovereignty or the welfare of her people, and that was to prevent those troops reaching the fort. Accordingly, orders were given to the officers in command of the other stations in the bay of Charleston to arrest or sink any vessel carrying United States troops to Fort Sumter. Yesterday morning a steamer, supposed to be the *Star of the West,* attempted to enter the harbor. A gun was fired across her bows from the battery on Morris' Island. She went on without regarding it and then she was fired into with such effect that she turned back and went to sea.

All revolutions are blunders. They are never intended. The huge blunder now marring the counsels of the Government of the United States seems to be, that the Union can be maintained by violence and war, and that South Carolina can be cowed by demonstrations of coercion....The people of South Carolina will fight, and will establish the Southern Confederacy.

Impasse over Fort Sumter

The New York Evening Post *applauded President Lincoln's decision to re-supply the fort, saying the "rebellion must be put down."*

Evening Post (New York), 10 April 1861

An Anonymous Writer: "Fort Sumter"

The telegraph last night bore to all parts of the Union the welcome revelation of the government's purpose to defend its property and maintain the laws. We know at last—what men have for four weeks cherished as their fondest hope—that we have a President who will not, like his predecessor, permit the Union to fall to pieces. We are assured, and those who best knew the Administration never doubted it, that Mr. Lincoln and his advisers will do what befits any government beset by rebels and traitors. He will defend against all odds the trust the nation conferred upon him on the 4th of March. He will maintain the Constitution of the United States, which but a short month ago he swore to "preserve, protect and defend."

Desirous now, as it has been from the beginning, to avoid by every means possible to an honest government the shedding of even rebel blood, the Administration frankly gives notice that its design is simply to provision a destitute garrison, famishing in a fort which is the undoubted property of the United State government, and must remain so and be defended as such until it is lawfully ceded away or by force of arms captured.

Supplies must be lodged in Fort Sumter at all hazards and against all opposition from armed rebels. It is carrying conciliation to its extreme when the government gives fair notice of its purpose, and contents itself with only sending the needed provisions. If the rebels fire at an unarmed supply ship, and make the perfectly proper act the pretext for shedding the blood of loyal citizens, on their heads be the responsibility.

The time has come when the government must assert itself. The people are wearied with five months of suspense and inaction. The interests of the country demand the settlement of the question without further loss of time. It can be settled only in one way. Rebellion must be put down; constitutional government must be maintained; and the laws which are expressly declared the "supreme law of the land" must be enforced.

On the other hand, the New York Journal of Commerce *said the Union risked war by sending ships to Fort Sumter.*

New York Journal of Commerce, 12 April 1861

An Anonymous Writer: "A Mission of Humanity"

This is the term applied by the friends of war, to the attempt to furnish Fort Sumter with supplies. It is, they say, a mission of humanity; an attempt to relieve a band of men from the dangers of starvation. Very well. We agree that Major Anderson and his command should not be starved to death in that fortress, where they remain by order of the government, doing their duty as faithful soldiers, acting under the command of their superiors. But is this the only mode in which humanity can reach them? And does not humanity demand also, that the terrible sacrifice of human life which will attend a war between the North and the South, shall be avoided? Humanity indeed!! That is a singular order of humanity which is shocked at the prospective hunger of an hundred men in a strong fortress, but demands the sacrifice of an hundred thousand on the battle field.

ATTACK ON FORT SUMTER

Most Southern newspapers claimed the North bore responsibility for starting the war. The Montgomery Advertiser *claimed the Confederacy had sought a peaceful solution to the problem.*

Montgomery Advertiser, 13 April 1861

An Anonymous Writer: "The War Begun"

The inexorable logic of events has at length brought the country to the verge of war, and it now becomes us to look the matter squarely and calmly in the face. The Administration of the Confederate States have done all that men could honorably do to bring about a peaceable solution of the questions which have arisen between this government and the one at Washington, but through the madness and perversity of the ruling powers at the North all efforts to that end have failed. We have asked nothing at the hands of Mr. Lincoln to which we were not fairly entitled. He has chosen to turn a deaf ear to our requests, to insult our government by refusing to receive its commissioners, and he has now taken the fearful responsibility of inaugurating a war the end of which no man can see or predict.

Our hands are free from the guilt of bringing upon the country the horrors which necessarily attend a bloody struggle between those who have heretofore been members of one common government.

As they had done in the debate over secession, secessionist newspapers in the South drew parallels in their struggle for independence with the patriots during the Revolutionary War. The Memphis Appeal *compared the attack on Fort Sumter to the Battle of Lexington and Concord.*

Memphis Appeal, 14 April 1861

An Anonymous Writer: "The War—The Past, Present and Future"

Charleston has become to the South, in eighteen hundred and sixty-one what Lexington was to our once common country in seventeen hundred and seventy-five. It is the scene of the first triumph which inaugurates the war of Southern independence....

Northern newspapers that had supported the president reacted with outrage to the attack on Fort Sumter. The Boston Advertiser *accused the Confederacy of starting the war and demanded that the North respond immediately.*

Boston Advertiser, 15 April 1861

An Anonymous Writer: "Cowardly and Unprovoked Attack"

Never was attack more cowardly and unprovoked that that of the seceders upon Sumter. Upon the mere rumor of an attempt to send in supplies under convoy of a few vessels, the opposing army opened their innumerable batteries upon the little garrison....The confederate States are determined to have war; and war now exists by their act....It is now a question of life and death for the nation. There is no excuse—we believe there is no disposition—for faltering or hesitation on the part of the Northern people. We are in the right; we are the strongest; we are the party in possession; we have on our side the prayers of freemen throughout the whole world, the sympathy of civilized humanity everywhere.

Some Democratic papers in the North, such as the Hartford Daily Times, *blamed the Republican Party for the attack, claiming "this horrible drama" could have been prevented.*

Hartford (Conn.) Daily Times, 13 April 1861

An Anonymous Writer: "The Black Day"

Friday, the 12th day of April, 1861, will be recorded as the Black Day in the history of the Republic. United States Forts firing upon United States Forts. American citizens directing the implements of death upon American citizens. The Civil War commenced. What a shocking record! O, how long will it be before this accursed state of things shall cease to exist in the memory of the People? No man can tell.

A few brief weeks ago this horrible drama could have been stopped. The troubles could have been settled as Washington, Franklin, Jefferson, Madison, and Adams, would have settled them—by the expression of kindly feelings among brethren—by the adoption of peace measures, of conciliation. It was only necessary to have said, "Our Territories are common property, purchased by the money and won by the blood alike of the North and South; let the line be drawn, on the Southern side of which no right of Southern men shall be questioned—and on the North of which, the freemen may erect free States at their pleasure. *Each and all enjoy your rights.*" Then peace would have smiled all over our land. The Union sentiment would have predominated at the South and throughout the North. No evils would have followed—but joy, and prosperity, and power, and influence in the cause of Liberty all over the world, would have been the happy lot of our great Republic. This would have been the spirit and policy of friends, settling the difficulties, and conceding the rights of every section of a friendly community.

"But no!" said Mr. Lincoln and his friends. Our *party platform* is in the way! And Mr. Lincoln incorporated into his Inaugural Address to the American people, a portion of a party platform—a platform, too, of a mere sectional party. Then this great country was humiliated, and one half of it, in a body, was grossly insulted. No other President "of the United States," elected to preside over the Executive department of the entire federal government—to "promote the general welfare" of the entire people, ever lugged into his Inaugural address a partisan dogma. But charity attributed it to the weakness of the man, and the people tried to forget the humiliation. They were not permitted, however, to forget. True it was, that for four weeks, the promise of PEACE was held out by the Administration, through their acknowledged organs, and the public mind was for the moment calmed. It was all false—all deception and a trick, unworthy of an Administration of a great and generous and free people. All this time of four weeks of hope, the Administration was preparing the implements of War, and fitting out the messengers of death! For what, pray let us know? *To sustain the Chicago Platform!* To uphold and perpetuate a Party based upon hostility to the sentiments, the institutions, and the vital interests of fifteen sovereign States of the Republic! For this object alone, the last hope of the Union men of the South, and the true friends of the Republic at the North, is to be crushed.

But, say the "yield not an inch" Republicans, "the Southerners fired the first gun." When, and under what circumstances? As our fathers in the Revolution declared their independence of Great Britain, so have seven States at the South declared their independence of the Federal Government of the United States. Of the sufficiency of their grievances, they claimed, that they must be the judges. In assuming this position, they asked that the forts made to protect their harbors and their cities be not used against their citizens. They claimed that the money of the South used in building forts in the Union had been sufficiently ample to erect all the fortifications in their midst. That their person and the soil of their sovereign States were fairly entitled to the protection of the fortresses built by the side of their own rooftrees, and for the special object of defending them and theirs. But on Friday an armed fleet, with men and cannon, and arms, appeared off Charleston harbor, to provision or to re-inforce a fort—certainly to perpetuate a rule over the people who had declared themselves independent—who had, to say the least, exercised "the Right of Revolution." Could that people wait till they were taken by the throat and held *in subjection?* Their position had been taken. That position was invaded by a powerful force, and to save themselves, they acted; for it is not the firing of a gun that makes war, but the pitching of military tents, the anchoring of armed ships, the array of armed bands around your soil and your homes, to force you into subjection, is war without the click of a gun-lock, or the smoke from the mouth of the hoarse cannon.

Now, in the end, this controversy must be settled by treaty. The paper settlement alone will bring peace. This could have been done two months ago with great advantage to the country. Every battle and every gun that is fired complicates it. We cannot hold the South *in subjection.* We have no "subjects" in this country. We are equals, or we have no REPUBLIC. The question must in the end be settled by a peace measure—by a Treaty finally.

War is the worst policy that can be devised in a case like this. Our Republic must be made up of friendly States, or it cannot exist. If there are any at the South who cannot and will not live with us peaceably, let them go by themselves in peace. *They have already begged for this favor,* but the Administration has resolved to drive them out in BLOOD. Then in blood will they wade out, and with them *all* of the slave States. But this policy is an enormity, and it will bring sorrow upon the People. Last Friday was a Black Day for our country. May He in whom is the trust of individuals and of Nations, guide our Nation to a better destiny.

One of the few newspapers in the South to claim that the Confederacy bore any responsibility for the attack on Fort Sumter was the Knoxville Whig, *edited by William G. "Parson" Brownlow. Brownlow had been controversial in the South for his support of the Union and editorials such as this made him more notorious.*

Knoxville Whig, 27 April 1861

William G. Brownlow: "Who Are the Aggressors"

There was no reason for this bloody, terrible, but cowardly assault. There was no excuse for it. There was not even a plausible pretext for it. It was the deed of men bent upon a diabolical revolution, hungering and thirsting for blood and slaughter. The Administration at Washington was unwise, stubborn, sectional, and ignorant of the state of public sentiment in the South; the Administration at Montgomery has been wicked, reckless, and awfully guilty.

QUESTIONS

1. Why would Southern newspapers compare their struggle for independence with that of the patriots during the Revolutionary War?
2. Why was President Lincoln's plan to announce the resupply of Fort Sumter with an unarmed ship such a masterful political move?
3. Is it surprising that Northern newspapers that had opposed Lincoln would support his administration after Fort Sumter was attacked? Explain.

NOTES

1. W.A. Swanberg, *First Blood: The Story of Fort Sumter* (New York: Scribner's, 1957), 144–49.

2. Richard N. Current, *Lincoln and the First Shot* (Philadelphia: Lippincott, 1963), 71–102.

3. Maury Klein, *Days of Defiance: Sumter, Secession, and the Coming of the Civil War* (New York: Knopf, 1997), 402–20.

CHAPTER 5

Preparing for War, 1861

Two days after the United States surrendered Fort Sumter, President Abraham Lincoln issued a proclamation calling for 75,000 militia to suppress the rebellion. An outraged North responded overwhelmingly to the president's call. Cities and towns across the North held war meetings to sign up volunteers. In New York City, an estimated 250,000 people turned out for a Union rally. Northern governors soon wired the War Department that they could easily exceed their quotas of troops.

Lincoln's call for troops covered all states still in the Union, including states in the upper South that had been considering secession. The president's proclamation angered many in these states that had opposed the rebellion. They now attacked Lincoln for being deceitful with the Confederacy and argued that their states could not furnish men to put down their neighbors in the South.

The outbreak of war also meant that the states of the upper South had a decision to make: stay in the Union or join the Confederacy. Their decision was crucial to the South's chances for successfully waging a war. The eight upper South states (North Carolina, Tennessee, Virginia, Arkansas, Kentucky, Maryland, Delaware, and Missouri) composed more than half of the South's population, including two-thirds of its white residents. They also generated three-quarters of the region's industrial production and three-fifths of its agriculture output.

No state in the upper South meant more to the Confederacy than Virginia. It had the largest population of any state in the South. Virginia's industrial production was nearly as large as that of the seven original Confederate states combined. As the home of Revolutionary leaders such as George Washington, Thomas Jefferson, and James Madison, Virginia also gave the Confederacy the kind of prestige that could attract other states in the upper South. Once news of Fort Sumter's fall reached Richmond, a large crowd marched on the state capitol while cannons fired a 100-gun salute. The crowd lowered the American flag from the capitol and ran up the Confederate stars and bars. On April 17, the Virginia state convention adopted an ordinance of secession. To recognize the state's importance to the Confederacy, the Confederate Congress made Richmond its permanent capital.[1]

Arkansas, North Carolina, and Tennessee soon followed Virginia's lead and voted to secede. But the four border states of Delaware, Kentucky, Maryland, and Missouri resisted appeals to act quickly. Their decision to leave the Union or stay in would have important consequences. Kentucky, Maryland, and Missouri would have added 45 percent to the military manpower of the Confederacy. In each state, secessionists constituted a minority but exerted a powerful influence.

Of greatest concern to the North was Maryland, largely because the state encircled Washington, D.C. on three sides. The state's largest city, Baltimore, had many Southern sympathizers, and they were angry over Lincoln's call for troops. On April 19, the 6th Massachusetts Regiment—the first unit to respond to the president's call—passed through Baltimore on its way to Washington. An angry mob, some carrying Confederate flags, jeered at the troops and threw stones at them. A riot soon ensued, and in the exchange of shots, at least four soldiers and nine civilians were killed. Hysteria gripped the city. Authorities, fearing that more troops would spark another outbreak of violence, cut Northern rail lines to the city. A delegation traveled to Washington to consult with alarmed federal officials, including President Lincoln. By April 28, the crisis had passed and the following day, the Maryland House of Delegates overwhelmingly voted against secession. Delaware, Kentucky, and Missouri also chose to remain in the Union.

Americans had a romantic idea of war in 1861. Local regiments paraded before cheering crowds of their friends and neighbors before boarding trains for the front. The Southern diarist, Mary Boykin Chestnut, wrote in 1861 that so far the war was "all parade, fife, and fine feathers."[2] Moreover, many on both sides believed they could easily defeat the enemy and the war would be over after a few battles. The armies of both sides were largely amateur operations. In both the North and South, companies often consisted of recruits of a single town, city, or county. Companies from neighboring towns combined to form a regiment, which received a numerical designation in chronological order of organization. Men elected many officers from their own ranks and state governors appointed the rest.

In appointing generals, the two presidents most often used two criteria: military experience or political considerations. Both sides initially turned to men who had been officers in the regular United States army before the war. In most cases, men went with the side their state had chosen, but the decisions could be difficult. The best-known example was Robert E. Lee, a West Point graduate and hero of the Mexican War. Lee was a member of one of Virginia's leading families, but he disliked slavery and had spoken out against secession. He was offered a Union command, but declined saying, "I cannot raise my hand against my birthplace, my home, my children." A few days later, he accepted an appointment as commander in chief of Virginia's military force.

As the two sides began mobilizing their armed forces, they also took every chance to proclaim the purpose and justice of their cause. Both sides believed they were fighting to preserve the heritage of republican liberty. The North believed it was fighting to maintain the best government on Earth, whereas the South claimed it was battling for the right of self-government. Southerners rarely mentioned defending slavery as an aim of the war, even though it was an essential aspect of Southern society. And among Northerners, only radical abolitionists initially argued that the war had anything to do with slavery. There was widespread support for slavery in parts of the North, and the Lincoln administration was concerned about northern unity.[3]

This chapter follows editorial reaction to events in the weeks after the attack on Fort Sumter as the North and South prepared for war. The *New-York Times* said the Confederate attack had led to a resurrection of patriotism in the North. On the other side, the *Chronicle & Sentinel* said the South must be ready to defeat a "wily and treacherous" enemy "full of hate" for the South. Not all newspapers took a warlike stance. The *Democratic Standard* said that the South should be allowed to peaceably leave the Union. Even though it supported peace, the *Arkansas State Gazette* argued that peaceable secession was impossible.

Newspapers also held different views of reasons for fighting the war. The *Public Ledger* said the Union must fight to preserve the republican principle of majority rule. In the South, the *Daily Picayune* and *Charleston Mercury* argued that the Confederacy was fighting to regain the constitutional liberties that had been usurped by the North. And the *Daily Argus and Democrat* argued that the war was being fought over the future of slavery. Finally, editors differed over the fighting ability of the other side. The *Daily Palladium* and *Albany Patriot* said their side would easily defeat the other. But the *New Orleans Bee* warned the South not to take its foe lightly.

LINCOLN CALLS FOR TROOPS

The New-York Times *cheered the patriotism that had enveloped the country in the days after the attack on Fort Sumter and argued that civil war could be positive for the country.*

New-York Times, 16 April 1861

An Anonymous Writer: "The Resurrection of Patriotism"

The cannon which bombarded Sumter awoke strange echoes, and touched forgotten chords in the American heart. American Loyalty leapt into instant life, and stood radiant and ready for the fierce encounter. From one end of the land to the other—in the crowded streets of cities, and in the solitude of the country—wherever the splendor of the Stars and Stripes, the glittering emblems of our Country's glory, meets the eye, come forth shouts of devotion and pledges of aid, which give sure guarantees for the perpetuity of American Freedom. War can inflict no scars on such a people. It can do them no damage which time will not repair. It cannot shake the solid foundations of the material prosperity—while it will strengthen the manly and heroic virtues which defy its fierce and frowning front.

It is a mistake to suppose that War—even Civil War—is the greatest evil that can afflict a nation. The proudest and noblest nations on the earth have the oftenest felt its fury, and have risen the stronger....War is a far less evil than degradation—than the national and social paralysis which can neither feel a wound nor redress a wrong. When War becomes the only means of sustaining a nation's honor and of vindicating its just and rightful supremacy, it ceases to be an evil and becomes the source of actual and positive good. If we are doomed to assert the rightful supremacy of our Constitution, by force of arms, against those who would overthrow and destroy it, we shall grow the stronger and the nobler by the very contest we are compelled to wage.

We have reason to exult in the noble demonstration of American loyalty which the events of the last few days have called forth from every quarter of the country. Millions of free men rally with exulting hearts around our country's standard. The great body of our people have but one heart and one purpose in this great crisis of our history. Whatever may be the character of the contest, we have no fears or misgivings as to the final issue.

Angered by the president's call for troops, the Chronicle & Sentinel *said the Confederacy must be ready to defend the South from "Lincoln and his black band."*

Chronicle & Sentinel (**Augusta, Ga.**), 18 April 1861

An Anonymous Writer: "The Plain Duty of Every Citizen"

Let us all, with one accord, prepare to welcome the invaders with "bloody hands to hospitable graves."

We have to deal with an enemy wily and treacherous, base, malignant and full of hate. It is impossible to know what are the full designs of Lincoln and his black band. Of one thing we may be assured: they will strike any and all the harm they have the power to do. Therefore we can lose nothing by being fully and thoroughly prepared at every point, and for any emergency.

Now we recommend that every man capable of bearing arms, regardless of age, and every boy sixteen years old and upwards, begin immediately to train and drill. All will not be needed for active service in the field.... Wherever thirty or forty or more men and boys can be got together conveniently in a neighborhood, let a squad be formed, and armed and regularly drilled once or twice a week. This is no ordinary time. None of us have ever seen the like of it before—let all then get ready. Arm and drill, arm and drill, should be the word now, all over the land.

PLEAS FOR PEACE

The Democratic Standard *in Concord, New Hampshire, said the North would never be able to conquer the South—and that the cause of peace meant the Confederacy should be permitted to leave the Union.*

Democratic Standard (Concord, N.H.), 4 May 1861

An Anonymous Writer: "Our Position"

It is proper that the position of every man, and every political press, should, in the present crisis, be distinctly defined. We have no hesitation in defining ours.

While we acknowledge the duty of allegiance and fidelity to the Government of our country, by whomsoever administered, we are against coercion. We are for peace. The South, which, in this scandalous civil war, will include every slaveholding State, cannot be reconquered. Her sons may be defeated on the field of battle; her cities destroyed; her fields laid waste; but they will not then be conquered. If defeated, they will flee to their mountain fastnesses and their morasses, and still carry on the war, until ultimately their invaders will be driven from their soil. They never will be conquered. Then why make war upon them? Why sacrifice thousands of precious lives and hundreds of millions of money, when in the end it will avail nothing?

No; let every true patriot in the land—republican, whig, or democrat—demand that this fratricidal strife shall cease. Let our Southern brethren go, if they cannot remain with us except by coercion at the point of the bayonet and the cannon's mouth.

We are for the peace policy. When our land is filled with widows and orphans, and our homes draped with mourning, as they will be in two short years, and we then find our brothers of the same race still unconquered, all will be for peace. Then why not make it now before all these tremendous sacrifices have been made?

We are for our country, or what remains of it. We are for its brilliant and glorious emblem—the stars and stripes. Its glory should never be bedimmed by bathing its folds in the blood of brothers. We are for maintaining the glory of this flag on the soil of our own country. We are not for the invasion of the South. We are for the defense of the North. If our brethren of the South invade the North, we are for repelling them. We are for defending the city of Washington until Maryland shall secede. As long as that State shall remain in the Northern Union, we are for defending the integrity of her soil, and that embraces the city of Washington. If she secedes, it will be useless even to defend Washington.

Such is our position. And this should be the position of the Democracy of the North. It probably will be; and not only their position, but that of hundreds of thousands of Republicans, before this war shall have been prosecuted two years.

The Arkansas State Gazette *in Little Rock opposed secession and urged peace between the two sides. But the paper recognized that it was impossible to have both in the climate that existed between the North and South.*

Arkansas State Gazette, 20 April 1861

An Anonymous Writer: "The Work of Coercion Commenced"

Speaking for ourself, we are opposed to the doctrine of secession, but the right to rebel against an oppressive government is one upon which all agree. Peaceable secession has proven to be what we thought it from the first—an impossibility. As well expect to pull a stout man's arm from its socket in his shoulder without pain as to sever the Union without violence.

Why Fight a War?

The Philadelphia Public Ledger *said the Union must fight to preserve constitutional authority and the republican principle of majority rule.*

Public Ledger (Philadelphia), 7 June 1861

An Anonymous Writer: "What Are We Fighting For?"

"What are we fighting for?" We are fighting for everything for which this Government was established. We are fighting to preserve our republican institutions in their purity; to maintain our Union in its integrity; to establish the authority of the Constitution and laws over violence and anarchy; to secure popular rights against aristocratic assumption; and to prove to the other nations of the earth whether we have a Government or not. The fundamental principle which is assailed in the present rebellion is the principle of equal rights as recognized under our Constitution. It is the underlying principle of our republic, and when that is destroyed, the principle which gives vitality to our democratic representative government is gone also, and with it the faith of mankind in popular government. We are fighting, therefore, to preserve the Government as it was established, on pure republican principles, in which artificial distinctions merely, shall not impair political rights....

[W]e are fighting for another great fundamental principle of republican Government—the right of the majority to rule. When the ballot-box was substituted for revolution, it was thought that all violent changes in established governments, all sudden overthrowing of political structures, would be obviated, for the will of the people could be peacefully known through the ballot, and their legally established rule be patiently submitted to. So long as it answered the purpose of maintaining power in the hand of the would-be-oligarchs, its decrees were acknowledged as binding; but so soon as it threatened to put power really in the hands of the majority, those who labor for their living, then the discovery is made that our institutions rest on a wrong basis, and that political equality is neither desirable for social prosperity, nor practicable for political permanency. We are fighting to expunge this great political error, and to prove to the world, that the free Democratic spirit which established the government, is equal to its protection and its maintenance. If this is not worth fighting for, then our revolt against England was a crime, and our republican Government a fraud.

The New Orleans Daily Picayune *compared the fight being waged by the South with that of the American patriots during the Revolutionary War.*

Daily Picayune (New Orleans), 4 July 1861

An Anonymous Writer: "Recurring to First Principles"

The Confederate States of 1861 are acting over again the history of the American Revolution of 1776. The actions of the British King, which were recited in the Declaration of Independence as "a history of repeated injuries and usurpation, all having in direct object the establishment, of an absolute tyranny over these States," have been repeated in spirit, and literally copied in many of the measures of the Government at Washington. The same despotic purpose to suppress political rights and destroy civil liberty by the employment of armies of invasion, "already begun with circumstances of cruelty and perfidy scarcely paralleled in the most barbarous ages, and totally unworthy of the head of a civilized nation," is as distinctly marked in the movements of the Federal Executive as it was in those of the British monarch, rendered more atrocious in character by the violent assumptions in the prosecution of the will of the American despot, of lawless powers which the people of England would never have permitted to the King.

The resistance of the South has been based on the same eternal principles which justified and glorified the patriots of 1776. What was won by their struggles, their long endurance, their heroism and their triumph, was the common inheritance of their children, in trust for the liberty and happiness of mankind. They established, as they thought forever, the great maxim of freedom that "governments derive their just powers from the consent of the governed," and that "whenever any form of government becomes destructive of these ends, it is the right of the people to alter or abolish it, and to institute a new government, laying its foundation on such principles and organizing its powers in such form as to them shall seem most likely to afford them safety and happiness.

These fundamental truths are still devoutly cherished in the Southern States of America. The people of the South are in arms to defend them against the aggressions and invasions of the degenerate sons of the illustrious patriots who went shoulder to shoulder with the men of the South, in wresting them, by battle, from the unwilling hands of a mighty monarchy. The North, inflamed by the same lust of dominion and the same arrogant confidence in superior strength, has renounced these free maxims for those which enlightened monarchy since abandoned, and is spreading its banners and arraying armies and fleets to reestablish, in the person of King Mob, the obsolete dogmas of the divine right of government to passive obedience.

In this frightful apostasy of a corrupt generation from the faith of their fathers, the people in the Confederate States of the South alone remain loyal to the principles of the Revolution—the great truths of the Act of Independence. They are the sole guardians left of constitutional liberty in America. They alone have kept unimpaired their inheritance in the glories of the Revolution, and their trust in its beneficent creed. To them now belongs of right the custody of all the hopes of human progress, of which the Fourth of July is the symbol in history, and it is by their swords that it is to be saved for mankind.

The Charleston Mercury *argued that the South was fighting for its freedom from the "remorseless despotism" of the North.*

Charleston Mercury, 19 April 1861

An Anonymous Writer: "For What Are We Now Contending?"

The matter is now plain. State after State in the South sees the deadly development, and are moving to take their part in the grand effort to redeem their liberties. It is not a contest for righteous taxation. It is not a contest for the security of slave property. It is a contest for freedom and free government, in which everything dear to man is involved. Shall we submit to the sectional and remorseless despotism of a majority of the Northern States, with no checks on their omnivorous rapacity? That is the question. Every man, every boy in the South answers No! And they will fight the foul usurpers and tyrants, if they dare the issue of war, as long as the streams run and the sun shines on our vallies [*sic*].

The Daily Argus and Democrat *in Madison, Wisconsin, said the war must settle the question of slavery in the United States and any peace short of that would not last.*

Daily Argus and Democrat (Madison, Wisc.), 4 May 1861

An Anonymous Writer: "The Abolition of Slavery the Only End of This War"

Till secession had become an actual fact—till the conspiracies of thirty years had ripened into actual rebellion, and treason to the government was organized and armed—there was no party at the north that sought or desired to weaken the Constitutional guarantees that protected slavery. On the contrary, all parties recognized its legal existence, and respected the established measures for its protection. A large party at the north were favorable to even extending and fortifying such measures of safety as those directly interested in the institution deemed necessary for its perpetuity. All their demands have been complied with. Measure after measure of rigorous and obnoxious legislation had been proposed, agitated, adopted and finally acquiesced in by a great majority of the North....

With the first gun from the rebels in arms perished every sympathy at the North with slavery. Never more, if peace were concluded tomorrow would slavery be granted another guarantee. On the contrary—those which it has possessed no longer exists; by the acts of the South itself they have forfeited. The war cannot now end but with the total extinction of slavery, which was the cause of the war; for this is the first and must be the last armed contest between the two sections of this Union. All cause for future quarrels, except the peaceful controversies of political parties, must now be abolished. And though it require a war of ten years, the sacrifice of a million lives and the entire devastation of every foot of slave territory, this result, and nothing that is less, must end. The North has the power to achieve it; and the conviction is universal that peace short of that would be an unsafe and delusive peace; that our children would be compelled to fight over the same battle; and the same battle will have to be fought over again as often as it is concluded by a less decisive event.

VIEW OF FOES

The Daily Palladium *in New Haven, Connecticut, claimed the South's armed forces were overrated. Although the Confederacy had captured defenseless U.S. government offices since the beginning of the year, the paper predicted the North would easily defeat the Rebels.*

Daily Palladium (New Haven, Conn.), 29 April 1861

An Anonymous Writer: "Southern Chivalry"

The people of the North have heard so much of southern chivalry for many years, that they have been impressed, in a rather indefinite way it is true, with the idea that there is somewhere in the South, a very considerable amount of chivalry which would neither brook a wrong or purposely commit one, and that this chivalry in defense of its honor would as soon walk into a grave as to sit down to a good dinner with a hungry appetite. While our people have never been in the slightest degree intimidated by their impressions of the existence of this fiery element of our national character, they have always been disposed to look upon it forbearingly, even when severely provoked by it, and to regard it as the result of climate and education, for which the impatient gentlemen under such influences should be very much indulgent. Hence they have had pretty much their own way in the government for more than seventy years. Personal apologies and national compromises have been tendered them whenever they required them, except when their demands were too outrageous to be even considered....

But we think the chivalry and even the bravery of the South, has been altogether over estimated. No one can doubt that there are brave men, and true hearted men in that section of the country. We have had proofs enough of that from the days of George Washington to this time. But at the same time, they have in all their communities, more cowards and mean men, in the proportion, probably, of twenty to one, than any other portion of our land. This fact has been illustrated from the days of the Revolution to this hour; and this character is found among their educated men as well as among their ignorant slave drivers. It is exemplified in their large and small towns as well as in the halls of our national Congress.

Their assault upon the National Government was as cowardly as their conspiracy was wicked. They believed they were assailing an impotent power, which, through the treachery of its pretended friends, they could surprise and overcome by a well-devised conspiracy, without any special hazard to themselves from bullets or scaffolds. They had so long trampled with impunity upon the rights and interests of the North; so often maltreated our citizens without atonement, that they imputed our forbearance to fear, and our desire to avoid a conflict with them, to an admission of their superiority in all the elements of a governing people. They did not like the brave men of the American revolution—or like the lovers of liberty in Poland, in Hungary, in France, strike for their rights in the face of despots armed to the teeth, and regardless of all consequences to themselves; but they have been stealthily and gradually sapping the foundations of the Government, creeping into places of trust in order to betray them; hanging, whipping, and otherwise outraging unarmed and helpless men, and turning to their own account the passions of the ignorant multitudes that follow them by falsehoods the most malignant ever devised by the most wicked of men. Such is the chivalry of the South, as it now is, and has been at least for the last dozen years.

The whole proceedings of these traitors, from the beginning of their last conspiracy to overturn the Government, has been characterized by the most contemptible cowardice. They have never threatened to attack any fortifications that were not almost in a defenceless condition for want of men and supplies. They have valorously assaulted Custom Houses and Post Offices, public mints and even a hospital of sick men, where there were none to defend; but we venture the prediction that they will not fight anywhere during the present contest, unless their advantage shall happen to be as ten against one.

If the Government maintains itself with the same energy and determination that it has exhibited since the attack upon Fort Sumter, we venture the further prediction, that this rebellion will be entirely suppressed with little or no fighting. The more troops we rally, the less prospect there will be of the loss of many lives in battle, for no battle will be fought unless we carry the war into the enemy's country, and that should be done. Our troops should protect the South from servile insurrection, from plunder, and from every evil not justified by the recognized rules of modern civilized warfare; but the traitors should be thoroughly subjugated, and at least a dozen of their leaders should grace a gallows within twenty-four hours after their capture. Fort Sumter should be voluntarily restored, or Charleston should be leveled with the ground after the women and children have had sufficient time to depart. Armistices and border State interference should have no consideration now, and in six months this warfare will be over; the honest people of the South who are now under a reign of terror from the conspirators, will deliver over their leading traitors for trial and execution, and the Union will have passed the fiery ordeal, and come out better and stronger than it ever was before.

Even before the war began, the Albany Patriot *showed no respect for the fighting ability of the North. The paper boasted that the county's women and children could easily whip Federal troops.*

Albany (Ga.) Patriot, 15, November 1860

An Anonymous Writer: "Afraid of What?"

We will insure the life of every Southern man from being killed in war by the abolitionists for a postage stamp. We will venture the assertion and take our salvation upon it, that you may take the muskets of the "Albany Guards," load them with Connecticut wooden nutmegs and place them in the hands of the women and little children of Dougherty county, and they can whip every abolitionist that has been here in ten years or will be here in ten years to come.

The New Orleans Bee *warned Confederates not to take the fighting ability of Northerners lightly.*

New Orleans Bee, 1 May 1861

An Anonymous Writer: "The War"

The North is bent on war. Facts demonstrate it. Every usage of war has been put in practice. The blockade of our ports, the stoppage of supplies to the South, the wanton and Vandal-like conflagration of Government stores and fortifications exposed to capture by the South, the efforts to control the navigation of the Mississippi, the deliberate persecution, insult and injury of all Southern sympathizers who unhappily fall into northern hands, the fell spirit of violence and despotism openly acknowledged by Administration sheets, the threats of invasion and extermination—all indicate beyond the possibility of a doubt the disposition and purposes of the North. We are to have war, and probably on an extended scale. We have no confidence in the well meant but fruitless attempts to arrest the progress of the conflict. Mr. Lincoln is aware that the South is arming only for defense, and asks nothing better than to be suffered unmolested to pursue the even tenor of her way. The responsibility of hostilities lies with him. He can suspend them whenever he pleases. He has no desire to call off his bloodhounds, and the war will therefore go on.

It is well, too, to guard against another common error—that of depreciating the adversary. Rank folly were it to deny the courage of the people of the North. They belong to the revolutionary stock, and have displayed their valor in many a battle field. They are as brave as the men of the South, and were their cause a just one, were they, as we are, defending their houses and firesides, their freedom and independence against ruthless invaders, they would be, as we trust we shall prove, invincible.

QUESTIONS

1. In what ways did the *New-York Times* argue that a civil war could be a "positive good" for a country?
2. Was it an effective argument for the *Daily Picayune* to compare the Confederacy's fight with the North to that of the Americans against the British during the Revolutionary War? Why or why not?
3. Why did the *Daily Argus and Democrat* claim that the war must be fought to end slavery?

NOTES

1. Emory M. Thomas, *The Confederate Nation, 1861–1865* (New York: Harper & Row, 1979), 93–101.

2. C. Vann Woodward, ed., *Mary Chesnut's Civil War* (New Haven, Conn.: Yale University Press, 1981), 69.

3. James M. McPherson, *Battle Cry of Freedom: The Civil War Era* (New York: Oxford University Press, 1988), 308–12.

CHAPTER 6

Battle of First Bull Run, 1861

The North and South spent the months following the attack on Fort Sumter readying for war. Neither side had armies or navies prepared for real fighting, and leaders used the time mobilizing manpower and equipment. Union and Confederate leaders also battled public attitudes about what fighting would involve. Many Americans of the era had a romantic idea of war, believing it to be exciting and glorious. Confident of success, they also believed that it would only take a battle or two to defeat the other side.

By the summer of 1861, many in the North were demanding that Union forces invade the South and crush the rebellion. The Confederate Congress scheduled its second session to begin in Richmond, Virginia, on July 20. Seizing on the event, the *New-York Tribune* coined the battle cry "Forward to Richmond!" and declared that the Rebel Congress must not be allowed to convene. Other newspapers picked up the cry. In the South, President Jefferson Davis believed the best strategy was to be defensive. He felt that the Confederacy could ultimately win the war by attrition and wearing out the enemy. But others in the Confederacy ridiculed his idea, including some newspaper editors who believed that South could easily defeat the North if given the chance.

Union General-in-Chief Winfield Scott did not believe that his troops were ready for an offensive against Richmond. But President Lincoln thought that by attacking the South immediately, the Union could achieve his limited war aims. Capturing the Confederate capital would discredit the secessionists, he argued, but it would not destroy the social and economic system of the South.[1] The president instructed General Irvin McDowell, who commanded the 35,000 troops outside Washington, to draw up a plan for attacking the Confederate army defending Manassas Junction. McDow-

PUNCH, OR THE LONDON CHARIVARI.—September 28, 1861.

A FAMILY QUARREL.

Family Quarrel. *The Civil War is depicted as a family dispute in this cartoon from the magazine* Punch *(September 28, 1861). The South shakes her fist at the North while each holds a symbol of the divided country, a torn U.S. map. In the background, a racist caricature of a childish slave is tiptoeing away from the quarrel.*

ell shared Scott's concerns that his army lacked proper training for an offensive. Lincoln, however, insisted that the time was right. In one of his most-often quoted remarks, Lincoln told the general, "You are all green, it is true, but they are green, also; you are all green alike."[2]

Manassas Junction, just 30 miles southwest of Washington, had assumed tactical importance because it was at the confluence of two railroads. The Orange & Alexandria Railroad was a natural line of advance for Union troops marching from the capital, and the Manassas Gap Railroad connected the two main Rebel forces in northern Virginia. General Pierre G.T. Beauregard commanded 22,000 Southern troops at Manassas Junction, but he would need the help of the 11,000 Confederates in the Shenandoah Valley under General Joseph E. Johnston. On July 16, McDowell's troops marched out of Washington toward Manassas Junction. A Confederate spy alerted Beauregard to the Federal advance, and he immediately sent for Johnston's troops. With 33,000 men, the Confederates established an eight-mile defensive line along Bull Run, a narrow, tree-choked river. McDowell's men tested several spots along the Confederate line until they found an undefended river crossing known as Sudley Ford.

Early in the morning of July 21, the main Federal column began marching toward the ford planning to cross the stream and sweep behind the Confederates. They encountered no resistance until a Confederate signal officer spotted the Union column and rushed men to block the advance until reinforcements could arrive. The Union assault initially crushed the outnumbered Rebels, but Federal troops did not pursue, which gave new Southern regiments time to arrive. By early afternoon, the Confederates had stabilized along a new front at Henry Hill.

For the next 90 minutes, fighting raged across the Henry family farm. There, Confederate commander Thomas E. Jackson earned his popular nickname "Stonewall." Confederate General Bernard Bee was trying to rally his broken brigade when he saw Jackson's fresh troops arrive. Bee reportedly pointed to Jackson's men and shouted, "There is Jackson standing like a stone wall. Rally behind the Virginians."[3] Unable to break the Confederate line on Henry Hill, McDowell tried to move around the Rebels. Heavy fighting continued with the Rebels receiving reinforcements, including the last brigade from the Shenandoah Valley just getting off the train. Seeing his advantage, Beauregard ordered a counterattack, and the screaming Rebels overwhelmed the exhausted Union troops. What began as an orderly retreat by the Federals soon turned into a panicked rout. The fleeing Union soldiers became entangled with frightened civilians, including some congressmen who had traveled from Washington to witness the battle. Confederate troops, who were almost as disorganized as the Federals, did not pursue. The first major land battle of the war was over.

About 420 Union troops were killed, and another 1,000 were wounded. More than 1,200 were captured. The Confederacy lost about 390 men killed and another 1,600 wounded. The South exalted in the victory at Manassas (or Bull Run as the battle was named in the North).[4] Confederate newspapers claimed the outcome was proof that the South could whip the Yankees in a fight. Some predicted that the Federals would never leave Washington again. The North was shaken by the embarrassing loss. But the despair of editors soon turned to determination to fight harder. Lincoln also was determined to learn from the defeat. The day after Bull Run, he signed a bill for the enlistment of 500,000 new troops. Three days later, the president signed another bill authorizing 500,000 more troops.

This chapter begins with one of the best-known editorial statements of the war, the *New-York Tribune*'s war cry, "Forward to Richmond!" Southern newspapers could be just as aggressive in calling for military action, as the editorial from the *Charleston Mercury* reveals. Following the Union defeat at Manassas, Northern newspapers urged leaders to learn lessons from the battle. Angry editors also said editors such as Horace Greeley should bear some responsibility for the defeat because they insisted the Union army should fight before it was ready. At the same time, Southern newspapers were reveling in the Confederate victory. Some urged Southern leaders to seize the advantage that the victory had provided and invade the North.

CALLS FOR FIGHTING

Following the attack on Fort Sumter, the New-York Tribune *was one of the most outspoken advocates for aggressive military action against the South. Editor Horace Greeley constantly prodded the Lincoln administration to greater activity and grew increasingly critical when the army continued to merely drill. The* Tribune *proclaimed that the nation should have a new motto: "Forward to Richmond!" The "Nation's War Cry," as it was called, appeared at the top of the editorial page every day from June 26 to July 6.*

New-York Tribune, 26 June 1861

An Anonymous Writer: "The Nation's War Cry"

Forward to Richmond! Forward to Richmond! The Rebel Congress must not be allowed to meet there on the 20th of July! BY THAT DATE THE PLACE MUST BE HELD BY THE NATIONAL ARMY.

The Charleston Mercury *urged the South to adopt an aggressive military strategy against the North.*

Charleston Mercury, 1 June 1861

An Anonymous Writer: "The War Policy of the South"

It is a fact, that at every collision of arms, every effort at resistance by the Confederate States has tended to strengthen and promote their cause. From the seizure of the forts and the firing is to the *Star of the West* in South Carolina to the last and bravest act of resistance in Virginia by the intrepid Jackson, fighting with us has been success. And yet, in every instance, we have been *forced* to fight. We have avoided battle. We have let our enemies take their own time to assail us. At this moment, in Virginia, we appear to be acting entirely on the defensive.

We are not generals in the field, and we do not intend to be so on paper; but there are a few plain principles and facts which any mind may understand, without having fought battles or won victories.

In the *first* place, delay is against us in the matter of numbers. The policy of the Confederate States, it seems to us, was and is—not to wait until vast masses are aggregated upon us, but to act promptly with such troops as we possess, and to demoralise and prevent the discipline of the troops of the United States, by vanquishing them.

For, in the *second* place, our raw troops are far superior to the raw troops of the United States. Our people are used to arms. They are accustomed to the gun and the horse. The people of the North can neither shoot a rifle nor ride a horse, unless trained. Is it good policy to let them be trained?

And in the *third* place, no soldiers, especially undisciplined soldiers, as the greater part of all the soldiers now in the field must be, can stand the eternal agitations of apprehended attacks in a defensive warfare. To be called out continually to prepare for battle, and yet not to fight, will chill the hearts of the bravest troops.

By assuming the position of the defensive we have lost Maryland, endangered Missouri, neutralized Kentucky, and are now making Virginia our battle field. Is this wise statesmanship? Is it efficient generalship? Fabian tactics are out of place. We trust the war policy of the South is about to become aggressive and efficient. It is time, and we are glad to see that our gallant Commander in Chief, after directing the preparations of the War Bureau for two months, has made Richmond his headquarters.

Northern Reaction

Some editors sought scapegoats for the loss. The Baltimore American *blamed the so-called newspaper generals, such as Greeley, who had prodded the military to action.*

Baltimore American, 22 July 1861

An Anonymous Writer: "The Defeat of the Federal Forces"

The terrible defeat experienced by the Federal army at Manassas Junction will doubtless now satisfy, to the full, those newspaper generals in New York, and elsewhere in that latitude, who have been so long vociferating for an "advance," and have been so eagerly clamoring for a "battle." Answerable at the bar of public opinion, they are not to be envied now for the terrible responsibility they have assumed of urging upon an old soldier like General Scott a degree of precipitation which has resulted in a disastrous defeat.

Horace Greeley reacted to the criticism by saying he would gladly serve as a scapegoat. In an editorial in the New-York Tribune, *he also said that in the future he would support the nation's military leaders.*

New-York Tribune, 25 July 1861

Horace Greeley: "Just Once"

If I am needed as a scapegoat for all the military blunders of the last month, so be it! Individuals must die that the Nation may live. If I can serve her best in that capacity, I do not shrink from the ordeal....

Henceforth, it shall be the Tribune's sole vocation to rouse and animate the American People for the terrible ordeal which has befallen them. The Great Republic imminently needs the utmost exertions of every loyal heart and hand. We have tried to serve her by exposing breakers ahead and around her; henceforth, be it ours to strengthen, in all possible ways, the hands of those whose unenviable duty it is to pilot her through them.

Northern newspapers did not downplay the seriousness of the defeat at First Bull Run. Many papers, such as the Philadelphia Inquirer, *said the Union could learn valuable lessons from the embarrassment.*

Philadelphia Inquirer, 25 July 1861

An Anonymous Writer: "The Lesson of the Repulse"

We have had our first vigorous grapple with entrenched rebellion, and for the time are baffled. In the moment of apparent victory came repulse; then retreat, disorder and panic. The part of true patriotism, in this trying moment, is not to repine and cavil at defeat, still less to supinely yield to it, but rather to glean from it its salutary lessons and nerve ourselves with fresh hope and courage.

We now know the full strength of this great rebellion. We have tested it in its own chosen stronghold, where it had gathered the bulk of its army. We find its spirit to be fierce, stubborn and desperate—the courage of men whose fears almost outweigh their hopes, and who have staked their all upon a last venture....

Let us take comfort in that we now know the worst. It is better that this rebellion should have the first victories than the last. It has gathered such an army as it can never gather again. It could not survive such a disaster as that from which we will instantly recover. We have only begun to draw upon our resources. This very seeming defeat will but be turned into a source of future triumph, if *we profit by its lessons.* Nations, as well as individuals, sometimes need the discipline of misfortune.

The Chicago Tribune *said the North would be resolved to fight harder as a result of the defeat.*

Chicago Tribune, 23 July 1861

An Anonymous Writer: "The Future"

Whatever may have been the extent of the disaster to Gen. McDowell's army on Sunday night, and it could not seemingly have been worse, the consequences will be only a mightier uprising of the people in behalf of their beloved Union and Constitution, a firmer resolve to conquer the traitors, a more gigantic preparation and a more nervous energy for the work to be accomplished. For every soldier driven back from Manassas to the Potomac, there are twenty who will march to contest again the ground which has been lost. Mortification may well mingle with our sorrow for the dead and wounded, *but despair never.*

SOUTHERN REACTION

Southern newspapers cheered the Confederate victory at First Bull Run. With great hyperbole, the Memphis Appeal *compared the route with other historic battles, including Napoleon's defeat at Waterloo.*

Memphis Appeal, 23 July 1863

An Anonymous Writer: "Great Victory at Manassas"

The victory on the part of the South is evidently complete, and the route of the enemy scarcely less overwhelming than that which lost Bonaparte the day at Waterloo. We can scarcely estimate the probable moral effect of this success of our arms upon the North, but have every reason to believe that it will cast a damper upon their energy, which will detract somewhat from the gusto they have so far exhibited for volunteering. It would not, perhaps, be going too far to surmise that it will be the battle of the present war, and will virtually break the backbone of the Washington government. Of such fearful contests it was that Mr. Webster spoke, when he, many years ago, truthfully asserted that "battles have been fought that *fixed the fate of nations.*"

Within a few days after the battle, some editors called on Confederate officials to follow up on the success of First Bull Run. The Richmond Examiner *argued that the Confederate army should take the fight to the North.*

Richmond Examiner, 26 July 1861

An Anonymous Writer: "Carry the War into the North"

We have whipped them in open field, and proved ourselves their masters in war; but it must never be said that the North invaded the South, and that the South could not retaliate the humiliation. There can be no lasting peace for the South with the Yankee until he is made to feel that the penalty of war with us is the certain invasion of his own hearth-stones. No terms of peace or armistice should be listened to until we have carried the war into the heart of his own country.

QUESTIONS

1. Do you think Horace Greeley bore some responsibility for the defeat given his newspaper's call to march on Richmond? Explain.
2. How did Northern newspapers show editorial leadership by encouraging readers to keep up the fight?
3. Why would a newspaper like the *Memphis Appeal* compare the Union defeat at First Bull Run with a historic battle such as Napoleon's defeat at Waterloo?

NOTES

1. James M. McPherson, *Battle Cry of Freedom: The Civil War Era* (New York: Oxford University Press, 1988), 335.

2. T. Harry Williams, *Lincoln and His Generals* (New York: Knopf, 1952), 21.

3. Arguments about exactly what Bee said and meant about Jackson began soon after the battle and continue. But there is no question that Bee gave Jackson the nickname. William C. Davis, *Battle at Bull Run: A History of the First Major Campaign of the Civil War* (Garden City, N.Y.: Doubleday, 1977), 196–98.

4. The North and South gave different names to several Civil War battles. In most cases, the Confederacy named the battle after the town that served as their base, and the Union used a landmark near the battle, usually a river or stream.

CHAPTER 7

Trent Affair, 1861

onfederate leaders made the decision to secede based partly on the belief that in the event of war with the Union, England and France would intervene militarily on the side of the South. The two European powers depended heavily on Southern cotton for their textile industries. Moreover, an independent South would economically weaken the United States, which had grown to become a major commercial rival for both England and France.

Soon after the Confederate government was organized, President Jefferson Davis's administration sent three envoys to major European capitals to negotiate treaties of friendship, commerce, and navigation. Even though the representatives offered significant trade concessions, the Confederacy did not receive the recognition it so badly wanted. By the fall of 1861, the Davis administration decided to take a different approach and send two special commissioners to London and Paris to secure official recognition of the South's independence. The new commissioners were James M. Mason, a former chairman of the U.S. Senate Foreign Relations Committee, and John Slidell, a prominent New Orleans lawyer.

On October 12, Mason and Slidell departed Charleston, South Carolina, on board the steamer *Theodora*, which ran the Union blockade. The two men traveled to Cuba where they booked passage to Europe on the British steamship *Trent*. Mason and Slidell had not kept their plans secret, assuming that they would be protected by international laws guaranteeing the protection of every nation's ships at sea. But when Captain Charles Wilkes, commander of the *San Jacinto*, learned that the envoys were on the *Trent*, he decided to stop them. He consulted works about international law in his cabin, but could not find any precedents for the action he contemplated. Although the law permitted him to seize enemy dispatches, he could not legally justify capturing the commissioners. So Wilkes decided to arrest Mason and Slidell as the "embodiment of dispatches." On November 8, the *San Jacinto* spotted the *Trent* and fired two shots across its bow, forcing the British ship to stop. The *Trent's* captain protested the American action, but eventually gave up the Confederate envoys and their secretaries. Wilkes let the *Trent* resume its voyage, and he took Mason and Slidell to Boston where they were imprisoned at Fort Warren.[1]

Northerners applauded the seizure of the Confederate commissioners as good news in a war that had not gone well for the Union to this point. The two Confederates were particularly hated because Mason had been a strong advocate of the Fugitive Slave Law, and Slidell had been one of the most outspoken advocates of secession. But the Lincoln administration was concerned about England's reaction to the arrest of the men on a British vessel. An angry Britain could decide to dispatch its navy to break the Union blockade, officials feared. Most of Lincoln's advisers believed that despite the contention of Wilkes, the captain had violated international law in seizing diplomatic envoys from a neutral ship. In the Confederacy, Southerners greeted the news of the seizure with a mix of outrage and satisfaction. On the one hand, they were angered by the arrest of two duly appointed Confederate commissioners. But they also recognized that the incident could help the South by generating support for British recognition of the Confederacy.[2]

Relations between Great Britain and the United States had long been strained. Once news of the seizure reached England, the British cabinet immediately created a War Committee. The British foreign secretary demanded that the United States immediately release the captives and apologize for violating international law. At the same, the British government banned the export of weapons and ammunition to the United States. It also sent more than 11,000 troops to Canada, bringing the garrison's strength in that country to 18,000 men. Finally, the British navy strengthened its fleet of ships in the western Atlantic. The rear admiral in charge of the fleet made plans to break the Union blockade of the South before implementing a blockade of his own around major Northern ports.[3]

President Lincoln initially rejected the British demands, and many members of Congress supported him. During several tense weeks in December 1861, the president and his cabinet debated how to defuse the crisis without appearing to bow to an ultimatum from the British. With the view of "one war at a time," Lincoln finally decided he had to release Mason and Slidell. Secretary of State William H. Seward drafted a letter to the British that, although not actually apologizing for the incident, admitted that Captain Wilkes had committed an illegal act.

On December 26, the Lincoln administration agreed to release Mason and Slidell, and six days later the commissioners left Fort Warren on board the HS *Rinaldo*. After changing ships in Bermuda, the commissioners finally arrived in England. For the United States, a major international crisis had been resolved, and a perilous conflict with Great Britain had been avoided. Mason and Slidell went on to serve in Great Britain and France until the end of the war, but they never secured the official recognition that Confederate leaders wanted so badly.

The *Trent* affair prompted a great deal of editorial reaction. Many Northern newspapers initially reveled in the news of Mason and Slidell's capture, but it did not take them long to reconsider the implications of the arrest. Editors in the South said the British should demand a full apology and the release of the envoys. Some of the region's newspapers also recognized that the crisis could actually prove to be good for the South.

When the British demanded the release of Mason and Slidell, many Northern editors argued the United States had little choice but to do so. And the Lincoln administration generally received praise for its handling of the diplomatic crisis. In the South, editors did not dwell on the opportunity the Confederacy had lost to gain support for official recognition by England. Instead, they claimed that by giving into British demand, the United States had suffered irreparable damage abroad.

SEIZURE OF MASON AND SLIDELL

In the days immediately following the seizure of Mason and Slidell, Northern newspapers, such as the New-York Times, reveled in the news of the captured envoys.

New-York Times, 17 November 1861

An Anonymous Writer: "The Capture of Slidell And Mason"

We do not believe the American heart ever thrilled with more genuine delight than it did yesterday, at the intelligence of the capture of Messrs. Slidell and Mason, recently of the Senate of the United States, the most prominent and influential actors in the rebellion, and on their way to England and France, to represent the rebels at the Courts of these countries. The capture of Beaufort may have created a deeper and more lasting impression, from a consciousness of the important results accomplished, but really no satisfaction is equal to that experienced when base and treacherous knaves meet their desserts....

These are the men who we have just caught and who are now safely caged. All thanks to Capt. Wilkes, who, consulting the dictates of common sense alone, marched straight to his object, unmindful of protest, convinced that an act which every honest heart must approve, could not be contrary to usage and law. In this, he was perfectly correct. The only mistake he committed was in not seizing the ship from which he dragged the traitors.

It did not take long, however, for some editors in the North to reconsider their strong words. The Pittsburgh Daily Post, *warned that to hold the commissioners would do the United States no good and risk war with Great Britain.*

Daily Post (Pittsburgh, Pa.), 19 November 1861

An Anonymous Writer: "The Exploit of Captain Wilkes"

The capture of Messrs. Slidell and Mason, on board a British steamer on the high sea, is an event the result of which no man can foresee. That these men were under the protection of the flag of Great Britain as much as was the commander of the vessel himself, is a fact that cannot be denied. That they were rebels against our government, and engaged at the moment of their arrest in the prosecution of a hostile purpose, is equally true but all this has nothing to do with the question between our government and that of Great Britain. The question is of a far higher significance.

Let it be borne in mind that no political offences or crimes are recognized in the Ashburton treaty, therefore Slidell and Mason do not come under its provisions. But even were this not so, or had those men been guilty of any crime whatever known to the laws, their capture would have been equally a violation of the sanctity of the British flag. The rendition of criminals can only be brought about by a regular process of law, and not by violent seizure: *the act of Capt. Wilkes, therefore, was an act of war.*

The whole country will applaud the zeal and pluck of Capt. Wilkes in this transaction; but cool and sober-minded men must nevertheless condemn it. He has brought the country into a bad scrape, and the sooner we get out of it the more gracefully we can do so. It will never do to rush wrong end foremost into a quarrel with Great Britain for the sake of a brace of traitors. We say this, not because Great Britain is powerful; but because we cannot afford, especially at a time like this, to persist in a wrong. This were to strike down at a blow all international law and comity, and throw the whole world into anarchy.

To hold these men as prisoners would, under the circumstances, do us no good, but, as we have endeavored to show, incalculable injury. Fortunately the outrage on the British flag was so flagrant that its disavowal can never be attributed to any other impulse than that of honor and fair dealing. But should there be the slightest hesitation about making the *amende honorable,* we shall lose all the advantages that we might derive from our magnanimity and our almost scornful indifference as to the whereabouts of this brace of rebels and mischief makers. If our government should restore them to liberty, and send them on their way, the sympathy of Europe would be changed to laughter.

Confederate newspapers reacted with outrage to the arrests. The Charleston Courier *said the British government should demand a full apology and the immediate release of the commissioners.*

Charleston Courier, 22 November 1861

An Anonymous Writer: "The Capture of Our Ministers"

[W]ho can doubt that the rights of Great Britain have been most flagrantly violated in the seizure of Messrs. Mason and Slidell?...Their seizure under such circumstances, upon a known vessel, with papers known to be genuine, must be held by Great Britain as an unmitigated insult. And not only in self-respect is she bound to *demand* a full atonement for it, but her *neglect* to do so would be such a departure from her neutrality, as would according to the law of nations, justify the Confederate States in going to war with her, if they were in a condition to do so.

Some Southern newspapers, such as the Charleston Mercury, *recognized that the* Trent *affair might help generate support for British recognition of the Confederacy.*

Charleston Mercury, 23 November 1861

An Anonymous Writer: "The Seizure of Our Commissioners"

Long before anything which may be said on this side of the Atlantic, on the seizure of our Commissioners on the high seas, from the British Packet, shall reach England, the British Government will have taken its position, as to the rights it involves. If the cotton famine shall have loomed up with those terrific proportions, which will inevitably be developed by time, the British Government will find, in the laws of nations, quite sufficient ground for a very impressive demand for reparation from the Government of the United States. If, on the contrary, the sufferers, prospective and immediate, of a deficiency of cotton, shall have been stupidly indifferent to their fate, and meet destitution and starvation with a passive resignation, the Government of Great Britain may treat the seizure of our Commissioners, as only an indelicate affair, requiring no stern demand for reparation. A gentle complaint, eliciting a polite disclaimer of any intention to offend, will close the matter. Which course Great Britain will pursue, it is difficult to anticipate. That she has acquiesced in a blockade, clearly illegal, according to the declaration of her Ministers in Parliament, is beyond dispute. How much further she will be prepared to acquiesce in the insolent illegalities of the United States, will be shown by time; but we are satisfied that one result will take place from the seizure of our Commissioners from the deck of a British Packet—*an immense impulse will be given to the cause of the Confederate States, in Great Britain.* Let the British Government construe the laws of nations as it pleases, with respect to this act, the people of England will feel that it is a moral outrage—a national insult and indignity. A man may have a guest in his house, who may be amenable to some Government inquisition—yet if he is seized at his table, before his family, and forcibly carried from his house, he must be indignant. His sympathies will be with his guest. Our Commissioners were under the British flag. Their errand was an errand of peace and good will towards the people of England. They were the bearers of probably the most magnificent offers of friendly and lucrative intercourse which have ever passed from another people to the people of England. Passing from one neutral port to another neutral port, in a British Packet—the packet is made to come to under the guns of a United States frigate—the packet is searched—and the Commissioners are seized, and forcibly carried off. Such an act every true Briton will resent. With or without law, he will feel that it is an insult, which no convenient law of nations, ever varying to suit the pretensions of the strong can allay or palliate. In its effect in promoting the cause of the Confederate States in Europe, it will be equal to a battle gained, and our Commissioners will do us better service as captives, than as Ministers at the Courts to which they were accredited.

What to Do?

During the first month that the envoys were in custody, President Lincoln kept silent on the Trent *question. But perceptive editors recognized that the administration clearly had a major dilemma on it hands. The* New Orleans Bee *gloated over the situation the North found itself in.*

New Orleans Bee, 19 December 1861

An Anonymous Writer: "The British Lion Aroused"

We rejoice at this manifestation. We rejoice at the dilemma in which the Yankees are placed. What will they do? Will they meanly yield after all their bravado—their official recognition and unstinted laudation of the act—their panegyrics of it contained in Cabinet reports and their huge vaunting and bragging generally. Let them surrender Slidell and Mason and their Secretaries, and truckle basely to the antagonist they affected to bully, and they will breed a schism among themselves which will end in their destruction, besides standing humiliated and disgraced among the family of nations. Let them refuse, and brave the wicked wrath of England if they can. Unable to subdue the South alone, can they have the folly and temerity to imagine they are able to contend with both the South and England? We should not wonder at any pitch of madness to which the besotted vanity of the Northern people may drive them. But a few days will tell the tale. Let them decide as they may, the South will be largely the gainer.

Word got out soon after the British sent a dispatch demanding the release of the envoys and an apology from the United States government. A new flurry of editorials, like this one in the New York Herald, *urged the Lincoln administration to give up Mason and Slidell.*

New York Herald, 21 December 1861

An Anonymous Writer: "Mason and Slidell to Be Delivered Up If Demanded"

In adopting this alternative of submission to these peremptory demands, the administration runs the hazard of disappointing the popular sentiment of our loyal States. But a little reflection will satisfy every intelligent mind of the wisdom of deferring a final settlement with England until we shall have made an end of this Southern rebellion. There have been some conjectures that arbitration may be resorted to; but it is better gracefully to yield to the exigencies of the crisis, and promptly relieve England of her convenient pretext for a quarrel, without the intervention of any third party. Let our government, then, meet the requisitions of Lord Lyons, in the restitution of Mason and Slidell to British protection, and in an acknowledgement of that, while Captain Wilkes would have been right in seizing the Trent steamer and in bringing her before a prize court for adjudication, he was wrong in limiting his proceeding to the seizure of his prisoners; and that we regret that his controlling considerations of international courtesy and leniency should have resulted in the very offence which it was his particular object to avoid.

Response to Mason and Slidell's Release

When the Lincoln administration announced that Mason and Slidell would be released, most Northern editors praised the decision. The New-York Times *said the North had "honorably escaped" a possible war with Great Britain.*

New-York Times, 30 December 1861

An Anonymous Writer: "Settlement of the Trent Affair"

A portion of our people will be disappointed at the result arrived at by our Government, in the affair of the *Trent*. But that feeling will have no deeper basis than a temporary and impulsive chagrin, that two such rebels as Mason and Slidell should have slipped through our fingers, in consequence of the interposition of the English Government on their behalf. And even this feeling will promptly yield to the profound satisfaction of the whole country, that we have honorably escaped the fearful perils of a war with England, which, whatever might have been its ultimate issue, would have given a certain triumph to the Southern rebellions. The *real* disappointment at the pacific settlement of this question will be felt in the dominions of Jeff. Davis. The rebels had taken fresh heart and hope, as well as they might, at the prospect of having the whole military naval power of Great Britain thrown into the scale on their behalf. The silent destruction of that hope will fall upon them like a thunderbolt. It will do more to dishearten and paralyze their efforts than any other event, short of an overwhelming defeat at the hands of the Union forces.

Many Southern newspapers maintained that by giving into British de-mands, the United States had shown itself to be a second-rate power in the world. The Richmond Daily Dispatch *claimed the national honor of the United States had been irreparably damaged.*

Daily Dispatch (Richmond), 1 January 1862

An Anonymous Writer: "The Yankee Back Down"

As will be seen by a telegraphic dispatch, the Yankee Government, which has been threatening at the most furious rate to "humble John Bull," has dropped down on its knees at the first roar of the British Lion, and released Messrs. Mason and Slidell. They have...themselves the scorn, contempt and laughing stock of all Christendom. Never did a nation before, with arms in its hands, make so pitiful, contemptible, and ignominious a surrender. It has signed and scaled the death warrant of its eternal disgrace and degradation. If John Bull had bombarded all its towns and overrun its whole territory, he could not have inflicted such an incurable damage on its national honor as it has visited upon itself with its own unclean and pusillanimous hands. What military prestige it may have had in the old Union is lost forever, and its own people must now despise their government, and the government its people. Nor need they expect exemption from the hostility of England by this tame and cowardly truckling to its power. Henceforth she will despise as well as execrate them; and feel no hesitation in breaking the blockade as soon as it suits her convenience.

QUESTIONS

1. Was Northern reaction to the seizure of the Confederate commissioners surprising given the state of the war in the fall of 1861? Explain.
2. Do you think President Lincoln used the reaction of newspaper editors in determining what he should do with the captured envoys? Explain.
3. Did Southern newspapers fully grasp what the release of Mason and Slidell meant to the Confederacy? Explain.

Notes

1. Norman B. Ferris, *The* Trent *Affair: A Diplomatic Crisis* (Knoxville: University of Tennessee Press, 1977), 3–31.

2. Gordon H. Warren, *Fountain of Discontent: The* Trent *Affair and Freedom of the Seas* (Boston: Northeastern University Press, 1981), 26–46.

3. Howard Jones, *Union in Peril: The Crisis over British Intervention in the Civil War* (Chapel Hill: University of North Carolina Press, 1992), 80–99.

CHAPTER 8

West Virginia Becomes a State, 1861–63

The state of West Virginia was born during the Civil War. Although originally part of Virginia, the 35 counties west of the Shenandoah Valley had always been different than the rest of the state. On the eve of the Civil War, the mountainous region contained only one-quarter of the state's white population and few slaves. Economically and culturally, residents were more connected to Pennsylvania and Ohio than to the Tidewater area of eastern Virginia. The plebian mountaineers of the west had long complained to the state government in Richmond that they were underrepresented and overtaxed.

Even before the war began, there had been growing sentiment for separate statehood in the region known as Kanawha. (The name came from the Kanawha Valley formed by the Kanawha and Little Kanawha rivers.) The secession debate only deepened the feelings in western Virginia where most residents opposed their state hastily leaving the Union. A Union meeting at Parkersburg declared that the election of Abraham Lincoln was no reason to abandon "the best Government ever yet devised by the wisdom and patriotism of men." Another large meeting in Greenbriar County said it was "unwise, impolitic, and unpatriotic" not to give the Lincoln administration a chance before seceding.

When the Virginia convention adopted an ordinance of secession on April 17, 1861, only 5 of the 31 delegates from northwest Virginia voted in favor of it. Within hours of secession, authorities in Wheeling were ordered to seize the U.S. Customs House, but a Unionist mob prevented the act from being carried out. A statewide referendum on the secession ordinance was scheduled for May 13. Meanwhile, delegates from western Virginia began organizing resistance. On the same day the statewide referendum was held, Union loyalists in the region began a three-day convention in Wheeling. Although some delegates supported an immediate proclamation of statehood for western Virginia, a majority favored another convention after the results of the statewide referendum on secession were announced. The results showed that voters in western Virginia rejected the plan to leave the Union by a margin of three to one.[1]

Unionists from 38 counties returned to Wheeling on June 11. Although a majority of delegates favored separate statehood, the U.S. Constitution stood in their way. Article IV, Section 3 required the consent of the state legislature to form a new state from the territory of an existing state. Recognizing that the existing Virginia legislature would not agree to the formation of a new state, the delegates set up a "Restored Government of Virginia" at Wheeling, on the basis of loyalty to the Union. The convention declared the new Confederate legislature in Richmond to be illegal and pronounced all state offices vacant. It appointed new state officials, headed by Francis H. Pierpont, an attorney and Republican leader, as governor. The U.S. Senate and House seats vacated by Virginia Confederates also were filled.[2]

While Unionists were debating the future of western Virginia, the Federal army was trying to defend Wheeling from Confederate threats. General George B. McClellan led the Union force, composed of regiments from nearby Ohio. McClellan told his troops, "Your mission is to restore peace and confidence, to protect the majesty of the law, and to rescue our brethren from the grasp of armed traitors."[3] On June 3, 1861, McClellan's troops routed the Confederates at Philippi. McClellan later forced Confederate commander Robert S. Garnett into battle at Corrick's Ford, where Garnett was killed—the first Civil War general to die in action. The campaign gave the Union control over western Virginia and allowed a reconvened Wheeling convention to meet securely beginning in August.

Delegates at the convention agreed to hold a statehood referendum on October 24. Voters approved the measure for a new state by an overwhelming majority of 18,408 to 781. A constitutional convention, which met from November 26, 1861, until February 18, 1862, drew up a state government and established new state boundaries containing 50 counties. To comply with U.S. Constitutional requirements that a new state must have the approval of the state from which it is carved, leaders of West Virginia turned to the "Restored Government" at Wheeling. That body gave its approval, and Governor Pierpont signed the statehood bill.

The issue of what to do with the 4 percent of the population in West Virginia who were slaves had prompted serious debate among the delegates. The constitutional convention came within one vote of approving gradual emancipation. But the West Virginia statehood bill had to be approved by the U.S. Congress, and the Republican-controlled Congress insisted that statehood be contingent on emancipation. After a great deal of debate, leaders agreed to a compromise. The new state constitution freed slaves born after July 4, 1863, and freed all others on their 25th birthdays. With that hurdle cleared, the statehood bill won congressional approval, and President Lincoln signed the statehood bill. On June 20, 1863, West Virginia joined the Union as the 35th state.

Union supporters in East Tennessee viewed the events in western Virginia with great interest. Their leaders were Andrew Johnson, a U.S. senator from Tennessee, and William G. "Parson" Brownlow, a former Methodist minister who edited the *Knoxville Whig*. The Unionists held two conventions in 1861, but their efforts to reconstruct Union governments in East Tennessee could not get far without northern military support. The Lincoln administration pressed the army to move into Tennessee, but the rugged mountains and lack of transportation facilities made that difficult. In the meantime, the Unionists in East Tennessee suffered for their loyalty to the United States. State officials imposed martial law and imprisoned hundreds of Unionists. Among those sent to jail was Brownlow, whose newspaper office was also seized. He later was freed and escorted to Union lines in March 1862.

This chapter follows editorial debate over the drive for statehood in West Virginia and the attempts to do the same in East Tennessee. Many newspapers in western Virginia supported the idea of separate statehood. Editors elsewhere in the Confederacy had a range of reactions about statehood. Not surprisingly, most Northern newspapers supported statehood for West Virginia. Brownlow used his *Knoxville Whig* to call for separate statehood in East Tennessee. He was vilified by Confederate editors elsewhere.

SUPPORT FOR SEPARATE STATEHOOD

During early debate about whether or not Virginia would secede from the Union, the Wellsburg Herald *suggested that western Virginia did not have to go along with the rest of the state. Wellsburg is now part of West Virginia.*

Wellsburg (W.Va.) Herald, **8 February 1861**

An Anonymous Writer: "Secession & Coercion Brought Home"

The section of country known as Northwestern Virginia having pretty generally elected delegates opposed to secession, and it being taken for granted that a majority of the counties in other portions of the State have voted the opposite, there arises a very pretty question.

The theory of a Convention of the people is, that it represents the sentiments of those represented in their original capacity, without reference to constitution or statute or any other law, other than such as nature and self-preservation prescribes for the good of individuals. The Convention, in its province, and for the time being, is superior to constitution and laws, which, indeed, are in effect abrogated that far. Theoretically, it is the supreme law of the land, and its will is to be enforced by the weight of superior numbers and strength. It is a government of force in the strictest sense of the term. At the same time that the people represented will be honor bound—not otherwise, for there is no law to bind them to do the will of the majority—should any portion of the people see fit to repudiate the action of their delegates, then the only way in which they can be brought to terms is by the use of force; in other words, by coercion, but without the basis of law for a foundation.

Premising that these principles are correct, the question arises, what will the people of Northwestern Virginia do in the event of the passage of an ordinance of secession. Will they submit to the will of a majority of the people of the State, agree to leave the Union at their dictation, do violence to their interests and their convictions of right, or will they repudiate the action of the Convention, remain in the Union, and let those who wish to, secede, and take the responsibility and risk of being coerced to go with the seceders (?) On every principle upon which this Convention is called, and upon every principle by which secession is justified, those of the citizens of Virginia who are unwilling to go with the majority will be justified in remaining under the stars and stripes, and by no process of reasoning known to the secessionist school can they be coerced into doing differently. This, then, opens the door at once for a division of the State, on strict Southern State rights grounds. The question, any way we look at it, is a pretty one, and we are much mistaken if it is not mooted both in the Convention and at home. Disguise it as we may, there is no doubt but there is a strong undercurrent in favor of a division of the State in the event of the secession of Virginia from the Union; and when circumstances have given our politicians backbone enough to enable them to speak above a whisper on the subject, it will be authoritatively felt. The feeling is latent among the people, a spark will inflame it into a blaze that will speedily consume all opposition. So long as Virginia remains faithful to the Union, there is no danger and little real disposition to take so decisive a step, but let the madmen take the initiative of secession from the Union, and the example will speedily be followed by those who are patiently waiting and fearing. Then we shall have the question of coercion brought home. Then we shall see whether the provisional government of Virginia has the moral or material force to maintain the integrity of her boundaries, or to drag its dissatisfied subjects from under the protecting flag of the federal Union.—Then shall we test the sincerity of the Southern dogmas in regard to secession and coercion.

If such an event as this should be rendered advisable, the Northwest should be careful not to be placed in the wrong position. It is not necessary that Western Virginia should secede, on the other hand it is a material point that Eastern Virginia should be compelled to stand the odium of such a step. If the West, or any part of it, even if only the Panhandle desires to remain in the present federal Union, all it has to do is to remain in *status quo*, let the balance secede, and, if necessary, call upon the federal Government for protection in its rights under the laws of the United States. If we have to split the old Commonwealth, let it go forth to the world and stand upon the record of history, that it was not the West, but the East, not the free labor, but the slave labor half that seceded from the Union, and in the same act demoralized and divided the good old State.

After Virginia approved an ordinance of secession, the Wheeling Daily Intelligencer *reiterated the complaints of western Virginia, that it was a "serf" to the eastern part of the state. It urged the region to remain loyal to the Union.*

Daily Intelligencer (Wheeling, W.Va.), 27 April 1861

An Anonymous Writer: "A Word to the Northwest"

There is a time for all things, or at least has been. There was a time for argument against secession in this State, but that time has now gone by. While there was the slightest ground to hope, we battled this delusion to the extent of our feeble abilities, and fought secession to the last hour. But the die is cast. The secession of Virginia is now a fact, reluctant as we were to believe it ever could become such; and it is no longer of use to argue the question of the right of secession. The argument has long ago been exhausted, the ground traveled over for the hundredth time, and on that phase of the question there remains nothing more to be said.

The time has now come for action—prompt, energetic, instantaneous action.—There is not a day nor an hour to be lost. What that action is to be, let a few plain statements determine. From time immemorial Western Virginia has been but the serf of the East—subjected to unjust taxation and unequal representation—causes which alone have heretofore been considered sufficient to justify separation in more instances than one. For years, as the West has grown into power, she has hoped that her rights would be acknowledged and her wishes respected, but hoped against hope, as it now appears. Four months ago we were commanded to go into an election for delegates to a convention, the known object of which was to place us and the rest of the State in apposition of hostility to the government to which we owe our allegiance, and which has always been the first to protect and the last to oppress us. The election resulted in sending the Convention a large majority of men who were opposed to the assumption of a right to change our relations with the United States Government. They went to Richmond, and from that day to the culmination of the catastrophe everything that could be conceived was done to buy away from their allegiance to the government, and duty to their constituents the delegates Western Virginia sent to Richmond. Finding everything else to fail, violence was resorted to by the desperate leaders who had foresworn the secession of Virginia, to dragoon our delegates into submission to their diabolical measures. A mob of ruffians was congregated in the Capital of our State, and a Convention of the sovereign people was subjected to its terrorizing presence. Our delegates from the Northwest, and the few from other parts of the State, who had the manliness to stand up unawed to the last, were threatened with every conceivable kind of personal violence if they did not join in the schemes of the conspirators. They were forced to go into a secret session, and bound by an oath not to divulge the passage of an ordinance of secession till the traitors had had time to seize the government property in the State. Under these influences, the ordinance of secession passed, and the mob was triumphant. Our representatives were obliged to fly for safety, some of them being constrained to procure passes from Mr. Letcher, once our Governor, now the mad leader of a yet wilder regime.

Without waiting for the action of the State on the ordinance—for the call for the Convention provided that the action of the Convention should be submitted to the people for ratification or rejection—the secession faction, with Letcher at its head, at once proceeded to make war on the Government, issues his mandate, calling upon the volunteer companies of Virginia to be ready at his beck to march upon the old and revered flag of their country, thus taking away from the people the opportunity of saying whether they desire to place themselves in such a position, and inaugurating at once a war in our midst against our Government, and against its supporters in Virginia, who are in many instances compelled to abandon the State to save themselves from violence. In addition to this, that arch traitor, Jeff. Davis, is invited to make our State the field of his operations, and our Capital the rendezvous of his Southern hordes of ruffians.

Men of the Northwest, this is where Virginia stands to-day—this is how you stand—this has been your treatment, these the indignities you have suffered. Will you submit to a repetition of them? Will you consent, and are you willing to have them doubled, quadrupled, carried beyond all power of endurance? Are you a free people? And would you retain your liberties? Are you agreed that the degredation [*sic*], wrongs and insults of the last few months shall be continued, repeated, re-repeated and intensified by a petty but most absolute tyranny for all time to come? If you are not, then you must make up your minds to act for yourselves, and without loss of time. Your position, if you have but the nerve to sustain it, is one of moral sublimity. The friends of the Union everywhere look to you and pray that you may have the moral courage to dare to stand up for your rights in the Union. You have the sympathy of the Union men in the two great States that join us, and all over the country, and you can have, so they assure you, the sinews that may be needed for the struggle. We conjure you, then, as freemen who must achieve their own enfranchisement, by all that you hold dear in the present, and anticipate in the future, by your duty as citizens of the best government on earth, by your fealty to the altars of liberty and your attachment to home and your own hearthstones, that you will forget past differences, if such there have been, and unite as one man in this hour of common danger, and act as becomes the momentous issues forced upon you.

The Philadelphia Press *urged western Virginia to not simply form a state but to "reform" the old state. It said residents must take a hard line against those disloyal to the Union.*

Philadelphia Press, 24 May 1861

An Anonymous Writer: "Northwestern Virginia"

North America has never afforded occasion for such action as that to which the people of Northwestern Virginia, and of other mountain regions of the Southern States, are called. They hold in their hands the future of the country. Upon their steadfastness and their wisdom hangs the hope of freedom. The *plains* of the South are dominated by the iron sway of military rule, and constitutional liberty is well nigh crushed out upon them; slaves and masters, bond and free, black and white, are yoked in common harness of slavery to their military oppressors. The *mountains*, thank God! Are yet free. May they be so, till the last syllable of recorded time....

Putting aside the idea of forming a new state, let Western Virginia boldly enter upon the work of reforming the old State. Whose opinions or feelings are with secession, or whose heart or head or hand fails him in unflinching loyalty to the Union, is against the work which the loyal men have before them to do. We must give way to one who can be trusted. Treason teaches at the other end of the state how to deal with its opposers. Loyalty may learn from reason how to deal with its enemies. Let no enemy, nay, let no lukewarm friend of the Union, exercise any executive or judicial function. The line is easily drawn. Whoever is on the other side of it is a public enemy, and so to be treated.

OPPOSITION TO SEPARATE STATEHOOD

As the secession debate in Virginia heated up following the attack on Fort Sumter, the Kanawha Valley Star *in Charleston urged the state not to split and to leave the Union as a whole. Charleston is now in West Virginia.*

Kanawha Valley Star (Charleston, Va.), 23 April 1861

An Anonymous Writer: "The Position of Western Virginia"

In utter disregard and contempt of every overture and prayer of Virginia, for peace, and without any authority of Congress, Mr. Lincoln and his advisers have declared war against the South. He has issued his proclamation for seventy-five thousand militiamen, and has had the audacity to call upon the border Slave States for a portion of them, designating three regiments as Virginia's quota. The various governors of the slave States have each responded promptly to the call, that they would furnish no men or money for the any purpose so wicked in its ends and so unconstitutional in its means as the proposed subjugation of the South. The free States have all offered their sinews of war and powers of destruction with eagerness and alacrity. The Virginia Convention has passed the ordinance of secession. Four hundred federal troops, stationed at Harper's Ferry, Va., after destroying ten thousand rifles and firing the public buildings, fled before the Virginians made their appearance. No doubt some of the gallant four hundred were familiar with John Brown's by-paths across the neighboring hills, and others of them may also have retained a vivid recollection of the latter end of the martyr. At any rate they decided and so acted that discretion was the better part of valor. The Virginians soon thereafter arrived, extinguished the flames and secured about four thousand rifles.

The Northern cities, in keeping with their usual fanaticism, are perfectly furious; any one who refuses to advocate coercion is in danger of losing his life. Federal soldiers are flocking into Washington city by thousands; negroes are in the ranks with white men. Civil war is commenced, and it behooves every man who loves his species now calmly to consider how can it be stopped. We have heretofore urged with all our little might, that prompt, decided and unanimous action by all the border slave States was the only possible means of preventing bloodshed and civil strife. For that, many men denounced us as traitors. We hope we may be pardoned for presenting once more with renewed energy and infinitely increased weight the same argument as applicable to our present disturbed condition. The immediate and unanimous voice of all the slave States in defense of themselves and the South, may yet cause the North to reflect before they rush headlong into this internecine strife. We are fain to believe that those in authority at Washington have made the issue simply to satisfy their party whether or not the Union is permanently divided. The Black Republican horde cried that the rebels must be demolished. In order to preserve his party organization at the North, Mr. Lincoln was forced to terminate the dreadful and doubtful inaction of his administration. The suspense caused by the delay and deliberation policy paralyzed every energy of the country as effectually as actual war would have done: it afforded no satisfactory response to those who persisted in reiterating the question "have we a government?" Mr. Lincoln drafted just about the same number of men from each of the slave States as he had votes last fall, respectively in them. If those States had sustained him, then his plan would have been to have subjugated the seven seceded states.

If the border States are not lost to every sentiment of honor and all knowledge of interest, if their people are not divided among themselves, Mr. Lincoln and his party will soon be convinced of the advantages of peace, and will speedily acknowledge our separate existence as a government. We are satisfied that the revolution is now a complete success; and no matter to what extremity the contest is pushed, we have no doubt of the ultimate and complete triumph of the South. We hope there will be no disertion [*sic*] or difference of opinion amongst our own community in regard to the great question before us. We are willing to forget all of the past that is unpleasant to any loyal citizen. Let each and all of us stand firm for Virginia, as a unit in this her greatest trial. Let no seditious one whisper any purpose of dividing the State. Virginia expects every man to do his duty.

With a statehood referendum pending, the Richmond Examiner *urged the Confederate army to begin a campaign to gain control over western Virginia. The paper argued that most residents remained loyal to Virginia and that Confederate control of the region would ensure that it remained part of the state.*

Richmond Examiner, 11 October 1861

An Anonymous Writer: "Hours Precious"

Never were days or hours more precious to an army or to a people than they are now to our army and our people in Northwestern Virginia. The season for military operations is nearly ended. Months have been lost in a costly and worthless campaign. Winter upon the mountains must soon seal the fate of a fourth part of the territory and the people of Virginia for many months and, possibly, forever. In about two weeks a vote is to be taken upon the question propounded to the people by the usurpers—whether the State of Virginia shall be divided and the State of "Kanawha" erected. Unless our army can advance every vote must be given within the enemy's lines. The number of votes recorded may be regulated by the Yankees and their tools, and it is easy to foresee that not a vote will be cast in opposition to their dictation. Yet the uniform history of Northwestern Virginia prior to the invasion has proved that a vast majority of the people are loyal to the Commonwealth, and we are convinced that not a tenth part of them would desire a division of the State if they were protected against invasion. A very large proportion of them are, at this moment, not only loyal, but exasperated by the oppression practiced upon them to such a pitch that they would furnish a numerous and resolute army to defend the country as soon as it shall be recovered. In this regard, it is believed, the popular sentiment is more encouraging than it has ever been before—and more favourable than it is likely to be at the end of a long winter of Northern domination without a sign of sympathy from the South....

There are traitors in Western Virginia, but they are not formidable in arms. Their bogus Governor and Attorney-General, and other great men, keep their families in Ohio and their trunks packed. Their common herd are panic-stricken at every report of approach of Secessionists. The bulk of the population being small farmers, scattered, unarmed, and obliged to remain with their families, while their country is invaded by the North, and unprotected by the South, take no part in the contest. In all this there is nothing to justify that shuddering honour which seems to have made some of our commanders quite willing to keep a mountain barrier between themselves and the "traitors" of Northwestern Virginia, as if it were a land of hobgoblins. Thousands of true-hearted men and women there pant for a sight of the Southern flag, and will take care of the "traitors" whenever out armies show themselves a match for the invading foes.

While the future of the Kanawha Valley was being debated, other Southern newspapers expressed anger at what the "westerners" were trying to do. The Charleston Mercury *argued that Virginia was better off without the western part of the state.*

Charleston Mercury, 21 May 1861

An Anonymous Writer: "The 'Pan Handle' and Pot Politicians"

We find that the politicians in Western Virginia persist in a scheme for setting up themselves, repudiating the "Old Dominion," and worse, proposing to make a bastard use of her vulnerable name. Now, we trust that Virginia will exhibit no resentment, and offer no opposition, to the proceedings of these patriots. We should think it her best policy; through her chief men, Legislature, and finally her Convention, to let them know that she is quite willing that they should go in peace; and that she has no desire to retain within her folds any counties who have been restive under her authority, and who are dissatisfied with her sway. If she declares herself thus readily, it will be quite probable that the more sensible counties will at once see the crime, the cowardice and miserable lack of patriotism which prompts this desertion of their State in the hour of her peril. Such a course will do more to shame the attempt, and paralyze the movement, than any other. Opposition and threats will only warm the measure into excitement, and yield fuel to a flame, which will die out, lacking it, in three-fourths of the counties concerned. And even should these counties take her at her word. Virginia will be the gainer, in the long run, by their defection. They contribute to her weakness, not her strength. They impair the patriotism of the eastern section, while feeding on her resources. Their mere numbers serve to neutralize, by the ballot, the superior intellect and moral of the eastern parts; and there is nothing in their history, their record, their intellect, their character, or achievement, which can, in the slightest degree, contribute to the fame, the name, the state, wealth, dignity, virtue or strength, of ancient Virginia. Theirs is a sort of fungus growth, a mere fecundity of weed, which is at once profitless and offensive. Let them make a State for themselves, if they can, and support it as they may; they will find the proceeding an expensive one, and the Old Dominion will be relieved of an incubus which has sucked no small portion of her substance, while adding nothing to her wealth, strength or reputation.

EAST TENNESSEE

One of the best-known Unionist papers in the South, the Knoxville Whig, *suggested that east Tennessee should form its own state if Tennessee should leave the Union. The paper's editor, William G. "Parson" Brownlow, used some of the same arguments that western Virginians used.*

Knoxville Whig, 26 January 1861

William G. Brownlow: "Let East Tennessee Secede"

If, by hook, or crook, in the course of coming events, Tennessee shall madly elected rush out of the Union, by the act of the State Convention, let the Delegates from East Tennessee, enter their protests, and secede from the rest of the State, and form an independent Mountain State, the State of Frankland, and we shall soon be reinforced by Virginians and Western Carolinians. We can never live in a Southern Confederacy, and be made hewers of wood and drawers of water for a set of aristocrats and over-bearing tyrants. We are candid in urging East Tennessee to withdraw from Middle and West Tennessee, if they shall be so reckless as to consent to go out of the Union.

Most Southern newspapers dismissed Brownlow's criticism of the Confederacy and his idea that east Tennessee should form a separate state. The At-lanta Southern Confederacy *argued that Brownlow should not be permitted to voice disloyal sentiments.*

Southern Confederacy (Atlanta, Ga.), 31 October 1861

An Anonymous Writer: "Brownlow"

This distinguished gentleman complains bitterly of his hard lot. He hates the Abolitionists and always has hated them; but he hates the Secessionists more. He is unyieldingly and eternally opposed to our present revolution, and never will acquiesce in it; and yet he clings to the South and calls it his country, and it his home.

Now, our opinion is, that every man has a right, in ordinary times, to entertain, and express freely, whatever views he may like on political subjects; but that no man ought to be allowed to remain in any country who will take sides against it, or who is not fully and unreservedly committed to its policy and fortunes upon a vital issue in times like this.

In such an issue as the present Mr. Brownlow should stand up for his country, right or wrong, or leave it. In our opinion, an honest man cannot do otherwise. When a man's country is at war, struggling for existence, whether the war was brought on rightfully or wrongfully, no man who loves it can remain in it and raise his voice for its enemies or inveigh against its policy. It is treason, and should not be endured; and no man who makes pretensions to honesty and patriotism should occupy such a position. Not even neutrality should be tolerated among us now—let alone hostility.

Questions

1. Why did the *Kanawha Valley Star* encourage the state not to split but, rather, to secede from the Union as a whole?
2. Do you think that Confederate occupation of western Virginia would have made a difference in the vote to form a separate state? Explain.
3. Why did the *Charleston Mercury* believe Virginia was better off without the western part of the state?
4. Do you agree with the argument of the *Southern Confederacy* that citizens must always support their country during wartime? Explain.

Notes

1. Edward Conrad Smith, *The Borderland in the Civil War* (New York: Macmillan, 1927), 185–202.

2. Ibid., 210–20.

3. Quoted in Richard Orr Curry, *A House Divided: A Study of Statehood Politics and the Copperhead Movement in West Virginia* (Pittsburgh, Pa.: University of Pittsburgh Press, 1964), 55.

CHAPTER 9

Emancipation Proclamation, 1861–65

The Confederate states had left the Union in large part over the issue of slavery, and the issue did not disappear once the war began. Radical Republicans and outspoken abolitionists took every opportunity to urge President Abraham Lincoln to end slavery. Personally, Lincoln hated slavery and had made that fact clear. But he also recognized that it was a sensitive subject politically in the North, especially in the Midwest where many people, including a sizable number of newspaper editors, sympathized with the South. The president believed that any move toward emancipation could undermine the Union cause in the Midwest and provoke border states, such as Kentucky, to join the Confederacy. Lincoln said preserving the Union should be the overriding goal of the war, and the issue of emancipation could be put off. However, General John Frémont, the commander of Union forces in Missouri, put the issue in the spotlight on August 30, 1861, when he declared martial law in the state and ordered the confiscation of property of all those who had taken up arms against the North, including the freeing of their slaves. Frémont's order alarmed Union supporters in Kentucky, and the president recognized that it could have dire political consequences. He ordered the general to modify his emancipation edict. But radical Republicans and abolitionists increasingly argued that freeing slaves should be one of the war's aims. They recognized that constitutional protection of slavery and Northern racism worked against them, so they began arguing that ending slavery was a military necessity. Their position was that slave labor was a critical part of the Confederate war effort and thus emancipation would hurt the South's ability to fight.

Lincoln gradually became convinced of the necessity for the forcible abolition of slavery. In July of 1862, he privately told two cabinet members of his plan to issue an emancipation proclamation. The president said it was "a military necessity, absolutely essential to the preservation of the Union. We must free the slaves or ourselves be subdued."[1] The cabinet supported the plan, but Secretary of State William H. Seward advised the president to postpone any announcement until after a major military victory by the North. The president agreed, putting the proclamation in a drawer.

Lincoln's plan was not known outside the administration, however, and he continued to come under criticism for not moving fast enough in freeing the slaves. One of his sharpest critics was Horace Greeley, editor of the *New-York Tribune.* In August, Greeley published what became one of the best-known editorials of the war, "The Prayer of Twenty Millions." The president eloquently responded to Greeley in an open letter to the editor that was first published in the *National Intelligencer.* In the letter, Lincoln reiterated that preserving the Union must be the main goal of the war. But he also hinted that he might support emancipation to accomplish that goal.[2]

The military victory Lincoln wanted took longer than he expected, but the president finally got it on September 17 when the Federal army defeated Confederate forces at the battle of Antietam. Five days later, the president issued the Preliminary Emancipation Proclamation, declaring that as of January 1, 1863, all persons held as slaves within any states engaged in the rebellion would be "forever free." In announcing the proclamation, the president was acting under his war powers to seize enemy resources. The Constitution protected slavery in states loyal to the Union, so he had no authority to free any slaves there. Even so, there was intense criticism from Democrats, and they made it their central issue in the 1862 midterm elections.[3] When the Democrats made significant gains in the election, some speculated that the president would not issue the final Emancipation Proclamation. Yet Lincoln did not give in to the pressure, and the proclamation he signed on New Year's Day 1863 in some respects went beyond the first one. It justified freeing the slaves as an "act of justice" and sanctioned the enlistment of black soldiers in the Federal army.[4]

The next step for abolitionists was a constitutional amendment abolishing slavery. The president and Republicans united in favor of a measure during 1864, and Lincoln interpreted his re-election that year as a mandate to abolish slavery in the United States. On January 31, 1865, after intense lobbying by the administration, the House of Representatives approved the amendment by a vote of 119 to 56. When the result was announced, spectators in the gallery cheered, and out in the streets cannons fired a salute. Within a week, eight states had ratified the Thirteenth Amendment and during the next two months, another eleven did so. Still, it was not until Reconstruction, when enough ex-Confederate states ratified the amendment, that it became law.

Horace Greeley. *New-York Tribune* *Editor Horace Greeley was one of the most influential editors of the Civil War. Early in the war, Greeley was a sharp critic of President Abraham Lincoln, and Greeley called on the president to abolish slavery in one of his best-known editorials, "The Prayer of Twenty Millions." (Division of Prints and Photographs, Library of Congress Collection)*

This chapter begins with an editorial from Frederick Douglass, one of the most outspoken supporters of the Emancipation Proclamation. The section ends with what some consider the most famous editorial about the slavery issue, "The Prayer of Twenty Millions," and the response to it, including Lincoln's letter to Greeley. Following Lincoln's preliminary announcement of the Emancipation Proclamation, a torrent of editorials came out either supporting or assailing the announcement. Editorials from the *Chicago Tribune* and the *New-York Tribune* are examples of the support Lincoln received. But there was plenty of opposition in the North, too, as the editorial from the *Crisis* shows. The editorial from the *Chronicle & Sentinel* typifies the sentiment of many in the Confederate press.

Similar sentiments were expressed when the president issued his final Emancipation Proclamation. Supporters argued that it took the war to a new level of significance, but critics in the North and South claimed that it was a dangerous move. Finally, the chapter ends with editorials on passage of the Thirteenth Amendment. The *Daily Dispatch* said the amendment sealed the South's separation with the Union, and the *New-York Times* editorialized on the meaning of the new law.

CALLS FOR EMANCIPATION

One of the most outspoken publications arguing that ending slavery should be a Union war aim was Douglass' Monthly, *published by noted abolitionist Frederick Douglass.*

Douglass' Monthly, July 1861

Frederick Douglass: "Notes on the War"

The very stomach of this rebellion is the negro in the condition of a slave. Arrest that hoe in the hands of the negro, and you smite rebellion in the very seat of its life. Change the status of the slave from bondage to freedom, and you change the rebels into loyal citizens. The negro is the key of the situation—the pivot upon which the whole rebellion turns....

To fight against slaveholders, without fighting against slavery, is but a half hearted business, and paralyzes the hands engaged in it.... [H]enceforth let the war cry be, down with treason, and down with slavery, the cause of treason.

When the president did not move fast enough for many people to end slavery, an exasperated Horace Greeley, decided to put the weight of public opinion against Lincoln by publishing an open letter to the president in the New-York Tribune.

New-York Tribune, 20 **August 1862**

Horace Greeley: "Prayer of Twenty Millions"

To Abraham Lincoln, *President of the U. States:*

Dear Sir: I do not intrude to tell you—for you must know already—that a great proportion of those who triumphed in your election, and of all who desire the unqualified suppression of the Rebellion now desolating our country, are sorely disappointed and deeply pained by the policy you seem to be pursuing with regards to the slaves of Rebels. I write only to set succinctly and unmistakably before you what we require, what we think we have a right to expect, and of what we complain....

[W]hat an immense majority of the Loyal Millions of your countrymen require of you is a frank, declared, unqualified, begrudging execution of the laws of the land, more especially of the Confiscation Act. That Act gives freedom to the slaves of Rebels coming within our lines, or whom those lines may at any time in close—we ask you to render it due obedience by publicly requiring all your subordinates to recognize and obey it.... As one of the millions who would gladly have avoided this struggle at any sacrifice but that of Principle and Honor, but who now feel that the triumph of the Union is indispensable not only to the existence of our country but to the well-being of mankind, I entreat you to render a hearty and unequivocal obedience to the law of the land.

Yours, Horace Greeley.

Lincoln responded to Greeley's letter with a letter of his own, first published in the National Intelligencer *a major supporter of the president.*

National Intelligencer (**Washington, D.C.**), **23 August 1862**

Abraham Lincoln: "A Letter from the President"

Executive Mansion
Washington, August 22, 1862

Hon. Horace Greeley:

Dear Sir:

I have just read yours of the 19th, addressed to myself through the New York Tribune. If there be in it any statements, or assumptions of fact, which I may know to be erroneous, I do not now and here controvert them. If there be in it any inferences which I may believe to be falsely drawn, I do not now and here argue against them. If there be perceptible in it an impatient and dictatorial tone, I waive it in deference to an old friend whose heart I have always supposed to be right.

As to the policy I "seem to be pursuing" as you say, I have not meant to leave any one in doubt.

I would save the Union. I would save it the shortest way under the Constitution. The sooner the national authority can be restored the nearer the Union will be "the Union as it was." If there be those who would not save the Union unless they could at the same time *save* slavery, I do not agree with them. If there be those who would not save the Union unless they could at the same time *destroy* slavery, I do not agree with them. My paramount object in this struggle *is* to save the Union, and is *not* either to save or to destroy slavery. If I could save the Union without freeing *any* slave I would do it, and if I could save it by freeing *all* the slaves, I would do it; and if I could save it by freeing some and leaving others alone, I would also do that. What I do about slavery and the colored race, I do because I believe it helps to save this Union; and what I forbear, I forbear because I do *not* believe it would help to save the Union. I shall do *less* whenever I shall believe what I am doing hurts the cause, and I shall do *more* whenever I shall believe doing more will help the cause. I shall try to correct errors when shown to be errors; and I shall adopt new views so fast as they shall appear to be true views.

I have here stated my purpose according to my view of *official* duty; and I intend no modification of my oft-expressed *personal* wish that all men every where could be free.

Yours,
A. Lincoln.

The New-York Times *was one of several papers that criticized Greeley for his letter. The paper said it was a bold assumption for the editor to claim to represent twenty million people.*

New-York Times, 25 August 1862

An Anonymous Writer: "President Lincoln's Letter to Horace Greeley"

The editor of the Tribune lately addressed a prayer to President Lincoln, in the name of "twenty millions of people." This was not considered very modest in our neighbor, for it was a bold assumption to claim to represent the views of so vast a constituency. With characteristic modesty and good breeding, Mr. Lincoln did not question the sublime sufficiency of his correspondent, but answered Mr. Greeley in a letter as brief and pithy as the epistle of the letter was long and diffuse....

The chief difference between Mr. Lincoln and Mr. Greeley seems to be this: that the former is President and was sworn on his own conscience, and must be governed by his own sense of oath, honor and duty, as to the time and manner of his actions. On the other hand, Mr. Greeley having clearer conceptions, it may be, of right, policy and statesmanship, wishes to substitute his own conscience for Mr. Lincoln's in the present National perplexity. The President not yet seeing the propriety of abdicating in behalf of our neighbor, consoles him with a letter that assures the country of abundant sanity in the White House.

PRELIMINARY EMANCIPATION PROCLAMATION

Newspapers that supported the end of slavery, such as the Chicago Tribune, *hailed the Preliminary Emancipation Proclamation.*

Chicago Tribune, 23 September 1862

An Anonymous Writer: "The President's Proclamation"

President Lincoln has set his hand and affixed the great seal of the nation to the grandest proclamation ever issued by man. He has declared that after the first day of January next all the slaves in then rebellious States *shall be free.* He has also directed all the officers of the army and navy to observe and enforce the emancipating sections of the Confiscation Act. He has further indicated his purpose to propose once more his scheme for the abolishment of slavery in the Border States, with a sufficient hint that if it be not accepted something worse will happen. Thus, it will be perceived, his proclamation aims at nothing less than complete emancipation, and the establishment of a Free Republic from the Atlantic to the Pacific, from the Lakes to the Gulf.

So splendid a vision has hardly shone upon the world since the day of the Messiah. From the date of this proclamation begins the history of the republic as our fathers designed to have it—the home of freedom, the asylum of the oppressed, the seat of justice, the land of equal rights under the law, where each man however humble, shall be entitled to life, liberty, and the pursuit of happiness. Let no one think to stay the glorious reformation.

Every day's events are hastening its triumph, and whosoever shall place himself in its way it will grind him to powder.

For New-York Tribune*'s Greeley, who had long dreamed of freeing the slaves in the United States, Lincoln's announcement was sweet news.*

New-York Tribune, 23 September 1862

Horace Greeley: "God Bless Abraham Lincoln"

It is the beginning of the end of the rebellion; the beginning of the new life of the nation.
GOD BLESS ABRAHAM LINCOLN!

Many Democratic newspapers in the North argued that Lincoln had exceeded his constitutional authority with the Emancipation Proclamation and predicted that it would strengthen Southern efforts to defeat the Union. The Crisis *in Columbus, Ohio, claimed that the action would hurt the Republican Party in the upcoming midterm elections.*

Crisis (Columbus, Ohio), 1 October 1862

An Anonymous Writer: "The Emancipation Proclamation"

For a year past we have tried to warn the country that a despotism of the worst and most dangerous character was in store for it if the leading radical free Negro abolitionists got the full control of the Government. We have carefully and continually warned the public against these efforts to disturb the whole order of society by proclamations, after the fashion of the South American and Mexican *Pronunciamentos.* We now have it in its worst and most odious form—in its most dangerous character, and yet some men will excuse and modify, and, like the sinners when Noah's flood was swelling to dangerous dimensions, still believed "it would not be much of a shower."

The deed is now done—the avalanche is approaching—the abolitionist is smacking his lips and thanking God that he has at last brought death and desolation close to every man's door. He is delighted with the scenes of misery and horror in anticipation, and is boastful that it is the work of its bloody hands.

Let every lover of this kind—every friend of a constitutional govern-ment—every advocate of the Union as it was, and of the States with the right to their own local governments, be on the alert. The elections are close at hand, and they will tell a tale for good or for evil. The Democrats desire a fair expression of opinion—to that they are entitled—to that they will look with deep anxiety.

If the doctrine of crushing out States is to be sanctioned, then we are in a new and fearful revolution. The abolition of slavery is a State question, and cannot be exercised by the General Government without a total revolu-tion in our whole governmental theory. Because, if the slaves were confis-cated in Kentucky or any other State to-day, such State would have the right to re-establish it to-morrow. Hence this proclamation strikes at the root of State existence! People of Ohio! Are you prepared for this! If you are not, be careful how you vote, and for whom you cast your ballots. The act of voting once committed it can never be recalled. Bear this in mind, and vote, and vote right. Now is the best of this whole Negro question, and your own exis-tence as free people!

At the same time, newspapers in the Confederacy ridiculed the president's proclamation. The Chronicle & Sentinel *proclaimed, "If you want our slaves come and take them if you can."*

Chronicle & Sentinel (Augusta, Ga.), 3 October 1862

An Anonymous Writer: "Lincoln's Proclamation"

This document, the last desperate resort of the Federal Government, seems about to cause more trouble and dissatisfaction at the North than dis-may at the South....

Not only are the moderate conservatives who have always opposed Lin-coln and his war policy, disgusted by the proclamation, both those who have hitherto unscrupulously supported him, like the New York Herald and its clique, are murmuring. They see in this attack, if it is successful, upon the institutions of the South, nothing but ruin for themselves, and an end to the rich harvests they have reaped from the products of Southern labor. It will lose Lincoln many friends, and gain him none but a few fantasies in Old and New England, to conciliate whom it was designed. As to the laboring masses, they will feel no inclination to support a policy designed to place them in competition with Negro labor, and to take the breed from them-selves and families.

The effect at the South will be only to increase the enmity and abhorrence of Black Republican rule. The designs they have hitherto masked under a cloak of conservatism are developed.... We are warned, but not alarmed. The proclamation is a mere declaration of designs well known long to have been entertained, and carried into effect wherever the Federal armies have penetrated. It is in reality of great benefit to us as demonstrating to those who fondly hoped that the premises of the Federal generals to respect the rights of property, will not hereafter be regarded. It will convince the wavering men of the border states that their only safety is under the Confederate banner. As for the more Southern States their answer to Lincoln, will be similar to that of Leonidas when the Persian demanded his arms. If you want our slaves come and take them if you can.

EMANCIPATION PROCLAMATION

There was a new round of editorials when the president issued his final Emancipation Proclamation on January 1, 1863. Newspapers such as the Boston Advertiser, *which had supported the president, extolled the virtues of what he had done.*

Boston Advertiser, 2 January 1863

An Anonymous Writer: "The Emancipation Proclamation"

The President's proclamation of emancipation will attract the eye of every reader. No instrument of more momentous import has ever been published since the Declaration of American Independence challenged the attention of the world: and this proclamation affects the welfare of as large a number of human beings as did that. It is brief and explicit. It is couched in terms which set at naught much of the criticism that has been wasted upon the measure by malcontents. The President issues the proclamation in his capacity as commander-in-chief of the army and navy of the United States, in time of actual armed rebellion against the authority and government of the United States, as a fit and necessary measure. By virtue of this power and for this purpose he orders and declares that all persons held as slaves in the disloyal States and parts of States, ARE AND HENCEFORWARD SHALL BE FREE; that the executive government, including the military and naval authorities thereof, will recognize and maintain the freedom of said persons. The President enjoins upon the people thus declared to be free, to abstain from all violence unless in necessary self-defence. He recommends to them, in all cases when allowed, to labor faithfully for wages; and announces that they may be received into the armed service of the United States, to garrison forts and to man vessels. The cry that the President would instigate the horrors of a servile insurrection is thus effectually disposed of. The proclamation bears on its face wherever it may go (and there is no nook or corner where it will not penetrate) the refutation of this calumny.

We are not among those who believe that the mere dash of the President's pen at the bottom of this new charter of freedom, secures to the full and at once the object in view, that it straightway crushes the rebellion and ends the war. On the contrary, we believe that we are now simply entering upon a new stage of the war, a stage in which our progress will be beset with difficulties and complications of a novel character, taxing to the utmost the power of the people and the wisdom of their rulers. But since the government has resolved upon this step, we gladly give to it the poor aid of our support; and we are not unmindful of the immense advantages in the prosecution of the war gained to us by this measure. Not to speak of the obvious advantages incident to the employment of Negroes in our own army, and in a measure, depriving the enemy of their services, in the first place we now strike the axe directly at the root of the tree of our national difficulties.

But Democratic newspapers, such as the Cleveland Plain Dealer, *questioned the president's authority to order the proclamation and warned of dire consequences.*

Cleveland Plain Dealer, 3 January 1863

An Anonymous Writer: "The Proclamation"

President Lincoln has issued his Proclamation. The slaves in many States are declared free, but advised to *remain where they are* and work for reasonable wages, which they no doubt will do. We have expressed our opinion of the Proclamation so many times that it will be useless to repeat it—Lincoln, by the Constitution, Commander In-Chief of the Armies of the United States, has exercised his war power, not as President, but as General. He justifies the act as a military necessity. Having failed to end the war and restore the Union by means of the magnificent armies generously confided to his Generalship and guardianship, having in fact suffered them to be decimated and their energy paralyzed by political Generals who seem to command the military Generals in the field, he has magnanimously resolved to risk what reputation he has left upon the issuing of a Proclamation of Emancipation and thus terminate the rebellion and the war, with one bold dash of the pen. Results will show the wisdom or folly of the measure.

Some Southern newspapers downplayed the proclamation, arguing that it was what the Union Army had been doing since the war began. The Mobile Register & Advertiser *said blacks would be stolen by the North and put to work for the army.*

Mobile Register & Advertiser, 15 January 1863

An Anonymous Writer: "What Will They Do with the Negroes"

Thus the slaves are only to change masters; they are to be stolen instead of freed; in place of being set at liberty...This is all the proclamation amounts to; it is harmless fulmination, the offspring of a malignant, but baffled and impotent hatred; the declaration of an intention to do on a grand scale what the Abolition army have been doing all along to the extent of their ability, that ability having hitherto been strictly limited to their own lines of occupation. Whether the Negroes would be gainers by such a change of masters is a question that has been sufficiently answered during the progress of this struggle. Wherever they have been decoyed or have fallen by the fortune of war into the hands of the enemy, they have been treated with the utmost barbarity, worked, whipped, starved and murdered by taskmasters, who, brutal and inhuman, have no interest in them beyond the immediate benefits of their labor. And such would continue to be their fate to the end of the chapter.

Slave insurrections were a great fear for many in the South, and some newspapers, such as the Richmond Examiner, *feared the proclamation would cause slaves to rise up against their owners.*

Richmond Examiner, 7 January 1863

An Anonymous Writer: "A Startling Political Crime"

The most startling political crime, the most stupid political blunder, yet known in American history, has not been consummated. The promised proclamation of Abraham Lincoln to decree the abolition of negro slavery, in all the States of the late Union not yet subjugated by the arms of the United States, is laid before the reader this morning....

To produce this last named effect—servile insurrection—is the real, sole purpose of this proclamation. No glowing words, no whining exhortation of good order to the slaves, conceal or disguise this horrid intention. No other translation of this paper will be given to it either in Europe or America. That it will fail to accomplish this vile end, and be void and entirely without effect in the Southern Confederacy, unless our armies should be not only beaten, but destroyed, are truths which need not be explained or argued before our readers. So far from being a cause of alarm, this proclamation is a subject of congratulation to the friends of the Southern cause. It exposes the true character of the enemy, beyond the possibility of misconception. It will obtain the universal condemnation and contempt of Europe, and fill every mind of the North that still retains the traces of humanity, with amazement, indignation, and horror. Its effect on the people of the South will be most salutary. It shuts the door of retreat and repentance on the weak and timid. Those who would turn back in their path, if there are any, have now no longer that miserable chance. Even submission now cannot procure mercy. The deed is done, and the Southern people have only to choose between victory and death.

THIRTEENTH AMENDMENT

Southern newspapers dismissed the Thirteenth Amendment. The Daily Dispatch *in Richmond said the new law sealed the South's separation with the Union.*

Daily Dispatch (Richmond), 7 February 1865

An Anonymous Writer: "The Thirteenth Amendment"

[T]he hand of Heaven has written on the wall the eternal separation of the United States, and no Confederate man will longer even desire to join together that which God hath put asunder.

The United States Congress has abolished slavery in the United States. We could laugh at their folly, if gratitude for the service they have rendered us did not forbid us to treat our benefactors with irreverence...Let them make good their laws by deeds instead of words. We are going to resist them henceforth as one man, and to defend our hearthstones and our lives as men do who have no hope but in God and in their own right arms. The "moral strength" of the Confederacy is this day restored as by a miracle.

Laus Deo! We shall maintain our cause, our institutions, the integrity of our soldiers. We ask no more for peace, nor do we expect it, nor will we have it whilst the foot of a Yankee soldier pollutes this soil, or a hostile Yankee flag is unfurled on this continent.

The New-York Times *hailed passage of the amendment as one of the most important acts in the nation's history.*

New-York Times, 1 February 1865

An Anonymous Writer: "The Abolition of Slavery"

The adoption of this amendment is the most important step ever taken by Congress, and its ratification by the requisite number of States will complete the most important act of internal administration performed by any nation for a hundred years. It perfects the great work of the founders of our Republic. The national feeling was not strong enough to enable them to abolish slavery at the outset of our career; but although slavery has grown in power with gigantic strides since that time, the growth of the sentiment of nationality has outstripped it, and slavery is now abolished, not only without danger to the Union, but as the only means of preserving and making it perpetual. The *rebellion*, however, is the cause of its abolition. That act of madness and treason touched the very heart of the nation, and aroused to vigorous action the patriotism and national pride of the American people. But for the rebellion slavery would have lasted fifty years—perhaps twice as long—and its destruction, even if it had been achieved by peaceful means, would have cost as much in treasure and in human suffering as the war has involved.

With the passage of this amendment the Republic enters upon a new stage of its great career. It is hereafter to be, what it has never been hitherto, thoroughly *democratic*—resting on human rights as its basis, and aiming at the greatest good and the highest happiness of all its people.

QUESTIONS

1. Why do you think Horace Greeley chose to write his editorial, "The Prayer of the Twenty Millions," in the form of a letter to the president?
2. Why did Copperhead newspapers in the North oppose the Emancipation Proclamation?
3. How did passage of the Thirteenth Amendment, in the words of the *New-York Times,* perfect "the great work of the founders of our Republic"?

NOTES

1. James M. McPherson, *Battle Cry of Freedom: The Civil War Era* (New York: Oxford University Press, 1988), 504.

2. *National Intelligencer* (Washington, D.C.), 23 August 1862.

3. Wood Gray, *The Hidden Civil War: The Story of the Copperheads* (New York: Viking Press, 1964), 100–108.

4. Roy P. Basler, ed., *Abraham Lincoln: His Speeches and Writings* (Cleveland: World Publishing, 1946), 689–91.

CHAPTER 10

McClellan Controversy, 1861–62

George B. McClellan was one of the most intriguing and controversial leaders of the Civil War. After the devastating defeat at First Bull Run, the Union general built the Army of the Potomac into one of the finest armies of the war. Dubbed the "Little Napoleon," McClellan enjoyed the admiration of his troops. However, his cautious nature led to questions about his military leadership. President Abraham Lincoln finally removed him from command after the battle of Antietam.[1]

McClellan was one of many Civil War generals to fight in the Mexican-American War where he won citations for distinguished service. He left the army to become a railroad executive, but when the Civil War began he received a commission to command the newly created Department of the Ohio. McClellan led Union troops to victory in the first land battle of the war at Philippi on June 3, 1861, following that up with two more triumphs. After the Federal defeat at First Bull Run, Lincoln summoned McClellan to Washington to rebuild the shattered Union army. Lincoln had signed a bill for the three-year enlistment of 500,000 men. From this group of raw recruits, McClellan created the Army of the Potomac, restoring morale and instilling discipline. At the same time, he established a rapport with his men that few Union commanders enjoyed.

But McClellan refused to be rushed into moving against the Confederate army in 1861. He overestimated the strength of the Rebels and used it as an excuse to remain on the defensive. By October, McClellan had 120,000 men outside Washington, more than twice the size of the Confederate force. However, McClellan was convinced that the enemy numbered 150,000 men. Critics began questioning his leadership, but McClellan still refused to move. Instead, the army went into winter quarters.

After prodding from the president, McClellan finally announced his plan for a spring 1862 offensive against the Confederate army. He proposed an amphibious assault against the Confederate capital using the Rappahannock River. Lincoln did not like the plan but gave his approval. The Peninsula Campaign, as it came to be known, began in March 1862 with nearly 400 vessels transporting more than 120,000 troops to the Virginia peninsula. The Lincoln administration was concerned that the plan would expose Washington to a Rebel counterattack. The president ordered a corps of 35,000 men detached from McClellan's army to protect the capital. McClellan later complained that the move hurt his chance for victory, but even so the Union force still far outnumbered the Confederates.

Confederate leaders anticipated McClellan's plan and moved troops from Manassas to an entrenched position behind the Rappahannock. The Union Army met its first serious resistance of the campaign near Yorktown. Only 13,000 Rebels defended the town, but they tricked McClellan into thinking they had far greater numbers. The Federal commander decided to lay siege to Yorktown, and this gave the Confederates time to bring in more forces to defend Richmond. Faced with insurmountable numbers, Rebel forces finally had to retreat from Yorktown up the Peninsula. By the end of May, McClellan had reached the outskirts of Richmond, so close that troops could hear the city's church bells.

Still pursuing a conservative strategy, the Union commander decided to lay siege to the Confederate capital instead of launching an outright attack. Confederate General Joseph Johnston launched a counterattack on May 31. At the battle of Fair Oaks, Johnston was wounded and replaced by Robert E. Lee. Lee recognized McClellan's cautiousness and launched a series of attacks known as the Seven Days' battles. Although the Confederate attacks were not successful, they put McClellan on the defensive, and he pulled back from Richmond. An exasperated Lincoln ordered McClellan to bring his army back to Washington.

After the failure of the Peninsula Campaign, McClellan was stripped of his authority, and he was ordered to support General John Pope's newly created Army of Virginia. By late summer, the Lincoln administration decided to launch a new offensive with Pope's army. But at Second Bull Run, the Confederates badly defeated Pope's forces.

Lincoln reluctantly turned to McClellan to rebuild the army again, and he did so. In the meantime, Lee decided to use the victory at Bull Run as a springboard for an invasion into the North. On September 5, Lee's army crossed the Potomac River and McClellan left Washington to follow the Rebels. A week later, Union soldiers found a lost copy of Lee's plan for the campaign. The remarkable stroke of good luck showed that the Confederate army had been divided into four parts that were miles apart. McClellan's larger army could crush the smaller forces before they could reunite. But once again, the cautious commander moved slowly, permitting Lee to concentrate his troops. The Rebel forces massed on the banks of the Antietam Creek near Sharpsburg, Maryland, and awaited McClellan's attack. The battle of Antietam on September 17 was the single bloodiest day of the war with both sides suffering enormous casualties. The Federal army stopped the Confederate invasion, but McClellan delayed pursuing the retreating Rebels and lost an opportunity to deliver a knockout. McClellan's critics again questioned his will to fight.

Lincoln visited the Army of the Potomac on October 1 and urged McClellan to move against the Confederates. Lincoln believed Lee's staggering army could finally be defeated once and for all. However, the general refused to move until his troops had fully recovered from the fighting at Antietam. After Antietam, Lincoln issued the preliminary Emancipation Proclamation, making the war a crusade against slavery. This put the president at odds with the conservative McClellan, who believed the Union should be restored with as few changes as possible. When it became clear the Union army would not fight the Confederates again soon, Lincoln gave up on his general. On November 7, he replaced McClellan with Ambrose E. Burnside, a favorite of the radical arm of the Republican Party. In explaining his decision to relieve McClellan, Lincoln told one of the general's supporters, "I said I would remove him if he let Lee's army get away from him, and I must do so. He has got the 'slows'."[2]

While awaiting a new assignment, McClellan contacted Democratic leaders who were considering candidates to run against Lincoln in the 1864 presidential election. A longtime Democrat, McClellan had the name recognition that supporters believed would make him a worthy opponent for the president, despite the controversy over his military leadership. The following year McClellan became the Democratic nominee, but Lincoln defeated him handily.

This chapter traces editorial views on McClellan. Republican newspapers that supported the president were often critical of the general, claiming he did not like to fight. Democratic newspapers backed McClellan, often citing his popularity with the troops. Southern newspapers generally did not take up the issue of McClellan, except to point out the problems it caused for the Union.

OPPOSITION TO McCLELLAN

The Chicago Tribune *claimed that McClellan, a Democrat, had purposely delayed attacking the Confederate Army after Antietam to keep from handing the Republican Party a victory on the eve of the congressional elections.*

Chicago Tribune, 8 November 1862

An Anonymous Writer: "McClellan to Thank"

The President has McClellan mainly to thank for the result of the October and November elections. The vote of censure upon the Administration is the work of the commander of the Potomac army. Had he pursued the rebels with vigor and resolution on the morning after the battle of Antietam it was in his power almost to have annihilated them. With bayonet, sabre, and grape shot his troops could have slaughtered the rebels by thousands, and thousands would have drowned in attempting to swim the Potomac, and whole brigades would have surrendered on the spot. A vigorous pursuit of the remnants that might have got across, would have resulted in their capture or dispersion, and the proud army of Generals Lee and Stonewall Jackson which has so long and successfully held the Potomac army at bay, would have ceased to exist. The effect of such a victory can easily be imagined. The whole country would have been electrified and rejoiced. The praises of McClellan and the Administration would be on every tongue. No party would have dared to set up against the Administration, and the Republicans would have swept every State at the polls.

The people will always cordially support the administration while it is achieving victories over its foes. No sacrifice is esteemed too great, if repaid with success. But it was not the purpose of "Young Napoleon" to do anything that would benefit the Republicans or strengthen the Administration with people. He has no disposition to be so accommodating.

The Baltimore American *said the Union "ought to have commanders who will move forward." McClellan had defied orders to move against the Confederate Army after Antietam.*

Baltimore American, 11 November 1862

An Anonymous Writer: "The Change of Commanders and the Reason for It"

[N]one have been more anxious than we have been that with the splendid opportunity afforded General McClellan, he should once and for all have silenced all who have complained of his slowness—of his backwardness to engage the Rebel army, Victorious at South Mountain and Antietam the country certainly expected him to follow up his successes.... The order to "advance" was imperative; the neglect to do so plain; and unless good and sufficient reasons—better than seem now to be presented—justify the five weeks inaction which has enabled the bulk of the Rebel army to run away in safety once more, all must agree that the Government ought to have commanders who will move forward....

The Chicago Tribune, *one of the most outspoken critics of McClellan, accused the general of being too timid to fight. The paper said the army was ready and needed a strong general to lead it.*

Chicago Tribune, 14 October 1862

An Anonymous Writer: "Army of the Potomac"

Poll the city of Chicago today, and nine-tenths of the people therein would vote to have Gen. McClellan move against the enemy, or give up his command and move to the rear, leaving "fighting Joe Hooker" in his place. They cannot endure the idea of another winter campaign on the Potomac, and they have no belief in the statement that our soldiers will not fight.... The rains and frosts of November will be as effectual a check to an advance, as apathy and treason have been. In a month, winter quarters for that army must be sought. It is now strong—unquestionably superior to that of the enemy. It is well provided with the means for an offensive movement. It is impatient of the restraint in which it is held. It has, in its loyalty, zeal and courage, the antecedent assurances of victory—if it is well led. Must it lie in tents, waiting the timidity of its generals, another winter? Must this great Republic, go to hopeless ruin on that rock...to prove, what yet remains an open question, that McClellan is a great commander.

Given his popularity with the troops, the Richmond Whig *argued that McClellan should have fought his reassignment. The paper had fun with the McClellan's nickname, the "Little Napoleon," and asked, "What would the real Napoleon have done under similar circumstances?"*

Richmond Whig, 17 November 1862

An Anonymous Writer: "The Little Napoleon"

McClellan's farewell to his troops is a protest against "the deep damnation of his taking off"—and appeals to them and the country for sympathy.

One cannot but help thinking how "little" there is Napoleonic in the manner in which he submits to the wrong and outrage which he evidently thinks has been done to him! What would the real Napoleon have done under similar circumstances? The army were his friends and partisans. The country had just declared in his favor by their voice at the polls. But with this immense leverage in his hands, he submits with lamb like humility to the edict of a despot powerless without the army. McClellan is a very little Napoleon!

SUPPORT FOR MCCLELLAN

A longtime supporter of McClellan, the New York Herald *claimed that the general was removed of command because he refused to support the Emancipation Proclamation.*

New York Herald, 10 November 1862

An Anonymous Writer: "The Removal of General McClellan"

[H]is unpardonable crime has been his persistent refusal to make the cause of the Union secondary to the cause of negro emancipation.... [T]his crowning offence has been covered up in the charges that he is too slow, too cautious, too timid, too lukewarm, too apprehensive of the strength of the army of the enemy, and with too little confidence of his own, and that he has lost too many opportunities for decisive victories....

But against these accusations history will answer that, after first disastrous battle of Bull [R]un, it was McClellan who reorganized the shattered army of the Union and saved the national capital...that McClellan, in his peninsula campaign, was thus victimized, and that against the overwhelming forces of the enemy his army and the national capital were again saved only through his admirable management...and, finally, that at Antietam he relieved Washington, Maryland and Philadelphia from the fearful dangers of a powerful rebel host, which had cut up the finest and most completely appointed army ever mustered on this continent....

The Johnstown Democrat *claimed abolitionist supporters, including members of the press, had tarnished McClellan's reputation. The paper said the general remained the "idol of the army and the people."*

Johnstown (Pa.) Democrat, 29 April 1863

An Anonymous Writer: "McClellan and His Enemies"

Notwithstanding the base and cowardly efforts of Congressional Committees, and the equally base and cowardly attempts of Abolitionist editors and politicians to blacken the justly earned fame of Major General Geo. B. McClellan, they have met with a signal, ridiculous, humiliating defeat.

Wherever the name of that illustrious, able, heroic soldier is mentioned in popular assemblies, it is received with spontaneous outbursts of enthusiastic applause. We are exceedingly rejoiced at this, because we have always believed that the dominant party in its course toward him, was influenced by a malicious spirit of persecution. Because it is a manifestation that the people appreciate at their true value and with gratitude, the invaluable services the General has rendered to the army and the country, and because it shows that they penetrate with a clearness and accuracy peculiarly characteristic of American citizens, the motives of those who seek to blast his now world-renowned reputation for military sagacity, prudence, foresight, and exalted patriotism.

His reports of the Peninsular campaign and his subsequent movements, embracing the brilliant and memorable battle of Antietam, are couched in plain, simple, unadorned language, which, while they carry conviction of his integrity and capacity to every honest, unbiased breast, furnish the best possible answer to the vindictive assaults of his enemies. Despite Congressional reports and a truculent party press, Gen. McClellan, (perhaps the only man in the country who was qualified to organize a respectable military force out of an armed mob after the first battle of Bull Run,) still remains the idol of the army and the people. The judgment of the army composed, as in the main it is, of intelligent, observant men, is not to be despised, but on the contrary, must be respected, and the discrimination of the people, when unblended by prejudice, is never at fault.

We predict that when the wretched time, serving politicians—who fatten upon the spoils thrown in their way by those who misrule and plunder this unfortunate nation, shall slumber in dishonorable graves, the name of him they vainly sought to brand as a traitor, will be blazoned in letters of imperishable lusture in his country's history.

The Cleveland Plain Dealer *called for McClellan's reappointment after the Union's army was defeated at the battle of Fredericksburg in December 1862. General Ambrose E. Burnside, who had replaced McClellan, re-*

signed his post and was succeeded by General Joseph Hooker. Hooker had bragged that he would defeat the Confederates, but suffered a humiliating defeat at Fredericksburg.

Cleveland Plain Dealer, 30 January 1863

An Anonymous Writer: "Another Commanding General"

The folly of appointing any other General but McClellan to the command of the Army of the Potomac must now be apparent to all but the blindest of partisans and the meanest of his enemies....

All the Burnsides, Hookers, and Meades ever born can never control and command that gallant army. It has an idol in its heart of hearts, and that idol is George B. McClellan. He alone can successfully command them.

It is painfully amusing to read the wretched apologies made for the removal of Hooker. He was removed for *incompetency*—why disguise the fact. Are the people so ignorant that they cannot tell a lion from an ass?...

McClellan has the faculty of controlling an army of hundreds of thousands. His mind is comprehensive, the grasp of his intellect keen and subtle. He is beyond question the greatest General of the day.... What we now need is a new Commander-in-Chief, and the General of all Generals for the position is George R. McClellan, and sooner or later—within two weeks or two months—he, we predict, will again command our armies.

The Richmond Examiner *found it remarkable that despite Democratic gains in the 1862 congressional election, the Lincoln administration would replace the party's favorite general.*

Richmond Examiner, 15 November 1862

An Anonymous Writer: "Abolitionist Government Bold"

One thing must be admitted, that this Abolitionist Government is very bold. It has not hesitated to take up the glove thrown down by the Democratic party, has dismissed the military hero of that powerful organization. We may rest assured that it will not any more hesitate to execute the tremendous project it has conceived for this winter's work.

QUESTIONS

1. Do you think criticism of General McClellan was justified? Why or why not?
2. Do you think the president was justified in removing McClellan from command, despite his victory at Antietam? Why or why not?
3. Do you think that General McClellan was responsible for the Republican defeats in the 1862 election, as the *Chicago Tribune* claimed? Why or why not?
4. Do you agree with the *Richmond Examiner* that it was bold of President Lincoln to replace a popular general after Republicans suffered defeat in the 1862 election? Why or why not?

NOTES

1. Thomas J. Rowland, *George B. McClellan and Civil War History: In the Shadow of Grant and Sherman* (Kent, Ohio: Kent State University Press, 1998).

2. Quoted in T. Harry Williams, *Lincoln and His Generals* (New York: Knopf, 1952), 177.

CHAPTER 11

Midterm Elections, 1862

As the summer of 1862 drew to a close, the North was in despair over the course of the war. Robert E. Lee's Confederate troops had defeated Union forces at the Seven Days' battles and General George B. McClellan's campaign against Richmond had become bogged down. The Union War Department called the army back to Washington and replaced the cautious McClellan with General John Pope. Lee then crushed Pope's troops at the Second Battle of Bull Run on August 30, and a confident Confederate army invaded Maryland. At the same time, another Southern force commanded by General Braxton Bragg marched into Kentucky to threaten Louisville and Cincinnati. "The nation is rapidly sinking..." wrote New York diarist George Templeton Strong. "Disgust with our present government is certainly universal."[1]

As important fighting was taking place, Republicans and Democrats were battling in the midterm elections of 1862. At stake were seats in the U.S. Congress, as well as the gubernatorial and legislative leadership of several key Northern states. Democrats scored major victories in the election of 1862. The party gained 35 seats in the House of Representatives, won gubernatorial races in New York and New Jersey, and took control of the state legislatures in Illinois, Indiana, and New Jersey. It is likely the Democrats also would have won gubernatorial and legislative races in the key states of Ohio and Pennsylvania if they had not been held in odd-numbered years.[2]

Several issues played important roles in the Democratic victories. Since the beginning of the war, Union authorities had arrested hundreds of Confederate sympathizers in the North. Most of those arrested were Democrats, including some prominent party members. Democrats, including their friends in the press, angrily denounced the arrests as violations of constitutional protections of free speech and a free press. The president's suspension of habeas corpus to enforce the draft also gave the Democrats another weapon with which to portray Lincoln as trying to assume unprecedented powers for the chief executive.

The Republican policy on slavery hurt the party in the midterm election. Radical Republicans had long wanted to make ending slavery one of the war's aims. But moderate members of the party, including President Lincoln, recognized that the issue could have political ramifications in Midwestern states, where there was widespread prejudice against blacks and slavery had considerable support. Lincoln eventually became convinced that slavery must be ended, and after the Union victory at Antietam on September 17, he issued the preliminary Emancipation Proclamation on September 22. Democrats effectively exploited the controversial order, arguing that an onslaught of free blacks would move north, compete for jobs, and disrupt the social system. The New York Democratic platform called the Emancipation Proclamation "a proposal for the butchery of women and children, for scenes of lust and rapine, and of arson and murder."[3] And an Ohio Democrat amended the party's slogan to proclaim "the Constitution as it is, the Union as it was, and the Niggers where they are."[4]

The outcome of the election also reflected the North's weariness with the war and frustration with how the Lincoln administration was waging it. After 18 months of hard fighting, many in the North could see no apparent progress in putting down the rebellion. Although the Union had scored several important victories in the Western theater, little of real significance had been accomplished in the East, aside from turning back the Confederate invasion at Antietam. Even then, General McClellan had seemed to squander a chance to destroy the retreating Rebels. Just weeks before the election, General Jeb Stuart's Confederate cavalry raided the North while racing around the Army of Potomac, seeming to underscore the military futility of the North.[5]

Although Democratic leaders, including their supporters in the press, proclaimed the 1862 election results a great triumph for the party, its significance was exaggerated. Republicans maintained control of both houses of Congress and made a net gain of five seats in the Senate. They also still controlled a majority of state legislatures and governorships.

Sobered by the election defeats, however, Republican leaders agreed they had to make changes. They recognized that military arrests had angered voters, and by the end of the year, many of those still in custody were released.[6] Republicans also recognized that they must maintain party unity and campaign more actively. The elections also taught Republicans the importance of procuring the vote of soldiers. Many states did not provide for soldiers voting on the field. But after the election, a number of states changed procedures to allow soldiers to vote by absentee ballot. Two years later, Union soldiers overwhelmingly voted for Lincoln's reelection.

Democratic leaders, including some in the press, speculated that the results of the election would force the president to suspend the Emancipation Proclamation. But Lincoln refused to change his plans. In fact, the final Emancipation Proclamation went beyond the first one to sanction the enlistment of black troops in the Union army.

This chapter follows editorial debate about the important midterm elections. Democratic newspapers in the North, such as the *Crisis, Jonesboro Gazette,* and *Dubuque Herald,* spoke out loudly against the Emancipation Proclamation, Lincoln's administration of the war, and what they saw as the abuse of constitutional powers by the president. Republican newspapers, such as the *Quincy Whig & Republican,* the *Chicago Tribune,* and *Philadelphia Inquirer,* accused Democrats of using racism to win the election.

Democratic papers reveled in the election results. The *Cleveland Plain Dealer* said the president had to replace the more radical members of his cabinet. And the *New York Herald* claimed that the results showed the country did not want the war to be about slavery. Even Republican supporters in the press said the president had to make changes. The *New-York Times* argued that Lincoln must show a stronger will to wage war against the South. The *Chicago Tribune* said General McClellan had to be replaced. After the election, Southern newspapers also weighed in and claimed that the election showed the Northern people were tired of the war.

Support for Democrats

The Crisis *was one of the most outspoken critics of President Lincoln's administration of the war. The paper expressed dismay at the casualties during the battle of Antietam.*

Crisis (Columbus, Ohio), 24 September 1862

An Anonymous Writer: "Horrors of War"

The past has been a most eventful week in the horrors of war, yet without any definite results commensurate with the number of battles fought, or the horrible destruction of human life. Were it the only purpose to depopulate the country by destroying the male portion of the human family, the success has been remarkably great on both sides. The horrors of this war on the fields of battle [in spite of the fact that one might be sure the government did not report the full losses] have no parallel in modern times....

The whole country in the region of the late battles in Maryland is filled with wounded soldiers, and the graves of the dead number in the thousands, if not tens of thousands. Every house, barn, stable and out building contains its full complement of maimed and dying, and still the cry of those at home is for more victims! The whole civilized world looks upon us with astonishment and cries out against such madness, as it appears to them.

The result of the bloody affray in Maryland is, that the Confederates have retreated across the Potomac toward Winchester. After taking Harper's Ferry and about 12,000 prisoners and more than a million dollars of public property, they abandoned it, and it is in possession once more of our troops....

What effect the Lincoln and Seward Proclamation freeing the slave may have on these bloody conflicts, time alone can develop. This we know: had this proclamation been issued sooner, many in the army would not have voluntarily gone....

The Jonesboro Gazette *urged voters to elect Democratic state legislators who would block what it claimed would be an onslaught of blacks moving into Illinois from the South.*

Jonesboro (Ill.) Gazette, 27 September 1862

An Anonymous Writer: "Keep Illinois from Being Overrun"

Democrats, recollect that you want to send men to the legislature who will take the means to prevent the State from being overrun by free niggers, and the labor of white men being reduced to free nigger prices.

The Dubuque (Iowa) Herald, *another vocal critic of the Lincoln administration, called on Democrats to "save this Union" from Republicans, who the paper claimed, were usurping people's Constitutional rights.*

Dubuque (Iowa) Herald, 8 October 1862

An Anonymous Writer: "Democrats, to Arms"

The time has come when we can no longer shut our eyes and hope for better things at the hands of the dominant party. This war is to be waged for partisan purposes. To save the Union is not a part of their design, but to divide and destroy it, is their aim. This war, which we are told by Abolitionists, is being conducted to put down the rebellion, is, in reality, to further their mad schemes of negro emancipation and negro equality. We who oppose those unconstitutional measures are denounced as traitors, and not only denied the meanest privileges, but our Constitutional rights are swept away. The Government is being destroyed, and on the ruins of the Temple of our liberties they are erecting a despotism as tyrannical as that of Nero.

These men have given us a little warning of their designs. They boldly talk of a strong Central Government, and even have hinted of a Monarchy! The doctrine of State rights they ridicule. The Constitution as it is they utterly disregard, and despise as a thing of the past, and hated by their entire party.

We have too great an interest in this Revolution to remain inactive while our liberty is being taken away, and having such an interest as is ours, shall we not have a voice in our own behalf? Are we to yield to these men, in devotion to the Union? Have we not a right to our opinion as well as they to theirs?—they, whose lives have been devoted to the labor of insidiously undermining the Government,—whose ancestors belonged to the tory party of the revolutionary war!—whose fathers burned blue lights at a later period— to guide a public enemy to our shores,—who belonged to the Hartford Convention, and denounced General Jackson,—who refused to vote supplies to our soldiers in the Mexican war,—who resisted the execution of the Fugitive slave law,—and who encouraged John Brown raids and Kansas freebooters,—in short, these men, who have ever opposed the Government, and favored mob law,—these men, who hated and despised the Government of Washington and Jefferson,—these men, who never drew a loyal breadth in their lives, come forward now, to charge us with treason!

Democrats! Our duty is plain. It is for us to save this Union and once more unite the people of this country. Let us rise in our might, and hurl these men from power!

Democrats, to arms! to the field! and put down these usurpers of the Government. The arms we must use are ballots, and our field is the platform of the Constitution.

SUPPORT FOR REPUBLICANS

The Quincy Whig & Republican *accused the Democratic Party of trying to revive a "dead and rotten party" by using racism to frighten voters into supporting the party's candidates.*

Quincy (Ill.) Whig & Republican, 17 September 1862

An Anonymous Writer: "A Dead and Rotten Party"

The Democratic Party is trying to galvanize a dead and rotten party into life by yelping "nigger! Nigger! NIGGER! Around its corpse.

The Chicago Tribune, *a loyal Republican supporter, said the election would determine the future course of the war—and "whether that precious blood that has been spilled shall have been spilled in vain." It called on Republicans to save the next Congress from Democrats who would end the war.*

Chicago Tribune, 21 October 1862

An Anonymous Writer: "To the Old Guard!"

We call upon you by the love you bear your sons and brothers in the field, to take hold of the work in earnest, and overthrow at the ballot box those would bring to naught the toils and sufferings of our soldiers and hand us over to Jeff. Davis and his traitor oligarchy.... The great edict of freedom to which the President has affixed the nation's seal, is yours to defend and uphold....

Since the war commenced—since the parricides first banded together to destroy their country and ours—there has been no moment of such imminent danger as this. The question of whether the precious blood that has been spilled shall have been spilled in vain; whether the vast treasures that has been poured out shall have poured out to no expense. Our friends are exposing their lives, wasting their youth, filling our hearts with anxiety in distant camps and fields, all that we may have a country, a flag, a constitution and the freedom which it guarantees. Shall Illinois now say, by her vote, that these sacrifices are worthless, this patriotism misguided?...

Reader, we make this appeal to you. If you love this land of your birth, the memory of your fathers, the heritage of free institutions, give your time and your strength to the work of saving this next Congress from the hands of Tories.

In an editorial published just before the election, the Philadelphia Inquirer *defended the the Lincoln administration's prosecution of the war.*

The paper said although the war was costly, preserving the Union was worth the cost.

Philadelphia Inquirer, 4 November 1862

An Anonymous Writer: "The Consistency of the War"

As we consider the sacrifices already made in this war, and attempt to estimate what more must be made for its prosecution, we find here and there a skeptic as to the policy of paying so dearly for the reduction of the Rebellion....

Now, among these various doubters about the war for the Union, we look in vain for an answer to the question, what would our independence as a distinct people be wroth with the independence of the Rebel States established? This war is immensely costly, but how much would the condition of peace cost in that event? To say nothing of honor, how much in men, in the actual expenditure of money, and in the direct and indirect interference with interests; and how much in safeguards vital to the Nation?...

There are other grave questions of profit and security which present themselves to even superficial reflection, upon the proposition of peace without union. But the merest suggestion of those referred to proves that is a thing not to be thought of. The war is to be prosecuted for the preservation of the Union and nothing less; its preservation at and necessary cost; by any necessary means. Peace without it must not be less hollow than shameful. The taxes imposed by such a peace would be immeasurable in amount; indefinite in duration. This would be our material loss. What would be the loss in honor, in hope, in the promise we have given the world of a free empire, we dare not dwell upon.

Reduced then to the homely calculation of dollars and cents—pride, reputation, duty to ourselves of this day, to our posterity, and to the cause of human freedom everywhere, all these considerations set aside—we have no choice but to carry on this war with its original purpose; to believe and to resolve that it must be prosecuted until the Union and Peace shall be restored together.

NORTHERN REACTION TO ELECTION RESULTS

Critics of the Lincoln administration charged that Radical Republicans in the president's cabinet had provided him with poor advice in waging the war and particularly in issuing the preliminary Emancipation Proclama-

tion. The Cleveland Plain Dealer, *an outspoken Democratic newspaper, said the president must replace his cabinet with new members.*

Cleveland Plain Dealer, 11 November 1862

An Anonymous Writer: "A New Cabinet"

The entire country has become thoroughly disgusted and almost disheartened at the manner in which this war has been conducted from its commencement to the present time. Miserable inefficiency and imbecility seem to weigh with leaden influence upon our counsels, as well as the movements of our armies. The Northern States have offered all the men and money that might be necessary to bring this war to a speedy and successful termination.

With unlimited means at its disposal, what has the administration accomplished? Our victories have been without result, and the sacrifice of thousands of our brave soldiers seems to have been almost without object. Assurances have been constantly given that important movements were about to be made, by which great things were to be done—all have ended in smoke.

No one has been benefited by this war but army contractors, who have succeeded in swindling the country to an alarming extent, and a host of officers whose pay has been ten times greater than it ever was previous to the war.

Now the people, who are the most interested and who have to pay the bills, ask what is the reason of this state of affairs, and how much longer it is to continue? What is the object of the war? Is it to save the country to endeavor to make it great, prosperous and respected once more; or is it simply for the Abolition of Slavery? The people now insist that something be done, without delay, and that political intriguers shall no longer have power to thwart our Generals in order to prevent them from becoming too popular.

Energetic action is now demanded—it is the only thing that can save the Republic. But so long as Mr. Lincoln retains his present Cabinet, things will go on as they have, and it will be folly to expect anything better. Timidity and feebleness in council are incompatible with vigor of action.

The men the President now has for advisers have been long enough in power to show what is to be expected of them. Now let us have a change.

Another Democratic paper, the New York Herald, *argued that the election results showed that the country did not want the war to be about ending slavery.*

New York Herald, 6 November 1862

An Anonymous Writer: "The Recent Conservative Revolution"

In these late elections we have all the manifestations of a great political revolution. Their results have astonished all parties, and completely confounded the abolition Jacobins.

From New York to Illinois the people of the great and powerful central division of the Union have spoken with a voice which cannot be misunderstood. It is the same voice which last year so emphatically endorsed the party identified with the administration. That party is so rebuked and repudiated, because of its pernicious measures of last winter's legislation and its enormous corruptions, while the original wise and patriotic war policy of President Lincoln is reaffirmed by the people. They call upon him to adhere to that policy. They demand that this war shall be prosecuted for the restoration of the Union, and that the wicked faction seeking to divert it into a war for the bloody extirpation of Southern slavery shall, by the President, be henceforth rejected and turned adrift.

The New-York Times, *generally a supporter of Lincoln, maintained that the election results showed a lack of confidence in the president's administration of the war. The paper said Lincoln had been indecisive too often, and that he must summon the will to win the war.*

New-York Times, 7 November 1862

An Anonymous Writer: "The Vote of Want of Confidence"

If we cannot have another President for over two years to come, and if an change in the in the head of the various department would, at best, reach only minor evils, in what other way is it possible for this vote of the people to gain its object than through a change in the spirit and purpose of president Lincoln himself....

In saying that President Lincoln must change his spirit and purposes, we, of course, recognize its difficulty. No man can easily take on a character that belongs to him neither by nature nor by habit. The very qualities which have made Abraham Lincoln so well liked in private life—his trustful disposition, his kindheartedness, his concern for fair play, his placidity of temper—in a manner unfit him for the stern requirements of deadly war.... His moral earnestness no man doubts. There is not a purer patriot in the land. And yet there is something beyond this which we miss—the high sacred vehemence, inspired by the consciousness of infinite interests at stake, and infinite responsibilities. It would be a signal blessing to the country, could "Old Abe's" patriotism, sterling as it is, be fired with something of the old Jacksonian passion—something glowing, thrilling, electric—that should be a stimulus not only to every faculty of his own nature, but to that of every man within the reach of his words. Yet, it is useless to talk of this, for nature has denied to his temperament all such susceptibility. But it is within his power to brace up his will; for if there is any thing in a man over which he has a control, it is his will. It is just this which the people have demanded of Mr. Lincoln, and he is a bound to do it, go against the grain though it may. We must have a fixed, steadfast, immovable determination that henceforth *all men and all things shall bend to the one sole object of making the speediest conquest of this rebellion.* That determination is certainly within the power of Abraham Lincoln. The people have demanded it, and it is his business to acquire it and maintain it.

There need be no apprehension that the people will not treat this change of spirit justly and liberally, when it appears. Once assured that the President will come up to the inflexible resolve to make short work of the rebels, they would give him their unlimited trust. He would at once acquire a moral power with them before which all of their predictions for this or that General, or for this or that line of procedure, would be as nothing. They have no favorite they would not give up if deemed necessary, nor any plan they would not forego. Knowing that *the right spirit* ruled, they would be slow to mark errors, and even hard reverses they would bear with composure, secure of final triumph. President Lincoln, notwithstanding the want of confidence just declared, has still but to will it to be master of the situation. The people know his honesty. They simply ask that his utmost capacities shall be brought to bear to make an end of the indecision and procrastination and general feebleness which, from the beginning thus far, have marked military operations, for which he is ultimately responsible. Let him boldly and thoroughly act up to this just responsibility. The people have enjoined that. They seek nothing more. They will take nothing less.

The Chicago Tribune *maintained that the election results were not a referendum on the president or his administration of the war. It claimed voters supported the war and argued that the president must get rid of military leaders like McClellan who were not willing to aggressively fight.*

Chicago Tribune, 10 November 1862

An Anonymous Writer: "Action Is the Word"

The country has decided, not that Abraham Lincoln in honesty, in patriotism, and in zeal is not worthy of the country's confidence; but that the men like McClellan, Buell & Co., who have so abused the public patience, are unworthy of a continuance of that support the President has accorded to them. It has decided that we must have war in earnest, or peace upon some terms the most honorable that can be obtained; at any rate, that the old policy of neglect and inaction in the field, shall give way to new and more energetic measures.

We believe that the voice of the people is for war. The avowal of a peace or compromise policy, on the part of the Democratic nominees for Congress, would, we think, have inevitably insured far different results from those that have been attained.

Their nominees, for the most part, are pledged to a continuance of hostilities until the territorial integrity of the country and its political unity are restored. We know that, in many cases, these pledges were intended to deceive, and that the President will contend against a powerful and almost openly disloyal faction as soon as the next Congress meets. But the people put faith in their sincerity, and cast their votes according to their convictions. And as much as we regret the disaster that has befallen the administration, we must confess, and, supporting Mr. Lincoln as warmly and as energetically as we do now and always have done, we confess with shame and mortification, that we have no reason to be surprised or shocked by the verdict that the people have rendered. There is an end to human endurance, and that end, a majority of the voters left at home had unquestionably reached.

Hence we declare that the disloyal Democracy means treason—treason perhaps ruled under the forms of law, or justified by some factitious necessity, but treason nevertheless; and that nothing but a series of vigorous and comprehensive measures instantly inaugurated and firmly pursued by the President, can save the country from disunion, and the North from the despotism which would surely follow that event. We mean that all men like McClellan ought to be, nay say must be, removed instantly; that in the places they will vacate, must be put soldiers who believe that war means war; that the doctrines of the Proclamation must be firmly maintained; that our armies rusting from inaction, must be pushed upon the enemy; that the aid of whatever and whoever promises to promote the Union cause, within the limits by which civilization bounds modern warfare must be invoked; and that, if necessary, the whole country from Mason and Dixon's line southward, must smoke redden with the destruction and death that our forces will carry with them.

SOUTHERN REACTION TO ELECTION RESULTS

The Richmond Examiner *claimed that the Republican Party had brought the United States to the brink of ruin by waging an unjust war. It said the party had "deceived, misled, [and] seduced" the people of the North throughout the war and voters had shown their disgust with the party.*

Richmond Examiner, 15 November 1862

An Anonymous Writer: "North Sick of Black Republican Rule"

The elections of the North, if they show nothing else, at least prove that the Northern people are growing sick of Black Republican rule....

Well may the people of the North at last begin to open their eyes to the deplorable results of their brief experiment of Abolition Government.... The greatest political power of the earth has been revolutionized and destroyed; and whereas before the advent of the Abolitionist party to power, the American Republic was the admiration of good men and the dread of vicious Governors throughout the earth, it is now become an object of pity or contempt, to all. The amount of suffering, bloodshed and expenditure already occasioned, is almost without parallel; and while two years ago our country was comparatively free from debt, and the people exempt from taxation, there has already been created by both parties to the contest, a debt that cannot fall short, in the aggregate, of three thousand millions of dollars; rendering necessary as heavy a system of taxation on this continent as ever cursed the old. The country has been checked in the full career of boundless and unparalleled prosperity; and reduced from affluence and abundance, to a state of exhaustion and privation, which it has not known before since the days of the first settlers of the forest and wilderness....

If the Abolitionists had suffered a popular defeat at the North, and had been driven from power, immediately after involving the country in civil war; even then, deplorable as the result of their brief possession of the Government had been, the calamity would not have been irreparable; for, however strenuously a large and controlling party at the South might have striven against reconstruction, it is probable that the Union sentiment of the section would still have been strong enough to accept terms of reconciliation with the North. But the possession of power for two years has enabled that party to infuse a bitterness, ferocity and brutality into the war, on their part, which must render re-union the most improbable of all political events....

Their acts prove them to have been from the beginning, and to be for the present and for the future, destroyers of the Union; yet they have the effrontery to denounce the South, who has been standing on the defensive throughout, as the enemy of the Union, and attempt to thrust upon her shoulders all the odium of their own policy and acts....

History will contemplate the career of this party with horror. There is nothing in the excess and madness of human passion or in the meanness of human nature, which she has ever had to contemplate, that can compare with the action and the temper of this party. In their war upon the South, they have not only inspired a hatred in her people deeper and more implacable than ever actuated an enemy; but they have incurred the hatred and contempt of all the world besides. They have done even more: they have disgusted the very people whom they have excited to become participants with them in this war. That people, deceived, misled, seduced and ruined, are now themselves turning upon this party; and on the first opportunity will drive it with righteous indignation and fury from the seats of authority.

The Charleston Mercury *did not believe the election results would signal an end to the war. But, the paper argued, the growing strength of the Democratic Party would be a distraction for Republicans and that would aid the South.*

Charleston Mercury, 10 November 1862

An Anonymous Writer: "The United States Elections"

The Black Republican party of the North drove the Southern States into secession, and made the war from which that section now suffers. The existence of the party is staked upon bringing the war to a successful termination. Failure to overpower the Confederate States and restore the Union, must be fatal to its popularity and power for all time. Hence the gigantic efforts put forth to achieve success, and the desperate measure through which the Administration proposes to bring the South to submission. The policy of the Black Republican party is, therefore, war—savage and relentless—at any rate, successful war.

The Democratic party of the North was not immediately responsible for secession or the war. Although it favors a restoration of the political Union and of the trade and business desirable from the Confederate States, it is opposed to the desperate policy of carrying on the war as proclaimed by Lincoln. Being a party of opposition and moderation, it must, to the extent of its power at the North, hamper and clog the policy of the rival Black Republican party. It must drift in the direction of practical antagonism to the war, as waged.

Taking this view of the subject, we are gratified at the Democratic success and Black Republican defeats in the late elections. We by no means expect this result to put an end to the war. But it is the elevation of the *expedient,* in place of the *fanatical,* as the governing principle of the Northern people. It is likely to bring distraction and division to the conduct of the war and among the people of the North, So far, so good.

QUESTIONS

1. Why would the so-called threat posed by the free black be an effective issue for Democratic newspapers to exploit?
2. Do you agree with the *New-York Times* that the election results showed a lack of confidence with President Lincoln's administration of the war? Why or why not?
3. Why would Southern newspapers be happy about the Democratic gains in the midterm elections?

NOTES

1. George Templeton Strong, *Diary of the Civil War, 1860–1865,* ed. Allan Nevins (New York: Macmillan, 1962), 253.

2. Joel H. Sibley, *A Respectable Minority: The Democratic Party in the Civil War Era, 1860–1868* (New York: Norton, 1977), 144.

3. James M. McPherson, *Battle Cry of Freedom: The Civil War Era* (New York: Oxford University Press, 1988), 560.

4. Frank L. Klement, *The Limits of Dissent: Clement L. Vallandigham and the Civil War* (Lexington: University of Kentucky Press, 1970), 107.

5. McPherson, *Battle Cry of Freedom,* 560.

6. Wood Gray, *The Hidden Civil War: The Story of the Copperheads* (New York: Viking Press, 1964), 109.

CHAPTER 12

Diplomacy, 1861–65

W hen the Civil War began, the United States was vulnerable to intervention by the two main European powers, Britain and France. Making the situation worse was that one of President Abraham Lincoln's first acts in response to the Confederacy's attack on Fort Sumter was a proclamation blockading Southern ports. Britain and France depended heavily on the importation of Southern cotton for their textile industries. In fact, Southern leaders made the decision to secede from the Union based, in part, on the belief that in the event of war, the two countries would intervene on behalf of the Confederacy to save "King Cotton." Intervention by the British or French might well have helped the South defeat the Union. Their powerful navies could have broken the Northern blockade and permitted the shipment of supplies to the Confederate armies.[1]

Confederate leaders focused their initial diplomatic efforts on securing foreign mediation or active intervention. Soon after the new government was organized, President Jefferson Davis's administration sent three envoys to major European capitals to negotiate treaties of friendship, commerce, and navigation. Even though the representatives offered significant trade concessions, they met a lukewarm reception. By the fall of 1861, Davis decided to take a different approach and send two "special commissioners," James M. Mason and John Slidell, to London and Paris, respectively, to secure official recognition of the South's independence. When the United States navy seized their ship, the British steamer *Trent*, it set off a diplomatic crisis for the North. After a month of tense negotiations, U.S. Secretary of State William H. Seward defused the affair by agreeing to release Mason and Slidell and conceding that the Navy had mistakenly seized the envoys.

When Mason and Slidell finally arrived in Europe, they sought to persuade the British and French governments to officially recognize the Confederacy and break the Union blockade. French emperor Napoleon III was reluctant to take any action before Britain took the lead. And Britain showed no interest in breaking the blockade even though cotton imports had been effectively stopped. With negotiations going nowhere, the South offered Britain and France special trade privileges and other inducements to break the blockade. But France maintained that Britain must act first, and British leaders would not even entertain recognition until the South had won decisive military victories. The Confederate defeats at Gettysburg and Vicksburg in 1863 dimmed prospects for a decisive military victory that would ensure Anglo-French intervention. In August 1863, Confederate leaders recalled Mason from London. Two months later, the Confederacy severed all relations with England by expelling British consuls in the South.[2]

On the other side, the North had to deal with the diplomatic fallout from its blockade of the Confederacy. Administration officials were concerned that anger over the blockade would lead to recognition of the Confederacy. Even so, they adopted a firm and, at times, threatening posture. Officials informed the British foreign secretary that if he insisted on seeing the Confederate envoys, he would risk the severance of diplomatic relations with the United States. They also announced that formal British recognition of the Confederacy would be construed as an attempt to overthrow the United States and would result in war. The bold threats worked as British leaders announced they had no plans to see the Confederate representatives.

United States diplomats also had to deal with France's interest in Mexico. Napoleon had long been interested in Mexico for the economic opportunities it could provide his country. Political turmoil in Mexico had forced the country to suspend payments on its foreign debts in 1861. By the end of the year, French, British, and Spanish troops had landed in Mexico to force its leaders to deal with the debt issue. Although the British and Spanish eventually left Mexico, Napoleon marched on Mexico City. Although it took him nearly two years, Napoleon eventually installed Austrian archduke Ferdinand Maximilian as Mexican emperor. United States officials recognized that the best means for the French to maintain a regime in Mexico was to join forces with the Confederacy. Diplomats assured the French that they would not intervene in Mexico if France and Mexico would remain neutral in the American Civil War. Although Maximilian made numerous pleas for the French to recognize the Confederacy, Napoleon never did.

Finally, United States diplomats had to be concerned with the South's efforts to purchase warships from Britain and France. The two countries had been leaders in the development of ironclads, and Confederate leaders believed that securing ironclads could help the South overcome the naval superiority of the North. Fortunately for the Union, the British and French had legal restrictions on the sale of ironclads, and diplomatic pressure from the

United States convinced the two countries to retain the ironclads for their own navies. The Confederacy did contract for the purchase of two wooden steamers from the British in 1862. One of the steamers, the *Alabama,* went on to become the most feared warship in the Confederate fleet, destroying or capturing 66 Union vessels before being sunk in 1864. The tremendous damage caused by the *Alabama* angered the Lincoln administration and led to a bitter diplomatic dispute with Britain that continued even after the war ended.[3]

This chapter follows editorial response to diplomatic issues during the war. Even before the first big land battle had been fought, the *Charleston Mercury* expressed great confidence that the need for cotton by England and France would mean the two powers would side with the Confederacy. On the other side, the *Charlestown Advertiser* claimed that England and France would not risk alienating the United States by recognizing the South. The *New York Herald* warned against angering the Union. When England held off recognizing the South, the *Richmond Examiner* said the British wanted to see the war continue to cripple both the North and South. The *Daily Constitutionalist* defiantly claimed that the Confederacy did not need foreign recognition and could stand on its own. The exploits of the CSS *Alabama* also prompted editorial discussion. The *New York Herald* claimed that England had violated its neutrality by selling the *Alabama* to the Confederacy, while the *South-Carolinian* reveled in the damage the warship was doing.

PROSPECTS FOR FOREIGN RECOGNITION OF CONFEDERACY

The Charleston Mercury *expressed utmost confidence that economic necessity would force England and France to grant foreign recognition to the Confederacy and intervene on its behalf.*

Charleston Mercury, 4 June 1861

An Anonymous Writer: "The Queen's Proclamation and the Blockade"

The blockade answers our purpose exactly. It will force Great Britain and France to choose between the friendship and commerce of the Confederate States, their natural and most *lucrative* customers, and that of the United States, their natural and most *injurious* rivals....The cards are in our hands and we intend to play them out *to the bankruptcy of every cotton factory in Great Britain and France or the acknowledgement of our independence.* If they chose to be bamboozled or intimidate by Yankees, let them take the consequences.

The Charlestown Advertiser *expressed confidence that England would not assist the South during the war. But the paper said that if England should do so, then the United States should move to annex Canada.*

Charlestown (Mass.) Advertiser, 29 May 1861

An Anonymous Writer: "British Sympathies"

Two of the chief powers which serve to bind people together are common interests and origin. Between England and the United States, the interests are identical, and the people of the North are the lineal descendants of the English.

Many speculations have been indulged in concerning the position Great Britain will take on American affairs, though, at the present time, she maintains strict neutrality. Cotton has been king in the past, and the events of the next few months will determine whether it shall be in the future.

That the sympathies of the great mass of the intelligent people of the Mother Country are with the Free States in the present great struggle to maintain the integrity of the Union, there can be no doubt. The politicians, who lead the two great political parties of the land, are making an issue of the matter, purely, we apprehend, for political capital. And probably the sympathies of the Manchester manufacturers will, in a great measure, be determined by their interests. Yet, aside from the interests of the manufacturers and the politicians, the administrators of the English Government have a position to take, and a part to play, which will either bind England and the United States closer than ever in ties of friendship and amity, or alienate them in sympathy forever, and which may maintain or even diminish the present extent of British Dominion in America. By her position in this matter she not only hazards her extent of empire, but also her national prestige.

It is hardly possible to conceive that a nation which for generations has stood foremost in the rank of civilized powers—pre-eminently distinguished for her enlightened philanthropy—will, for a temporary interest, sacrifice an enviable fame, acquired at the cost of treasure and blood, ignore the power of her moral prestige and cover herself with shame, by extending to that relic of barbarism—the Slave power of the South—her sympathy and fellowship, to say nothing of more material assistance.

It is impossible that she will so stultify and malign her past glorious history. A belief may be reasonably entertained, that to maintain her noble position she will submit to sacrifices of material interests, and, if the hand of industry be paralyzed, and the thousands of her industrial population, depending on the cotton crop of the South for support, should temporarily come to want, the same generous philanthropy which now supports the magnificent charities of London, and, but a little while ago, bought the bondman from chains and slavery, will again manifest itself in behalf of her own people, should the evils apprehended come upon them. That the struggle now going on between the North and South has become a war for supremacy, on one hand, and obedience, on the other, is evident, and must result in the entire submission or annihilation of the North or the South. The South can never subdue the North, and should England see fit to aid the Confederate States, to assist them in establishing their independence, and endeavor to force the United States to recognize it, the North, already imbued with the war spirit, might turn its attention to foreign conquests, and, as a retaliatory measure, make an irruption into Canada and create disaffection and rebellion, with a view to the annexation of Canada....

The New York Herald *said that European powers should learn from history and not intervene on behalf of the South. The paper warned England and France to "beware ruffling the pinions of the American eagle."*

New York Herald, 30 November 1862

An Anonymous Writer: "The Lessons of History"

There exists, in some respects, a striking analogy at the present moment in the position of the United States and the monitory, if not threatening, attitude assumed towards us by France and England. A war is pending in our midst in which a late wealthy and still proud aristocracy have raised the banner of revolt against the principles of republicanism and democracy enunciated and consecrated in our national constitution. The authors of this war may be compared with the aristocracy and old *noblesse* of France, though they have thus far succeeded, chiefly by violence and terrorism, in drawing into their train a larger mass of the people than perhaps the former were able to do.

Essentially, however, the same political elements are again placed in hostile array against each other. It is the element of aristocracy and despotic government again in this our civil war pitted against the principles of democracy and popular ascendancy. There is the same anxiety for foreign aid and intervention on the one side, and the same repugnance to foreigners intermeddling with our domestic affairs on the other side, as reigned among the supporters of aristocracy on one side and the people of France on the other at the time referred to. The people of the North feel the same indignation as the French people did then at the mere idea of foreign rulers and potentates interfering to put down the principles of democracy and the republican government which they had established. Let the cabinets of France and England take a lesson from the page of history.

What was the result of the intervention of England and the other Powers of Europe in the domestic affairs of France? They raised up a Napoleon, whose family still rules over France by the profession of attachment to democratic principles and to the principles of the first Revolution. They restored the Bourbon family for a brief interval only, and all their labor of intervention, all their wars and conflicts of a quarter of a century, were so much labor, blood and treasure wasted and thrown away. Let them profit, then, by these indelible lessons of the past. All the efforts and intervention of all the Powers of Europe, were they even combined in one gigantic, unanimous league against us, would, beyond doubt, ultimately fail in vanquishing the cause and destroying the principles of democracy in America. The democracy of the United States, dormant and crashed down to the ground in the South, are powerful and strong enough in the North, not only to raise up their oppressed brethren in the South, not only to put down the proud, fire eating aristocrats of the same region who are now in rebellion against our rights, our laws, our constitution and our principles, but they are mighty and powerful enough to resist and finally to overwhelm and destroy all the Powers of Europe, if they should madly combine against us to assist a Southern aristocracy in destroying our Northern democracy. They need not look even for the partial success which they obtained in Europe when, after twenty-five years of war and bloodshed, they succeeded for a short time in restoring the Bourbons and the old *noblesse*—the Southern rebels of France. If they throw down the gauntlet against us they will meet with a people more powerful in every attribute than when they rushed against republican France. We possess wealth and resources, armies and fleets, which were wholly lacking to France, when, newborn from centuries of despotism and oppression, she first formed herself into a republic. We are already a veteran republic—a powerful people—inured to democratic principles from early infancy, unwilling to resign them, fully able to maintain them against the fire-eating madmen in our midst, or against meddling intervention from across the Atlantic.

We repeat, the cabinets of Europe, and that of France especially, will do well to pause in their counsels, to profit by the teaching of the past, and to beware of ruffling the pinions of the American eagle—to beware of the wild and mad idea of crashing by their intervention the democracy and principles established here among us in the New World.

RESPONSE OF BRITAIN AND FRANCE

The Richmond Examiner *suggested that England had not supported the South because it wanted to see the war continue to the "mutual ruin" of both the North and South.*

Richmond Examiner, 8 November 1862

An Anonymous Writer: "Behind England's Mask"

The greatness of America is a recent revelation to Europe. With the North and the South confederated under the old government the United States possessed a military power and an abundance of resources of which her citizens, even in the excesses of their self-complacency, never dreamed. But few minds in Europe had any idea of the power of the young giant of the Western World. One or two of their public men...might have apprehended, by the force of their genius, the military magnitude of America. But it was generally a dim speculation in Europe. Our boasts of military prowess were frequently ridiculed by the English press and passed as trans-Atlantic bluster. But this war has shown that even these boasts fell far short of the reality; it has revealed to the world an enormous power that overshadows whatever there is of military display in modern history, and has amazed the most arrogant nations of Europe.

Within eighteen months of this war, the North and South have raised armies larger than those of the first Napoleon; iron-clad fleets have been launched capable of destroying the combined navies of England and France; two millions of men have been put in the field; and yet the internal system of the industry of the country and the ordinary pursuits of peace have been but little interrupted, unless from the exceptional cause of the blockade of the Southern seacoast. Had the North and South continued as one nation there could scarcely have been any limits to the achievements of their military power. England could never have checked it. We could have overrun the continent, taken Canada in the teeth of a combination of all the European powers, and crushed England alone as an egg-shell under the hammer.

The bloody and unhappy revelation which this war has made of enormous military resources has naturally given to Europe, and especially to England, an extraordinary interest in its continuation. Nothing could be more contrary to the wishes and policy of England than that the war should end in re-uniting the North and South, and consolidating and renewing in rivalry to her, a military power which is now wasted in internecine strife. That the Union never shall be restored is a foregone and settled conclusion with the British Government. It would not now hesitate for a moment to recognize the South, unless firmly persuaded of our ability and resolution to carry on the war, and unless it had another object to gain besides that of a permanent division in the nationality and power of her old rival. That object is the exhaustion of both North and South. England proposes to effect the continuation of this war, as far as possible, to the mutual ruin of the two nations engaged in it by standing aside and trusting that after vast expenditures of blood and waste of resources the separation of the Union will be quite as surely accomplished by the self-devotion of the South, as by the less profitable mode of foreign intervention. To the advantages she hopes to gain from this separation, she desires to add those which she expects from loss and ruin to both North and South in a long war. Her present policy of neutrality with reference to the war is founded in the confidence that, the South is able to achieve her independence, and that the prolongation of hostilities does not risk her subjugation.

In this unchristian and inhuman calculation, England has rightly estimated the resolution and spirit of the South. We are prepared to win our independence with the great prices of blood and suffering that England has named. But we understand her in this matter. Behind her mask of conscience and pharisaical precision, there lurks a hideous and devilish purpose.

The Daily Constitutionalist *said the first two years of the war had shown that the South could "stand alone" without the support of European powers. It urged the Confederacy to recall its commissioners from England and France.*

Daily Constitutionalist (Augusta, Ga.), 30 January 1863

An Anonymous Writer: "Our Foreign Relations"

The Confederate States have, from the beginning, occupied a most unusual position towards foreign governments, the nature of which was such as to require the utmost delicacy, caution and prudence, in their intercourse. These States, from the very birth of the Confederacy, have been ceaselessly engaged in a war of uncommon magnitude and character, during all which time their seaports have been blockaded. It was of vital interest that our Government should maintain the best possible terms with foreign powers; for from the subjects of those powers, only could we obtain anything...which we could not produce at home. We were, comparatively, very ill prepared for waging war, especially such an one as has marked our whole short history; but we undertook it because it was unavoidable, trusting to the merits of our cause, the soldier-like qualities of our population, the unity of our people, and the blessing of Heaven.

The wisest and most far-seeing among us never dreamed that the war could ever assume such vast proportions as it has. Almost everything that has occurred has produced wonder and surprise. We have astonished ourselves, the enemy and mankind—not that we could beat the Yankees, with anything like a fair showing, in a stand up fight, (for that we always counted on,) but that we should have been able to endure so much, sacrifice so much, and never once look back, or contemplate again the idea of Union. Not the least astonishing thing to us was, that the Yankees, the most perfect idolators of money, should make war upon us at all, when it should have been plain to them that every dollar they spent, in their attempts to force us back into a Union which we had deliberately abandoned, was just so much money wasted, actually destroyed, beyond hope of recovery. Another thing which has surprised us no little, is the cool indifference with which the great nations of Europe have thus far looked on, with folded arms at the great struggle, upsetting all our predictions, and proving the fallacy of all our calculations in regard to them. Notwithstanding we went into the contest, relying upon ourselves solely, and determined to fight to the bitter end alone, till we confidently hoped that we should receive at least the moral support of the leading European powers, and perhaps their positive aid.

Of course, then, it became our policy to maintain the best relations we could with those powers, to treat them with the utmost courtesy, and to leave no stone unturned to secure their good will. Besides our dependence on Europeans for such limited supplies of necessity articles as might run the blockade, which made our Government desirous of securing the utmost friendly feeling with these Governments, and loath to do any act which might tend to prevent that desirable end, there was another important consideration controlling us. Europe had always misunderstood the South— was really ignorant of our capacities, and especially of our character. As a part of the great American Republic, of course we were in disfavor. But we were also a slave-holding people, and the state of our society was regarded a little better than that of semi-savages. While one portion of Europe regarded us as a slothful, reckless, wasteful set of spendthrifts: another portion looked upon us as a parcel of ferocious nabobs, without culture or conscience, lustful of empire, and slavery propagandists, seeking territory to be annexed. Our war-like capacities were never doubted by any. In this aspect of matters it was very important, then, that our Government should be wary, cautious, plausible and pacific. And so it has been. We sent Commissioners to Europe to explain our position, intentions and views; to give information as to our capacities to maintain ourselves in war, and our sources of wealth and profitable commerce in peace. Rather than give any ground of complaint, we have also allowed European consuls, appointed to the United States, and exercising their functions by virtue of the right granted by that Government, to reside in our seaports, there to look after the persons and interests of the subjects of their Governments.

Surely no one can doubt that our Government has done all that could be reasonably expected of it. It has done nothing in the spirit of subserviency or hypocrisy; but it has been ultra-courteous, that there might be no chance to mistake our friendly disposition. But the second year of a great war is drawing to its close, whose history demonstrates to the meanest capability our power to maintain ourselves, and our right to be acknowledged as an independent sovereign-power. Still European nations fail to admit this right, and to acknowledge us; and still their commercial agents exercise their functions...from our enemy, in our own midst. Is it not high time that an end be put to all this, and that our Government assert its own dignity and honor? We believe the voice of the country demands it, and that the demand is just, and ought to be heeded. It is useless longer to submit to shame, by wearing the appearance of supplicants for foreign recognition. We can manage to get along as well without foreign nations as they can without us. We have cast off swaddling clothes, and proved our ability to stand alone. Let our Commissioners return from Europe.

CSS *ALABAMA*

The New York Herald *claimed that England had violated its neutrality by selling the CSS* Alabama *to the Confederacy.*

New York Herald, 10 October 1862

An Anonymous Writer: "English Treachery—Gross Violation or Neutrality"

At the very commencement of our civil troubles, and almost before the conflict of arms had been really entered upon, the British government, with most unseemly haste, recognized the rebel confederacy as a belligerent

Power, accompanying that act with a proclamation of neutrality. It was not only in a moral cut in a material point of view, that this attitude of England was an advantage to the rebels. It placed them before the world in a position to which, certainly, they were not then entitled, and it opened the British and colonial ports to their privateers and smugglers. But, as if these were not sufficient proofs of sympathy with the rebellion, England endeavored to pick a quarrel with us in the Trent affair, and, failing in that, has ever since been encouraging and lending aid to the rebels in every possible way. The vessels that have run the blockade of the Southern ports have been English, the ordnance and small arms which the rebels have been procuring abroad have been English, and it has been at English ports that the rebel privateers have received shelter, protection and outfits.

The case of the *Alabama,* which is now committing depredations on our trading vessels off the Banks of Newfoundland, affords the latest proof of the treacherous part which England has been systematically acting towards us. This vessel was built at Liverpool, notoriously for this very business. She was fitted up and armed there by English means, under the eye of the English authorities, and sent to sea with a crew largely composed of Englishmen. She carries on her piratical trade with St. George's cross flying at her masthead, only changing that ensign for the pirate's flag when its victims are allured within her power. In this way she has destroyed and burned at sea, within a week, no less than ten merchants and whaling vessels, including one the cargo of which was owned in England. Is this the neutrality which the British government proclaimed? Is this friendship which it manifests towards a nation with whom it professes to be on terms of peace and amity? The English government might just as well throw off at once the hypocritical garb which it has been affecting to wear, and show itself at once in its true colors, as the avowed enemy of the American republic. It is easier to deal with an open enemy than with a concealed foe.

Our government should at once, in this matter of the Alabama, make reclamation on the English government for all the losses which our people have sustained, or may sustain, through the operations of that British Confederate privateer. It may not be politic to insist upon those reclamations at this time; but they can be filed by, to be brought to light and urged with the whole power of the nation as soon as we have put down the rebels and restored the republic to all its former greatness. When that time comes we will be much surprised if our government does not, in retaliation for the villainous treachery of England, seize and hold Canada until full and satisfactory retribution be made for this and all other covertly hostile acts which, in our time of tribulation, we have experienced at the hands of the British Government.

The South-Carolinian *reveled in the damage done by the CSS* Alabama *and claimed the warship was making naval history.*

South-Carolinian (Columbia), 6 March 1864

An Anonymous Writer: "The Alabama"

How many vessels, in the course of her errantry upon the main, the Alabama may have destroyed, we have not the means of computing, but enough to justify the assertion that the history of naval wars contains no similar instance of a single ship effecting what has usually been the work of half a national marine....[F]or many months the Alabama has baffled the whole Yankee navy, and ...has made Yankee navigation so dangerous as seriously to injure and considerably to diminish Yankee commerce....

QUESTIONS

1. Why is using the phrase "beware ruffling the pinions of the American eagle" an effective bit of editorial writing?
2. What reasons did the *Daily Constitutionalist* give for arguing that the Confederacy did not need the support of European powers?
3. Do you agree that England violated its neutrality by selling the *Alabama* to the Confederacy? Why or why not?

NOTES

1. Frank L. Owsley, *King Cotton Diplomacy: Foreign Relations of the Confederate States of America,* 2nd ed. (Chicago: University of Chicago Press, 1959), 1–50.

2. D.P. Crook, *The North, the South, and the Powers, 1861–1865* (New York: Wiley, 1974), 319–43.

3. Charles M. Robinson III, *Shark of the Confederacy: The Story of the CSS Alabama* (Annapolis: Naval Institute Press, 1995).

CHAPTER 13

Prisoners of War, 1861–65

When the Civil War began, neither the North nor South was prepared for fighting of the massive scale that ensued. And certainly neither side knew how to deal with the thousands of war prisoners that the fighting produced. Feeding, housing, guarding, and transporting prisoners of war required a tremendous amount of resources and planning. Both sides struggled with the task, and, as a result, conditions in prison camps could be atrocious and, often, lethal, especially in the South. The North and South both accused the other of mistreating its prisoners of war.

Early in the war, the Confederacy recognized that it would have difficulty feeding large numbers of Union prisoners. Confederate leaders sought a formal agreement for exchanging prisoners. Since the Lincoln administration refused to admit the right of the South to secede, Lincoln and his cabinet were reluctant to agree to an exchange cartel for fear of seeming to recognize the Confederacy as a legitimate government. But after early battles, thousands of captured Union soldiers were packed into inadequate Southern prisons. The administration felt increasing public pressure to get the men out of the prisons where it was alleged they were being abused. On July 22, 1862, the Union and Confederacy agreed to an exchange cartel. Based on the exchange agreement between the United States and Britain during the War of 1812, the cartel specified a man-for-man exchange of all prisoners.[1]

The exchange agreement effectively emptied prisons on both sides, but it broke down during 1863. The Emancipation Proclamation and the Union's decision to enlist black troops angered the South and raised fears of slave insurrections. In response, the Confederacy approved a policy to re-enslave or execute captured black soldiers and their white officers. Outraged Northern leaders stopped the exchanges, and Confederate prisoners were held as hostages to keep the South from implementing the policy. With the suspension of the cartel, tens of thousands of soldiers captured during the major battles of 1863 and 1864 poured into Northern and Southern prisons, taxing the resources of both sides.

To handle the influx of prisoners, the Union opened or expanded prisons in Elmira, New York; Chicago; Indianapolis; Columbus, Ohio; Johnson's Island, in Lake Erie; and other locations. The Confederacy opened or expanded prisons in Richmond; Salisbury, North Carolina; Macon and Andersonville, Georgia; and elsewhere. As the fighting intensified, the number of prisoners soon overwhelmed the South, which was finding it increasingly difficult to supply its own troops, much less those of the enemy. The Union blockade, and the fact the war was largely fought in the South, meant that the Confederacy had difficulty providing the necessary food, clothing, and shelter for Federal prisoners.

The most infamous Southern prison camp was Andersonville in southwest Georgia. The Confederacy hastily built the prison, officially known as Camp Sumter, in early 1864 to hold soldiers previously held at Belle Island near Richmond. By August 1864, 33,000 prisoners were packed into the 26-acre stockade, which had a small stream running through it. Overcrowding, poor sanitation, exposure, and inadequate food contributed to the disastrous conditions for prisoners. In all, approximately 13,000 of the 45,000 Union soldiers at Andersonville died. Although many in the North claimed that the South deliberately mistreated prisoners at the camp, there was no evidence to support the charges.[2]

Stories of starvation and disease in Confederate prisons camps began making their way north. A special exchange of the sickest prisoners in April 1864 outraged the North as the emaciated men who returned home seemed to confirm Union fears about the treatment of prisoners. In retaliation, Union Secretary of War Edwin M. Stanton cut the rations of Confederate prisoners. The cut in rations, combined with a large increase in the number of Southern captives, led to deteriorating conditions in Northern prisons and more cases of sickness and death.

The fate of African American Union troops captured by the Confederacy is difficult to determine. Even the number of black captives is unknown because the South refused to acknowledge them as legitimate prisoners and so kept few records. Confederate soldiers massacred hundreds of black soldiers at infamous battles such as Fort Pillow and the Crater before they could be captured. Others were returned as slaves to their old masters or sold to new masters. The treatment of black prisoners concerned the Lincoln administration. The president ordered an eye-for-an-eye retaliatory measure, but that proved difficult to put into practice.[3]

The treatment of all prisoners increased pressure to renew the exchange cartel, but Union General Ulysses S. Grant argued that exchanging prisoners would strengthen the Confederate army more than it would strengthen the Federal army. President Lincoln also remained concerned about the treatment of captured black soldiers. In January 1865, a desperate Confederacy agreed to the exchange of all soldiers, including blacks. During the next three months, several thousand prisoners a week were exchanged. After the South surrendered in April, the remaining captives on both sides were released.

In all, approximately 215,000 Confederate soldiers and 195,000 Union soldiers were held as prisoners during the war. Of those, the best estimate is that about 26,000 Rebels and 30,000 Federals died while in captivity (although some historians believe the Union number is too low). The figures account for about 9 percent of the total deaths during the war.[4]

The various problems associated with prisoner of war issues produced a great deal of inflammatory rhetoric in both the North and South. Newspapers on both sides defended the way their government treated prisoners and also accused the enemy of mistreating their prisoners. The controversial subject also produced letters to the editor. Included in the readings is a letter from a Confederate soldier imprisoned at Fort Warren near Boston, accusing the federal government of denying soldiers anything but the most basic provisions. The poet and author Walt Whitman also weighed in on the treatment of prisoners with a letter urging the North to exchange more soldiers.

TREATMENT OF WAR PRISONERS: SOUTHERN VIEWPOINT

The Daily Dispatch *in Richmond defended the Confederacy's treatment of Union prisoners claiming the government was doing all it could for the soldiers, especially given the South's own limited resources.*

Daily Dispatch (Richmond), 13 November 1863

An Anonymous Writer: "The Yankee Prisoners"

The persistent lies of the Yankee journals about the starvation and cruel treatment of their prisoners in Richmond are only intended to blow up the war spirit in the North.... [A]ll is done for the support and comfort of the Yankee multitude which the Confederate government is capable of doing.... [I]t is our people that are in danger of starving in order that these prisoners may be fed.

To anyone willing to listen to reason and truth, it must be apparent that thirteen thousand Yankee prisoners thrust upon a community already over-crowded...cannot expect to, with the best dispositions on our part, to fare sumptuously every day. We know people once in affluence, who would be glad to be assured of as liberal a daily provisions as these Yankee prisoners. It may be that their food is plain, and not abundant, but it is as good, and as plentiful as...we can supply.

The Richmond Examiner *took a harsh view of the overwhelming number of prisoners in the city. It criticized the Union's unwillingness to exchange prisoners and said if the Union was not willing to take the men, then they should be left outside in the weather "where the cold weather and scant fare will thin them out."*

Richmond Examiner, 30 October 1863

An Anonymous Writer: "What Shall Be Done with Them?"

The proper authorities are debating the question of the removal of the twelve thousand Yankee prisoners from Richmond to some other point not so circumscribed for food, and where it can be had at less expense, and in greater abundance without affecting the necessities of the people....

The Yankee Government, under the laws of civilized warfare and the cartel, are entitled to these men, and if they will not take them, let them be put where the cold weather and scant fare will thin them out in accordance with the laws of nature.

In a letter to the Charleston Mercury, *a Confederate soldier held at Fort Warren described his captivity after being freed. The soldier, who identified himself as "A Voice from Fort Warren," claimed the treatment of prisoners worsened in the fifteen months he was held. He urged the South to retaliate by treating Union prisoners in the same way.*

Charleston Mercury, 7 November 1864

A Voice from Fort Warren: "The Fate of Our Prisoners"

To the Editor of the Mercury: Since our arrival in Dixie, ten days ago, after a confinement of fifteen months in Fort Warren, Boston Harbor, we have received congratulations on all sides and many expressions of sympathy for our sufferings under the hardships of prison life, and have conversed freely with editors and others; but, save in the efforts now being made to forward supplies to our brothers in captivity we see no signs of a movement in the right direction—no voice has been raised to force the issue of fair treatment to those we left behind us. May this be heard and heeded. For the first few months of our imprisonment we were allowed to purchase, and receive from friends at the North even luxuries, but ever since the visit last winter, of the Yankee Commissary of Prisoners, Colonel Hoffman, 3d Infantry, the reins have been gradually drawn tighter and the rations reduced, so that for the past six months neither tea, coffee, sugar or lights have been furnished, and more recently the privilege of either receiving or purchasing such essentials—or in fact anything else eatable has been denied. And, in a country where it is dark at 4 p.m., you may imagine how cheerless the long evenings must be without lights. Somehow the increased restrictions upon us seemed invariably to follow closely upon the published accounts of the kindness and courtesy extended to Yankee prisoners at the South, especially in Charleston. Now it was certainly aggravating to us to read such accounts and then contrast that treatment with our own privations. It is but just that our people should send supplies to our brothers in captivity; but should they not first be assured that they will be distributed as intended?...And should the Yankees in our hands be allowed to purchase or receive, while our friends are denied? We say No—most emphatically, No. Shut down at once...and treat them as the dogs that they are until we learn that our friends are allowed to purchase for themselves, or receive what friends either North or South may send them, and also to bring away with them, when released, all the clothing thus purchased or received, as the order now is to confiscate all but one suit on the person, and one change of underclothing....Why extend our sympathies to the Yankees in our hands, when the like is denied to our brothers at the North? Will the knowledge of that help to cheer them in their dreary confinement, or tend to relax their bonds? Not in the least. Retaliation in kind is what alone will touch the senses of our brutal foes, and since they force us to it let it be worked with a will. No lights, no vegetables, no vinegar, pickles or pepper. No tea, coffee and sugar from any source, and no interviews with prisoners, until the reins are slackened in Northern prisons, and see if that will not have some effect. Fort Warren was a paradise, compared to other Yankee prisons; and yet the last

usage there was such as to make us yearn for opportunities of retaliation, with a strong disposition to include in the same category some of
those who so foolishly expend their sympathies on Yankees at the
South. If they will feel so kindly disposed, why not let them go North
where there is such a wide field? These are not the times for the practice or exhibition of such sensibilities. Do what will help our own boys
in Northern prisons, and let the Yankees fare as they may. They have
no love for us, and only laugh in their sleeves at Southern sympathy
and gullibility. Remember the hard lot of our own friends, this winter,
at cold, cheerless North, doing their own washing and cleaning, and
trudging knee deep in snow after their fuel and water, with only shoes
on—for boots are not allowed to be purchased, and they are not permitted to go on the side walks—and then see if you can send delicacies
and servants to wait upon the merciless invaders in our hands. And the
half has not been said of what might be uttered by

A VOICE FROM FORT WARREN.

A writer for the Charleston Mercury *visited Andersonville and described
the prison in an editorial. He admitted that conditions at Andersonville
were bad but said "every effort" was being made to treat the prisoners hu-
manely. The "Royal Ape" he refers to is President Lincoln.*

Charleston Mercury, **26 August 1864**

An Anonymous Writer: "The Yankee Prisoners at Andersonville"

Andersonville was an interesting and novel spectacle to me. The Yankee
prisoners within the stockade, about 30,000 in number, when closely
viewed, resemble more in their motions a hive of bees seen through a glass
opening than anything else I can think of. The area of the stockade is being
rapidly increased by General Winder, who is evidently desirous of doing all
in his power to make them comfortable. They have thousands of little huts
and tents, variously constructed, which seem to protect them from the
scorching rays of the sun and the inclemency of the weather generally. Gen.
W. informed me that very soon the lumber would be procurable to put up
temporary shanties for their comfort.

A fine but small stream of water runs through the stockade, supplying
them with water for bathing and other purposes. I saw hundreds of them

bathing in this stream at once. Others, not engaged in bathing, were waling [*sic*]about among their fellows....I learn that many of them have bartered away nearly all their clothing for tobacco. On the whole, their condition, bad as it is, and bad as it deserves to be, seemed better than could have been expected. In spite, however, of every effort to treat them with humanity, their mortality is great, averaging about one hundred per day. About 2000 are in hospital. Over 36,000 have been received since the establishment of Andersonville as a military prison.

The prisoners are said to be very docile, but greatly exasperated at the Royal Ape for not exchanging them. They were greatly elated last evening at finding a paragraph in one of our newspapers stating that a general exchange of prisoners would soon be resumed. The defences of Andersonville are admirably planned by the skillful veteran, General Winder. Formidable batteries of artillery bear directly on the prisoners, in the event of an emeute; and strong works, with artillery, defend the place against hostilities from without. A strong force of infantry is there also. Raiders would find themselves woefully mistaken if they were to attempt the liberation of the prisoners.

TREATMENT OF WAR PRISONERS: NORTHERN VIEWPOINT

The New-York Times *was one of the biggest critics of Southern prisons. In this editorial, the paper compared conditions at Libby Prison in Richmond to the infamous Bastille in France.*

New-York Times, 31 March 1864

An Anonymous Writer: "The Richmond Prisons—How Prisoners Are Treated on Both Sides"

A chapter will be written by some future historian on the horrors of the "Libby Prison," which will almost equal in fearful interest the records of the Bastile [*sic*]. We shall hear of brave and enthusiastic young men who entered those gloomy walls, and who gradually, as month after month passed away of the dreary and filthy confinement, became depressed in spirit and broken in body, until when release came at last, it came too late. There will be stories of petty persecutions of brutal indignities practiced on persons helpless and weak, of cruelties, of hopes deferred month by month, of weariness and sickness, and the lonely death of gallant men, which will make, in the fu-

ture, that Richmond prison, or the place where it had been: one of the most
painful places in the American memory.

No civilized nation at the present day insults or tortures its prisoners.
This is left alone to savages. But the Confederate authorities and their subordinates have, from the beginning, acted toward our unfortunate men,
taken as prisoners of war, as if they were New-Zealand savages with a fresh
capture of unlucky white men. They have invariably robbed their persons.
They have tortured them with long and painful journeys, made on foot,
under the burning sun or amid rain and sleet, while the captors rode. They
have shut them up in such quarters as are not seen outside of the barbaric
prisons of Asiatic rulers—dark, stifling, smoky, filthy, and full of vermin.
Their scanty fuel, and still scantier rations of mouldy bread and corn meal,
have been often cut short, as if the Confederate Government, fearing the
opinion of the world, and not venturing on a cold-blooded massacre, would
try the secret and more sure method of unhealthy quarters and bad food—
of typhus and starvation. Then, in the prison itself, all that can annoy and insult brave men is continually tried to break the spirits and worry out the life
of these unfortunate prisoners.

Nothing in all the records of modern prisons is so brutally and savagely
cruel, as the treatment of our officers and men in the Libby Prison by these
Richmond authorities. It sickens us at heart to think that such cowardly and
base cruelty could exist among a people which had even called itself Christian. And then to hear from these torturers of the helpless the claim of
"chivalry" or superior military honor! We all recognize now what is the soil
from which all this crop of brutality and cruelty springs. We see that nothing
but Slavery could harden the heart of any man, with even the exterior of a
gentleman, so that he could insult and starve a prisoner. We know that no
one but a man long used to rob the laborer of his wages, and to lash the
women who served him, could first cheat a helpless captive of his own race,
of the scanty sustenance sent him from the North, and then coolly shoot him
behind prison bars, as we know to have happened.

The North has been too cool by far to these astounding brutalities. The
recent returned prisoners inform us that to one-half of the twelve thousand
unhappy men, who, till lately, were in the various Richmond prisons, the
long-delayed release will soon come too late. Filthy rooms, bad food, insult
and disappointment will accomplish what the rebels would gladly effect by
quicker and sterner methods. The great executioner is rapidly equaling the
cartel of prisoners, North and South. Here the rebel prisoners have better
fare than they have been accustomed to for years, cleaner clothing, and a
more invigorating climate. No insult or oppression touches them; on the
contrary, they receive unbounded sympathy from the thousand half-sympa-
thisers with treason among us. They return invigorated in constitution, and

all ready for service again. Our doctors and inspectors will tell us how many Federal prisoners go into immediate service, and how many never return.

Such a state of things as this ought not to exist. It is a shame to our manhood that brave men, who have fought for our flag, should be thus left to the mercies of such utter barbarians. In some way the powerful hand of our Government ought to be extended over them.

Retaliation is a terrible thing, but the miseries and pains, and slow-wasting life of our brethren and friends in those horrible prisons, under brutal officers, is a worse thing.

No people or Government ought to allow its soldiers to be treated, for one day, as our men have been treated for the last three years. It weakens our cause and disgraces our character. Nothing will check enlistments so much, and nothing so enfeeble the arms of our soldiers in the field.

The condition of Union prisoners who returned to the North during the exchange cartel outraged the New York Herald. *The newspaper said if the Confederacy could not properly care for the captives, it should request supplies from the Union.*

New York Herald, 31 October 1863

An Anonymous Writer: "Horrible Treatment of Union Prisoners at Richmond"

The detachment of paroled Union prisoners which arrived at Annapolis on Thursday last, from Richmond, confirm, and more than confirm, the worst that has been rumored or feared of the treatment of our unfortunate soldiers in the prisons of the rebel capital....These poor men state that they were not only kept without food, but were exposed, for a larger portion of their time, to all the inclemencies of the season, in their scanty clothing, and without shelter of any kind.

This is, indeed, a horrible state of things, and utterly without palliation or excuse on the part of Jeff. Davis and his infamous jail keepers. We know that the people of Richmond, from their bread riots, are themselves reduced to the verge of famine; we know the rebel army of Lee is half starved, shoeless and in rags; for a correspondent, writing from that army to the Richmond Enquirer, makes a boast of it that, if they gained nothing else in their late grand march to Manassas and back again, they have gained some few pairs of shoes, which were taken from the feet of their Yankee prisoners. But if the rebels are too poor to feed their prisoners, or to give them shelter, they know that an honest confession of this inability to any Union officer, with an intimation that supplies will be accepted from Washington, would instantly be answered by a shipload. The failure of the enemy to adopt this course fully justifies the conclusion that they have deliberately adopted the policy of starving their Union prisoners of war to death, from that ferocious hatred which springs from a devilish despair.

Now, what is to be done? There are ten or twelve thousand Union soldiers still held to this trial of starvation at Richmond. They must not be permitted to perish. But what is to be done? That which should have been done long ago. Those prisoners at Richmond must be rescued by force of arms; and this can be done. The Army of the Potomac can do it, and do it at very short distance, if relieved of the duty of guarding Washington for a time. And to relieve this army for this urgent duty of the capture of Richmond, the President has only to call upon Pennsylvania and New York for fifty thousand militia for sixty days' service. In answer to such a call the troops, we believe, would be in Washington (fifty thousand) in ten days. Thus relieved, the army of General Meade, shipped to the peninsula, could be in Richmond before the end of November. We have not a doubt of it. We believe, moreover, that this movement would at once bring about the collapse of the rebellion from Virginia to Texas.

We earnestly call upon President Lincoln to move in this way to the rescue of our starving soldiers at Richmond; for such an enterprise will make our liberating army invincible in their righteous wrath, and superior to all impediments.

The poet and author Walt Whitman wrote a variety of letters, editorials, and poems on the war. Whitman, a regular visitor to the New York hospitals for soldiers, was especially concerned about the condition of soldiers, including those who became prisoners of war. In a letter to the New-York Times, *he sharply criticized the federal government for not exchanging more prisoners with the South.*

New-York Times, 27 December 1864

Walt Whitman: "The Prisoners"

To the Editor of New-York Times:

The public mind is deeply excited, and most righteously so, at the starvation of the United States prisoners of war in the bands of the Secessionists. The dogged sullenness and scoundrelism prevailing everywhere among the prison guards and officials (with, I think, the general exception of the surgeons,) the measureless torments of the forty or fifty thousand helpless young men, with all their humiliations, hunger, cold, filth, despair, hope utterly given out, and the more and more frequent mental imbecility, I have myself seen the proofs of in so many instances, that I know the facts well, and know that the half has not been told....But there is another and full as important side to the story. Whose fault is it at bottom that our men have not been exchanged? To my knowledge it is understood by...those among us who have had longest and nearest contact with the secession exchange officers, that the Government of the latter have been and are ready to exchange man for man as far as the prisoners go, certainly all the whites, and as I understand it, a large proportion of the blacks also.

Under the President (whose humane, conscientious and fatherly heart, I have abiding faith in,) the control of exchange has remained with the Secretary of War, and also with Maj.-Gen. Butler. In my opinion the Secretary has taken and obstinately held a position of cold-blooded policy (that is, he thinks is policy) in this matter, more cruel than anything done by the Secessionists. Ostensibly and officially saying he will not exchange at all, unless the Secession leaders will give as, on average terms, all the blacks they capture in military action, the Secretary has also said, and this is the basis of his course and policy,) that it is not for the benefit of the United States that the power of the Secessionists should be repleted by some 50,000 men in good condition now in our hands, besides getting relieved of the support of nearly the same number of human wrecks and ruins, of no advantage to us, now in theirs.

Maj.-Gen. Butler, in my opinion, has also incorporated in the question of exchange a needless amount of personal pique, and an unbecoming obstinacy. He, too, has taken his stand on the exchange of all black soldiers, has persisted in it without regard to consequences, and has made the whole of the large and complicated question of general exchange turn upon that one item alone, while it is but a drop in the bucket. Then he makes it too much a personal contest and matter of vanity, who shall conquer, and an occasion to revenge the bad temper and insults of the South toward himself.

This is the spirit in which the faith of the Government of the United States toward fifty thousand of its bravest young men—soldiers faithful to it in its hours of extremest peril—has been, for the past year, and is now, handled. Meantime, while the thing has been held in abeyances in this manner, considerably more than one-fourth of those helpless and most wretched men (their last hours passed in the thought that they were abandoned by their Government, and left to their fate), have indeed been exchanged by deaths of starvation, (Mr. Editor, or you, reader, do you know what a death by starvation actually is?) leaving half the remainder closely prepared to follow, from mental and physical atrophy; and even then the remnant cannot long tarry behind....

In my opinion, the anguish and death of these ten to fifteen thousand American young men, with all the added and incalculable sorrow, long drawn out, amid families at home, rests upon the heads of members of our own Government; and if they persist, the death of the remainder of the Union prisoners, and often worse than death, will be added.

Walt Whitman.

QUESTIONS

1. Were you surprised by the *Richmond Examiner* editorial urging the South to leave prisoners outdoors in the winter where they would be thinned out "in accordance with the laws of nature"? Why or why not?
2. Do you think it was effective for the *New-York Times* to compare Libby Prison to the Bastille in France? Why or why not?
3. Do you think Walt Whitman makes an effective argument for the need to exchange prisoners? Why or why not?

NOTES

1. William B. Hesseltine, *Civil War Prisons: A Study in War Psychology* (Columbus: Ohio State University Press, 1930), 22.

2. Ovid L. Futch, *History of Andersonville Prison* (Gainesville: University of Florida Press, 1968).

3. James M. McPherson, *Battle Cry of Freedom: The Civil War Era* (New York: Oxford University Press, 1988), 793–94.

4. Hesseltine, *Civil War Prisons*, 254–55.

CHAPTER 14

Peace Movements, 1861–65

Movements for peace both in the North and South began soon after the fighting started. In the Confederacy, Unionists, who had always been opposed to the South leaving the federal government, led the peace movements. In the North, the so-called Peace Democrats, also known as Copperheads, led the peace movements. With support for the war so widespread in the South, Unionists initially stayed underground where they formed secret organizations such as the Heroes of America and the Peace Society. The Copperheads were far more visible.

In January 1863, Democrats led by Clement L. Vallandigham of Ohio launched a peace movement in Congress. Vallandigham, who had been defeated in the 1862 Congressional election, used his farewell speech to sharply criticize the war and propose peace negotiations. He argued that the Confederacy could never be conquered and that the war had only brought "defeat, debt, taxation...the suspension of habeas corpus, (violations) of freedom of the press and of speech...which have made this country one of the worst despotisms on earth for the past twenty months."[1]

The peace movement enjoyed its greatest support in the Midwest states of Ohio, Indiana, and Illinois where many residents sympathized with the South. There was even talk of a "Northwest Confederacy" that would ally with the South against New England. Democratic newspapers throughout the Midwest, most notably the *Cleveland Plain Dealer* and *Chicago Times,* supported the platform of the Peace Democrats.

Fearing civil unrest from the peace movement, General Ambrose E. Burnside, commander of the Department of the Ohio, issued General Order No. 38. It declared that any person committing "expressed or implied" treason would be subject to a military court trial and punishment by expulsion or death.[2] Vallandigham, who was trying to drum up support for the Demo-

THE COPPERHEAD PARTY.——IN FAVOR OF *A VIGOROUS PROSECUTION OF PEACE!*

Copperhead Party. *The Copperheads, or Peace Democrats, threatened the Union, as depicted in this cartoon from the magazine* Harper's Weekly *(February 28, 1863). The Copperheads got their name from the pennies they wore, but they were often depicted as the poisonous snakes of the same name. Here they are shown looking menacingly at Columbia who carries a sword and shield.*

cratic gubernatorial nomination in Ohio, defied the order in a speech in which he called the war "wicked, cruel and unnecessary." Soldiers arrested Vallandigham at his home in May 1863, and he was convicted by a military tribunal of "expressing treasonable sympathy." He was sentenced to a federal prison for the rest of the war, but President Abraham Lincoln commuted his sentence and banished him to the South. Peace Democrats decried Vallandigham's arrest, claiming that it violated constitutional protections of free speech.

In the South, opposition to the draft and general weariness with the war fueled the moves toward peace. Confederate governors Joseph E. Brown of Georgia and Zebulon B. Vance of North Carolina fought conscription at every turn, even taking their battles to the courts. The Northern peace movement in 1863 precipitated a strong peace movement in North Carolina where more than one hundred rallies were held across the state during the summer. Supporters urged the Confederate government to begin peace negotiations and suggested reunion on the basis of proposals offered by Northern Democrats.

One of the most outspoken leaders of the peace movement was William W. Holden, editor of the *North Carolina Standard* in Raleigh. He called for negotiations to "arrest this awful evil," advocating a peace that would "preserve the rights of the sovereign states and the institutions of the South." Holden's repeated calls for an end to the war led to "peace meetings" throughout the state. But his message angered many in the South, including Confederate officers who feared it would hurt army morale. On September 9, 1863, Georgia troops passing through Raleigh broke into the *Standard's* office where they scattered Holden's papers and dumped out printing ink and type. Governor Vance arrived on the scene and urged calming, probably preventing the printing presses from being destroyed.[3]

Peace factions also developed in other Southern states, most notably Georgia. The Georgia peace movement was unusual in that it was led by the state's two top leaders: Governor Brown and Vice President Alexander H. Stephens. Both men were strong supporters of states' rights and had become disenchanted with President Jefferson Davis for his support of conscription and suspending the writ of habeas corpus. In January 1864, Brown and Stephens introduced resolutions in the Georgia Legislature urging Davis to initiate peace negotiations with the North after every Confederate victory. The two leaders did not receive the support they wanted, but they continued their calls for peace throughout the remainder of the war. Brown became so unhappy with the Davis administration and its lack of action toward peace that he called a special session of the Georgia legislature in February 1865. He wanted Georgia to take the lead in calling for a convention of Confederate states to seek the removal of Davis from the presidency. However, Brown could not generate any support for his proposals.[4]

Diplomatic efforts to end the war began during the summer of 1864 when commissioners from both sides met at Niagara Falls, Canada. *New-York Tribune* editor Horace Greeley wrote President Lincoln that the country "longs for peace" and told him of word that two Confederate envoys were at Niagara Falls, Canada, supposedly bearing peace proposals from Davis. Lincoln asked Greeley and John Hay, the president's private secretary, to meet with the envoys. Lincoln insisted in a letter that he was willing to discuss any proposal for "the restoration of peace, the integrity of the whole Union, and the abandonment of slavery." But the Confederate commissioners refused any peace on those terms and the talks broke off. One final attempt at peace was attempted later in 1864, but ended with the unsuccessful Hampton Roads Peace Conference on February 3, 1865.

This chapter begins with editorials on Vallandigham and his controversial peace movement. Many newspapers weighed in on his arrest and conviction, including the *Chicago Times* and *Chicago Tribune*, which took opposing sides.

The peace movement in the South was likewise controversial. The *North Carolina Standard* advocated peace in repeated editorials, such as the one published here. However, the *Southern Recorder* strongly opposed any moves toward peace. The Niagara Falls peace conference sparked another round of editorials. The *New-York Tribune* defended the failed conference, arguing that any means of shortening the war was worth pursuing. But the New York *Evening Post* argued the efforts were foolish and futile. There was also disagreement among the Southern press over the consequences of the failed conference at Niagara Falls.

PEACE MOVEMENT IN NORTH

The Dubuque Herald, *an outspoken Democratic paper, expressed outrage at Vallandigham's arrest and accused the federal government of exercising arbitrary power against its citizens.*

Dubuque (Iowa) Herald, 10 May 1863

An Anonymous Writer: "The Arrest of Vallandigham"

Mr. Vallandigham was arrested by brute force, protected by a show of military authority. He does well and is deserving of the gratitude of the people for refusing to recognize that power. If by its decree he falls, Heaven help the executioners. Justice may be slow, but it is sure. If for an eye, an eye is not rendered, it will be because an outraged people call to mind the later injunction of "do good to those who persecute and despitefully use you." Each successive attack upon the liberties of the people, borne as these latter attacks are borne, shake our confidence in their patriotic integrity. They only deserve liberty who prize its blessings, and they tyranny, who crouch before its blows. To think that the champion of a peoples, rights, bold, inflexible, honest and unselfish, should be torn from their midst—for words uttered in their defense is to believe them unworthy of the sacrifice. Put the question honestly to yourself—your own heart, whoever you may be, Democrat or Republican—whether if these things are to be permitted, you are not the playthings of arbitrary power? That Mr. Vallandigham may be released argues nothing. It may cast a deeper odium on the authors of his arrest, but it palliates nothing. The act was tyrannous, and if committed three years ago would have been the signal of an uprising too terrible to dwell upon. How long will the American people bear these wrongs?

On the other hand, the Chicago Tribune *said Vallandigham deserved a harsh sentence. Moreover, the newspaper argued the government should arrest other enemies of the country.*

Chicago Tribune, 7 March 1863

An Anonymous Writer: "Now Let Them Be Punished"

Let Vallandigham be punished. The work can begin on no better or purer sample of that Northern traitor.... Thousands of loyal men will wait now to witness the amplest justice done to Vallandigham. There should be no empty threatening this time—no chance for his cheap and unharmed martyrdom.... With better and sterner work in the field, it is time for a more thorough handling of the home enemies of the Government. Let Vallandigham head the list, and all the people will say amen.

The New-York Times, *another Vallandigham critic, applauded his conviction. The paper urged the court to make an example of him and send him to the South "to join that noble company of traitors."*

New-York Times, 13 May 1863

An Anonymous Writer: "Where Shall Vallandigham Go?"

We published on Monday morning the charges upon which Mr. Vallandigham was recently tried by Court-martial in Cincinnati. We have no doubt that the evidence offered was sufficient to establish their truth. There remains the question, what sentence the Court will pass on him. If we could have our choice in the matter, it would be that he be sent South beyond our lines. Taking his life might seem too hard, imprisonment would quite likely make a martyr of him, but every one will recognize the fitness of sending him to Dixie, to join that noble company of traitors whose praises he has sounded so loudly, and to receive from them in person that meed of praise which they have so steadily bestowed upon him at a distance.

It is quite time that he should appear upon another stage. He has appeared before our Northern people in the character of a pacificator quite often enough. He has inculcated everywhere he has gone, the doctrine that nothing could be gained by war. Let him go now and try what he can do in that line on the other side. Let him urge upon the rebels the manifold evils of the war which they are waging, and the utter impossibility of accomplishing anything by battle....

On the whole, we are inclined to think that sending him South now would do more good to our cause, than his presence has done us harm heretofore. Not that he will say anything to help us—not that anything he could say would have the slightest influence upon the rebel leaders, for as soon as he crosses their lines, he is squeezed orange. But the fact of our ejecting him will be one which must be widely spread, and it will speak most convincingly to every one who hears it of the determination of the North, which is hardening from flint to adamant, to suppress this rebellion, and to grind to powder all those who would sustain it....

The Democratic Chicago Times *condemned Vallandigham's expulsion from the United States, calling it the "funeral of civil liberty." The editorial and others like it led General Burnside to suspend the* Times *for several days until President Lincoln reversed the suspension.*

Chicago Times, 27 May 1863

William Storey: "Mr. Vallandigham"

As one reads the account of the expulsion of Mr. Vallandigham beyond the Federal lines, the ceremony seems like the funeral of civil liberty. Guilty of no offence save devotion to the Union and an intense desire for its restoration—charged with no offence save the exercise of the right of freedom of speech given to him by the same power which made Abraham Lincoln President and that speech a prayer for the safety of the constitution and denunciation of the ruthless invasions of it—he suffers for his fearless faithfulness, unbending integrity and stern patriotism. He has violated no law; he is punished because of his maledictions of those who do violate law—of those who daily pollute their souls with perjury in breaking their solemn oaths to "preserve, protect and defend the constitution of the United States."

PEACE MOVEMENT IN SOUTH

The North Carolina Standard *in Raleigh was one of the most of outspoken advocates of peace in the South. Editor William W. Holden argued that the Union was ready to negotiate terms for ending the war.*

North Carolina Standard (Raleigh), 19 June 1863

William W. Holden: "Tired of the War"

The people of both sections are tired of the war, and desire peace. We desire it on terms honorable to our own section, and we cannot expect it on terms dishonorable to the other section. We believe in fighting as long as we are invaded, and in driving the enemy from our soil—in taking prompt advantage of such victories as we achieve, not in invading the enemy's country, for we are not strong enough for that, but in dislodging him from his positions on our own soil; but while we believe in this policy, as the best and only policy for the present, we also hold that the friends of peace in both sections should give utterance to their views, and should thus pave the way for negotiations, to which both sections must at last come, as the only means for closing the contest. If we could negotiate *now*, so much the better. Thousands of valuable lives would be saved, and much devastation and ruin would be stayed. Is there any inconsistency in this? What are we fighting for? Not for war, surely, but for peace.

The Southern Recorder, *located in the Georgia capital of Milledgeville, argued strongly against moves toward peace by the South.*

Southern Recorder (Milledgeville, Ga.), 4 October 1864

An Anonymous Writer: "Peace Negotiations"

We are in the fight and must carry it on to the bitter end; until we can close it with honor. It is no time for us to propose negotiations, or to ask forbearance. The sword can be sheathed after victory.

Another Georgia newspaper, the Chronicle & Sentinel, *claimed the South should "employ all the arts of policy for the attainment of peace."*

Chronicle & Sentinel (Augusta, Ga.), 8 November 1864

An Anonymous Writer: "Peace"

It becomes us a wise and christian people, engaged in a struggle for all that is dear to man, and only seeking our rights, to bear the sword in one hand and the olive branch in the other. To extend the hand of fellowship to any party at the North which is opposed to the continuance of the war. To give a favorable reception to any proposition for its termination, compatible with our independence. To offer any terms or inducements to the people of the North, consistent with our own honor, to cease hostilities. In a word, to employ all the arts of policy for the attainment of peace, just as we employ all the arts of strategy for the achievement of victory. Policy must concur with valor in bringing this bloody and disastrous war to a close. Negotiations must end what the sword has begun.

The New York Herald *and other newspapers in the North found great satisfaction in the controversial peace movement gripping the South. The* Herald *said it showed the cracks in the South's armor of unity.*

New York Herald, 4 November 1864

An Anonymous Writer: "The Rebellion within Rebellion"

It is clear that the immense unity of purpose that once gave such strength to the rebellion is gone.... It is torn with the disintegrating influences of personal jealousy, and its leaders pursue one another with such bitter recrimination that at times it appears as if they existence of common enemy were forgotten.... This is the state of affairs that immediately precedes the closing struggle on so many of the great pages of history.

NIAGARA FALLS CONFERENCE

Horace Greeley, who was one of the representatives at the Niagara Falls Peace Conference, used the New-York Tribune *to defend the meeting and said any attempt to hasten peace was worth the effort.*

New-York Tribune, 25 July 1864

Horace Greeley: "Peace Efforts"

It seems to us that the time, if it has not already come, must be near at hand, wherein the North and the South will be ready to exchange glances otherwise than over the crests of their rival intrenchments along the sights of their respective muskets—a mode of regard not conducive to geniality of temper, graciousness or manner, or comeliness of visage. In that day, the South will be made to comprehend that the North requires the extinction of Slavery in no envious, inimical spirit—requires it because its continued existence involves the cherishing of inbred through smothered jealousies, antagonisms, antipathies—because cordial Union, lasting Peace, are attainable only through homogenous institutions, based on Liberty for All. And, if the superficially abortive effort at Niagara shall have served to hasten by but a week this most desired consummation, it will by no means have been made in vain.

Others ridiculed the Niagara Falls affair in the press, including the New York Evening Post, *which used unusually harsh language to criticize Greeley, among others.*

Evening Post (New York), 25 July 1864

An Anonymous Writer: "The Peace Negotiations"

[W]e are only sorry that men can be found on the side of the Union foolish enough to aid in distracting attention from the war by such proceedings. If peace comes at all, it will only be after the next movements of Grant and Sherman, which, if we are not over confident, will drive the rebellion into a very narrow corner; and it will come then, not from…any body purporting to represent the desperate cabal at Richmond; but from gentlemen of position, intelligence and statesmanship, who will speak in the name of the abused people of the South. The government at Richmond is a conspiracy which can never yield but with its life, and our only hope of reconciliation and unity is from the returning good sense of the masses whom it has betrayed and ruined. Let us have no more of this inexpressibly sickening and irresponsible "negotiation."

Southern newspapers disagreed over the consequences of the Niagara Falls affair for the North. The Richmond Examiner *argued that participating in the event sent the message that the South was so weak that it would do anything to secure peace.*

Richmond Examiner, 26 July 1864

An Anonymous Writer: Creating Wrong Impression

To exhibit an ex-Senator and member of Congress of the Confederate States thus timidly crawling by a round-about way to the footstool of the Emperor of the Yahoos, whining and sniveling about peace and "liberal negotiations," and haughtily refused even admittance to the sovereign presence will serve not the peace, but the war party; because it will be used to create the impression that the Confederacy must be in the agonies of death when two distinguished legislators make so pitiful an attempt to reach the ear of offended majesty.

The Richmond Sentinel *claimed that the failed mission strengthened the peace movement in the North by proving that Lincoln was not interested in peace with the South.*

Richmond Sentinel, 26 July 1864

An Anonymous Writer: Peace Not Possible with Lincoln

The peace men of the U. States will be satisfied that no peace can be obtained as long as Lincoln presides over the destinies of the United States.

QUESTIONS

1. Do you believe that a newspaper such as the *Dubuque (Iowa) Herald* or the *North Carolina Standard* is being disloyal when it advocates peace? Explain.
2. Can you imagine a newspaper editor today being part of peace negotiations as Horace Greeley was? Explain.
3. Do you find it surprising that some Confederate newspapers would advocate peace with the North? Why or why not?

NOTES

1. James M. McPherson, *Battle Cry of Freedom: The Civil War Era* (New York: Oxford University Press, 1988), 592.

2. *War of the Rebellion: A Compilation of the Official Records of the Union and Confederate Armies,* Series 1, Volume 23, Part 2, p. 237.

3. William C. Harris, *William Woods Holden: Firebrand of North Carolina Politics* (Baton Rouge: Louisiana State University Press, 1987), 127–55.

4. Joseph H. Parks, *Joseph E. Brown of Georgia* (Baton Rouge: Louisiana State University Press, 1977).

CHAPTER 15

Black Soldiers, 1861–65

When the Civil War began, President Abraham Lincoln had no plans to use black troops in the Union Army. African American leaders regularly called on the president to enlist black soldiers, arguing that it would strike another blow at slavery. But the cautious Lincoln feared that any federal program would arouse prejudices in the North and alienate the important border states that might be tempted to join the Confederacy.

Still, the president looked the other way early in the war when Union commanders in Kansas, Louisiana, and South Carolina experimented with enlisting freed blacks. Major General Benjamin Butler became desperate for men after the U.S. Navy captured New Orleans in 1862. Butler used his authority to enroll 24,000 free blacks who had been members of Confederate militia units. Confederate leaders angrily decried the practice, and it set off a heated debate in the North over the use of African American soldiers.

In the face of increasing pressure by abolitionists and some in Congress, Lincoln became convinced of the wisdom of using blacks militarily. In the preliminary Emancipation Proclamation of 1862 and the final proclamation of 1863, he declared slaves in areas still in rebellion to be free. The president also urged slaves to escape from their masters and join the Union army. Individual Northern states had the authority to enroll black troops just as they had been doing with white soldiers. But this piecemeal approach proved to be ineffective. So in May 1863, the War Department established the Bureau of Colored Troops to oversee recruitment of black troops and screen applications for officers in African American regiments. The bureau recruited in Northern cities, as well in sections of the Confederacy occupied by the Federal army. By the end of the year, approximately 50,000 African American troops had enlisted in the Union army. That number tripled the following year, and by the end of the war approximately 180,000 blacks were serving in the armed services.

The 166 regiments in the United States Colored Troops (USCT) included 145 infantry, 7 cavalry, 12 heavy artillery, 1 light artillery, and 1 engineer. More than 80 percent of the black troops came from Confederate states, and most were former slaves. The great majority of USCT officers were white, but because they were rigorously screened, many were considered better officers than those in white regiments. Most had invaluable combat experience.

Black regiments served in every theater of the war. They participated in 38 major battles and 449 smaller actions. African American troops won perhaps their greatest acclaim at the assault on Fort Wagner. The earthen fort was one of the principal defenses of Charleston, which had become one of the Union army's prime targets by 1863. After one assault of the fort was beaten back with severe casualties, another was made on July 18. The 54th Massachusetts Colored Infantry, the North's showcase black regiment, spearheaded the assault, gaining the fort's parapet and holding it for an hour until falling back. But the assault came at a frightful cost as the 54th Massachusetts lost nearly half its men, including Colonel Robert Gould Shaw, the regiment's commander.[1] Black troops also suffered the greatest casualties at the Battle of the Crater at Petersburg in 1864. But black troops also had the honor of being among the first regiments to enter Richmond after the Confederate capital was captured in April 1865.

Even so, black troops in the Union army suffered from myriad forms of discrimination. They were paid three dollars a month less than white soldiers. Moreover, African American soldiers had three dollars deducted from their monthly pay for clothing while whites paid nothing. Congress approved equal pay for black troops in 1864, but the increase applied only to men who had been free at the start of the war. Union commanders often assigned black regiments to the most unhealthy posts. Black soldiers also suffered from substandard medical care. As a result, an estimated 29,000 African American troops died from disease, nine times as many as those lost to wounds, and a far higher proportion than white soldiers who died in hospitals. Only about 100 black soldiers obtained commissions as officers, and more than 70 of them suffered such cruel racial harassment that they eventually resigned. Few white Union soldiers would willingly take orders from African American officers.[2]

Black troops faced added dangers from the Confederate army. Authorities in Richmond warned that African American soldiers captured would be put back into slavery or executed. Confederate officials eventually backed down from the policy when President Lincoln threatened to take retaliatory measures against Confederate prisoners of war. Still, there was little to stop Rebel commanders from murdering captured black troops.

The most infamous treatment of black soldiers by the Rebel army took place at the battle of Fort Pillow in 1864. The fort was held by 236 black and

295 white troops. A Confederate cavalry division, under the command of Nathan B. Forrest, surrounded the fort and demanded its surrender. When the Union commander refused, the cavalry swarmed into the fort. Although Northern and Southern accounts at the time differed, most historians now believe the Rebel soldiers were guilty of various atrocities, including murdering most of the garrison after it surrendered. The battle became known as the "Fort Pillow Massacre." Afterwards, many black troops went into action shouting "Remember Fort Pillow."[3]

An estimated 37,000 black soldiers died in service to the Union during the war. Sixteen African Americans received the nation's highest military honor, the Medal of Honor. They affirmed one leading Confederate official's declaration regarding black troops. Arguing against using slaves in the Confederate army, former Georgia Governor Howell Cobb said, "The day you make soldiers of them is the beginning of the end of the revolution. If slaves will make good soldiers, our whole theory of slavery is wrong."[4]

This chapter surveys editorials dealing with the use of black soldiers by the Union Army. *Douglass' Monthly* made one of the first and most eloquent pleas for the use of black troops. Once an enlistment plan was approved, Northern newspapers reacted variously. Yet, editorial writers had high praise for black troops who saw conduct. And Northern papers, such as the *Philadelphia Inquirer*, were outraged when they learned about the massacre of African American troops at Fort Pillow. On the other hand, the *Richmond Examiner* claimed the North had committed similar outrages against the Confederacy.

Reaction to Enlistment Plan

From the beginning of the war, Frederick Douglass regularly called upon the federal government to enlist black men. This editorial appeared in Douglass' Monthly *after Massachusetts announced it would begin enlisting troops for a black regiment. It became one of his best-known appeals and was reprinted in many newspapers and on broadsides.*

Douglass' Monthly, March 1863

Frederick Douglass: "Men of Color, To Arms!"

When first the rebel cannons shattered the walls of Sumter, and drove away its starving garrison, I predicted that the war, then and there inaugurated would not be fought out entirely by white men. Every month's experience during those two dreary years, has confirmed that opinion. A war undertaken and brazenly carried out for the perpetual enslavement of colored men, calls logically and loudly upon colored men to help suppress it. Only a moderate share of sagacity was needed to see that the arm of the slave was the best defense against the arm of the slaveholder. Hence with every reverse to the National arms, with every exulting shout of victory raised by the slaveholding rebels, I have implored the imperiled nation to unchain against her foes her powerful black hand. Slowly and reluctantly that appeal is beginning to be heeded. Stop not now to complain that it was not heeded sooner. It may, or it may not have been best that it should not. This is not the time to discuss that question. Leave it to the future. When the war is over, the country is saved, peace is established, and the black man's rights are secured, as they will be, history with an impartial hand, will dispose of that and sundry other questions. Action! action! not criticism, is the plain duty of this hour. Words are now useful only as they stimulate to blows. The office of speech now is only to point when, [w]here and how, to strike to the best advantage. There is no time for delay. The tide is at its flood that leads on to fortune. From East to West, from North to South, the sky is written all over "NOW OR NEVER." Liberty won by white men would lose half its luster. Who would be free themselves must strike the blow. Better even to die free, than to live slaves....

In good earnest then, and after the best deliberations, I now for the first time during this war feel at liberty to call and counsel you to arms. By every consideration which binds you to your enslaved fellow country-men, and the peace and welfare of your country; by every aspiration which you cherish for the freedom and equality of yourselves and your children; by all the ties of blood and identity which makes us one with the brave black men, now fighting our battles in Louisiana, in South Carolina, I urge you to fly to arms, and smite with death the power that would bury the government and your Liberty in the same hopeless grave....

This is our golden opportunity—let us accept it—and forever wipe out the dark reproaches unsparingly hurled against us by our enemies. Win for ourselves the gratitude of our Country—and the best blessings of our posterity through all time. The nucleus of this first regiment is now in camp at Readville, a short distance from Boston. I will undertake to forward to Boston all persons adjudged fit to be mustered into the regiment, who shall apply to me at any time within the next two weeks.

Frederick Douglass.
Rochester, March 2d. 1863

Nashville was one of the captured cities in the South where the Union army recruited black soldiers. The Nashville Daily Press *described the reaction*

to the sight of African American troops parading in a Southern city. The
major referred to was George L. Stearns, who was in charge of recruiting
black troops in the Department of the Cumberland.

Nashville Daily Press, 3 October 1863

An Anonymous Writer: "Negro Troops"

The regiment is the one, we understand, recently recruited in this city by
Major Starnes [Stearns]. These soldiers were armed and equipped as the
law directs, and attracted more attention than any body of troops that ever
kept time to martial music in Nashville. They were officered by white men,
but the novelty of armed Negro troops elicited many remarks about the policy of the Administration in raising them—both *pro and con.*

The New-York Times *said that while admitting blacks into the army was*
a noble goal, the North also must keep in mind that it could inspire the
South to fight harder.

New-York Times, 9 January 1863

An Anonymous Writer: "The Employment of Enfranchised Negroes as Soldiers"

President Lincoln, in his Proclamation, declares that emancipated slaves
"of suitable condition will be employed in the armed service of the United
States." This declaration, made by the highest military authority, and announcing a policy which the Government has decided to adopt, renders it
desirable that the public should look at the matter a little more attentively
than it has yet done. In the first place, let us say that there are insuperable
objections to raising a negro army for the mere purpose of proving that negroes can fight, and if such be the object of the supporters of the project,
they should think twice before they push it any further.

We admit that the task of vindicating the military reputation of a whole
race, and proving them to be possessed of those martial qualities which,
whether rightly or wrongly, all nations in all ages have agreed to consider
the greatest, if not the only claim, to respect, is a noble and inspiring one.
We admit that if we could prove within the next year, by actual experiment,
that the African race can defend themselves in arms we should have solved,
in the eyes of the world, the great problem of their use and their destiny;

and we admit also, that the duty of solving this problem devolves in a great measure on us, because we have had a great share in raising the doubt and mystery which at present surround it. But it must not be forgotten that the time is past when we could afford to carry on this war for the purpose of elucidating a theory, or loosening an ethnological knot. We might have undertaken such a task two years ago, when we had no debts, when our resources in men and in material were still untouched, and when the subjugation of the South promised nothing more exciting than a sort of military promenade. But the disasters and losses which have since occurred have thrown so much doubt on the issue, that whatever our desires may be, we are forced by the necessity of the case to concentrate our attention upon the winning of victories in the field. Though we were ever so well disposed to do other things, the only thing we dare now attempt to do, is to overcome the armed resistance of the enemy. Upon our doing this successfully depends, so far as we can see, not only the safety and welfare of our own country, but the cause of popular government all over the world. In other words we fight simply to conquer. Of the remote consequences of our triumphs, the stern and inexorable necessities of the crisis forbid us now to think.

The sole question to be considered, therefore, in employing negroes as soldiers, is what its immediate effects will be on the fortunes of the war. If after mature consideration, it should appear that their services will not be as valuable as those of the same number of white men, they ought not to be embodied, because it would be a waste of arms, and officers, and transports, and ammunition, and money. But if we cannot raise as many white men as we need or can use, then the negroes ought, if they make even tolerable soldiers, to be enlisted and employed, unless their uses will produce a stronger spirit of resistance in the South and of discontent in the North, than their aid will counterbalance. In other words, we are bound, in embodying them to consider whether their appearance in the field will add more strength to Southern resistance than to our power of attack. If it should appear that such would be the case, it would be our duty, as well as our interest, to discard them. But if, on the contrary, we should be satisfied that they would furnish assistance sufficient, or more than sufficient, to overcome the additional *animus* which their presence would infuse into the contest on the side of the enemy, there is no consideration worthy of the least attention which is not in favor of using them. In all wars of invasion, the feelings of the people are worthy of the closest study, in a military point of view, as they materially affect the success and duration of the operations. There was a time when it might have seemed advisable to consult Southern prejudices for other and more sentimental reasons. But no one but a fool or a visionary, will deny that that time is now past. The state of Southern feeling or opinion is for us, at this supreme crisis, simply a question of strategy. If we try to look at it any longer in any other way, we shall simply seal our own fate. Nobody will pity us.

The Democratic Watchman *in Bellefonte, Pa., was one of many Democratic newspapers that claimed white soldiers in the Union army would refuse to fight alongside black troops.*

Democratic Watchman, 6 March 1863

An Anonymous Writer: "Negro Soldiers"

If Negro regiments and brigades are put into the army of the Potomac, we would not be surprised to see those same soldiers who fought so desperately at Malvern Hill, Williamsburg, Westpoint, Fair-oaks [*sic*], Mechanicsville, Gaines Mills, South Mountain and Antietam, throw down their arms and refuse to fight at all, or turn their cannons and bayonets against the enemies of the Union who are now holding sway in Washington.

One of the first black regiments was the 1st South Carolina, commanded by Colonel Thomas Wentworth Higginson. The regiment received praise from various quarters, including the New-York Tribune, *for a successful raiding expedition into St. Mary's, Georgia.*

New-York Tribune, 11 February 1863

An Anonymous Writer: "Negro Soldiers on Duty"

The bravery and good conduct of the regiment more than equaled the high anticipation of its commander. The men were repeatedly under fire, were opposed by infantry, cavalry, and artillery, fought on board of a steamer exposed to heavy musketry from the banks of a narrow river—were tried in all ways, and came off invariably with honor and success. They brought away property to a large amount, capturing also a cannon and a flag, which the Colonel asks leave to keep for the regiment, and which he and they have fairly won.

It will not need many such reports as this—and there have been several before it—to shake our inveterate Saxon prejudice against the capacity and courage of negro troops....No officer who has commanded black troops has yet reported against them. They are tried in the most unfavorable and difficult circumstances, but never fail. When shall we learn to use the full strength of the formidable ally who is only waiting for a summons to rally under the flag of the Union?

Col. Higginson says: "No officer in this regiment now doubts that the key to the successful prosecution of this war lies in the unlimited employment of black troops." The remark is true in a military sense, and it has a still deeper political significance. When Hunter has scattered 50,000 muskets among the negroes of the Carolinas, and Butler has organized the 100,000 or 200,000 blacks for whom he may perhaps shortly carry arms to New Orleans, the possibility of restoring the Union as it was, with Slavery again its dominant power, will be seen to have finally passed away. The negro is indeed the key to our success.

TREATMENT OF BLACK SOLDIERS

The massacre at Fort Pillow prompted plenty of editorial reaction especially in the North, where newspapers such as the Philadelphia Inquirer *expressed outrage at the event.*

Philadelphia Inquirer, 3 May 1864

An Anonymous Writer: "The Fort Pillow Massacre"

There cannot be a nation on the face of the earth but what will look upon these acts and the people who perpetrated them with loathing and horror. The individuals who committed these terrible outrages against the well established and universally recognized laws of humanity, if they could be caught, should be tried and punished with death; they have placed themselves out of the pale of the rules of warfare, and like murderers they should be executed. But these criminals must be captured by us, or we must adopt measures which will force the Rebels to surrender them to us. The most obvious way to do this is to hold a like number of prisoners in our hands as hostages for the return of the murderers. The question is one full of embarrassments. The crimes of these wretches demand swift and sure punishment, but the teaching of common humanity revolt at the thought of visiting the deserved punishment upon those not engaged in the massacre....The Rebels are at war with us and they are our bitter enemies. They have, no doubt, adopted this system of murdering prisoners in order to deter us from the employment of colored troops; but their design will fail, and retributive justice must speedily overtake them.

The New-York Times *supported a Congressional investigation into the events at Fort Pillow and said the Confederate army should not be permitted to treat African American troops inhumanely.*

New-York Times, 18 April 1864

An Anonymous Writer: "Our Negro Troops—The Reported Rebel Massacre"

Both the Senate and House passed a resolution, on Saturday, calling for immediate inquiry into the circumstances of the Fort Pillow Massacre. Even before this action, the Secretary of War had appointed officers to make investigation into the matter. It is essential that this should be done, and it is well it should be done very promptly. The black soldiers reported to have been butchered in cold blood to the number of three hundred, were men regularly and legally enlisted into our army. They were in the National uniform, defending the National flag and the National integrity, and were fully entitled to the protection guaranteed to all our soldiers. We cannot permit the rebels to massacre them. We cannot pass over this and like massacres by Forrest's rebel gang—if the circumstances be as they have been represented. Jeff. Davis has undertaken to dictate to us very often in this war; but we cannot possibly permit his insolent dictation to go as far as this. The blood of these slaughtered men is on our skirts as well as on the skirts of the rebels, if we permit them to be killed while we stand by, when it is in our power to protect them; and Heaven and history will hold us responsible.

The Richmond Examiner *said the "virtuous wrath" of the North about what happened at Fort Pillow ignored what the newspaper claimed were similar outrages committed against the Confederacy.*

Richmond Examiner, 23 April 1864

An Anonymous Writer: "Fort Pillow"

The exploit of General Forrest at Fort Pillow, which diffused a warm and soothing glow through the veins of every good Confederate, "chills the blood" of the Philadelphia *Inquirer*, and "makes it heart sicken." For the sake of humanity that benevolent journal trusts their [*sic*] may be some exaggeration, some mistake in the narrative of that storm and slaughter. The tender-hearted writer is unwilling to think so ill of his species, as to believe that even "the fiends who are endeavoring to destroy the Union" could be guilty of killing the garrison on the storm of an indefensible position....

This burst of virtuous wrath over the crimes perpetrated by Confederates may well make us reflect, and put us upon a course of stern self-examination. Evidently, in the eyes of the strictly moral Yankee, we have entered upon an evil and vicious course of conduct. It is clear that they cannot allow their own methods of warfare to be any precedent for us. At Charleston, for example, although they have not stormed that city, and cannot take it by siege, mine, starvation or bombardment, they feel it to be their duty, at any rate, to throw Greek fire amongst the non-combatant population of the city in order to bring them to a wholesome sense of their crimes....One cannot but infer that there is some great intrinsic difference in the cause on the one side and on the other, turning that which is held legitimate warfare on their part into barbarous murder when perpetrated by us, and a difference there certainly is, which, to the careless observer, would seem rather in our favour. We are not invading their country, nor holding, nor seeking to hold, any place which belongs to them; we are not blockading their rivers, nor shelling their beach, nor pillaging their property; are not trying to starve them to death and to break their hearts by more hunger and hardship; only desire in short to have nothing whatsoever to do with them any more forever. Under these circumstances it might be too hastily concluded that we may lawfully permit ourselves at least as strong measures for defence as our enemies use for offence. But in fact the true difference—and it alters the whole case—is that our Northern brethren are in the position of officers of the law fringing criminals to justice; we in the position of burglars and brigands resisting the authorities; and the sheriff may do to the highwayman what the highwayman must not do the sheriff. The constable may shoot, or starve out, or smoke out, or blow up, the resisting burglar, because he has a lawful warrant; but if the burglar perpetrates these enormities upon the constable, it chills the blood and sickens the heart.

Soldiers in the black 55th Massachusetts Regiment refused to accept less pay than white soldiers received. A member of the regiment wrote a letter to the Weekly Anglo-African *(New York) in which he lamented the hardships the pay discrimination caused soldiers and their families.*

Weekly Anglo-African (New York), 30 April 1864

An Anonymous Writer: Unequal Pay

Headquarters 55th Reg. Mass Infantry,
Palatka, Fla., April 10, 1864

Mr. Editor:

This regiment was mustered into the United States service about the 18th or 20 of June, 1863, consequently we have been ten months working for Uncle Sam, not taking into account the time when some us were sworn in.

The only thing that engrosses our mind now, is the old and troublesome subject of pay.

We have been promised that we would be paid, and a paymaster came (last November) to pay us. He offered us $7 per month. We enlisted for $13 per month, with the promise (and I wish the public to keep this fact before them, to see how these promises are being fulfilled) that we should be treated in all respects like white soldiers, our bounty, rations, and emoluments being the same. The same inducements were held out to us as to all Massachusetts volunteers....

We do not look upon Massachusetts as being responsible for our sufferings; but upon the government of the United States, and how a government with such a lofty reputation can so act, is beyond our conception or comprehension. We know, and the world knows that had we been white men the whole land would have been up in blaze of indignation in regard to the great injustice done us.

How the authorities expect our families to live without the means to buy bread, pay house rent, and meet the other incident expenses of living in these terrible times, we know not; but if it does not exert its well known power it certainly will not be held guiltless in this matter.

Are our parents, wives, children and sisters to suffer, while we, their natural protectors, are fighting the battles of the nation? We leave the government and Congress to answer.

That they *do* suffer we have abundant evidence.

I have seen a letter from a wife in Illinois to her husband, stating that she had been sick for six months, and begging him to send her the sum of *fifty cents*. Was it any wonder that the tears rolled in floods from that stout-hearted man's eyes?

How can it be expected that men will do their duty consistently with a soldier's training, under such circumstances?

Patience has an end, and with us will soon cease to be a virtue. We would be contented and happy could we but receive our pay.

I have been asked by officers, not connected with our Regiment, why we did not take our pay when we could get it. My answer was that our pay has never been sent to us. True, money has been sent here, but it was not our pay. When the United States authorities shall send us $13 per month, which is our just due, we will take it, *and not until then, will we take one cent....*

Our debasement is most complete. No chances for promotion, no money for our families, and we little better than an armed band of laborers with rusty muskets and bright spades, what is our incentive to duty? Yet God has put it into our hearts to believe that we will survive or perish with the liberty of our country. If she lives, we live; if she dies we will sleep with her, even as our brave comrades now sleep with Col. Shaw within the walls of Wagner.

More anon,

Bay State

On the subject of the North's discrimination against African American troops, the Chicago Tribune *said there was no reason why black soldiers should be paid less than white soldiers.*

Chicago Tribune, 1 May 1864

An Anonymous Writer: "Treatment of Black Soldiers"

Congress is still pottering, every now and then, over the question of paying black soldiers; being in deadly fear lest they should receive—not the fair amount they may be worth—but as much as the white soldiers of the same rank and services. If the white men get ten dollars per month, the black may have seven; but if whites receive sixteen, the blacks are allowed thirteen. A late law reported to the House from the Senate equalizes the pay, as the dispatch leaves us to infer, but tacks on a provision, that three dollars of the black man's wages shall be reserved for his family or dependent relatives.

Now, what earthly reason can any man show for any such provision? Why not reserve three dollars of the other men's wages for a like purpose? Have white men no wives and children; or mothers and grandmothers? Or do all the wives and children of white men take care of themselves; or are they taken care of by husbands and fathers? It is time this fooling with the black man was done with. If he earns wages, why not pay them to him? If he earns as much as a man of any other color, why not pay him as much?

QUESTIONS

1. Do you think President Lincoln was wise politically to move slowly in enlisting black troops? Why?
2. Why would a black publication, such as *Douglass' Monthly,* be in favor of enlisting African American soldiers?
3. Why was it important for newspapers to editorialize about the Fort Pillow massacre?
4. What were the arguments of the *Chicago Tribune* for paying black soldiers that same amount as white soldiers?

NOTES

1. James M. McPherson, *Battle Cry of Freedom: The Civil War Era* (New York: Oxford University Press, 1988), 686–87.

2. Benjamin Quarles, *The Negro in the Civil War* (New York: Russell & Russell, 1953), 183–213.

3. Robert Selph Henry, *"First with the Most" Forrest* (Indianapolis: Bobbs-Merrill, 1944), 248–69.

4. Cited in Robert F. Durden, *The Gray and the Black: The Confederate Debate on Emancipation* (Baton Rouge: Louisiana State University Press, 1972), 183–85.

CHAPTER 16

Battle of Gettysburg, 1863

By May 1863, General Robert E. Lee believed the time had come for the Confederate army to invade the North again. Lee's forces had just won an impressive victory at Chancellorsville, but the Union army still posed a threat on the Rappahannock. The general believed that by defeating the Federals in their own backyard, he could resupply his army, bring foreign recognition to the Confederacy, and strengthen the growing peace movement in the North. The victory at Chancellorsville, in which Lee daringly split his forces, also convinced the general that his army was capable of most anything. "There never were such men in an army before," Lee said. "They will go anywhere and do anything if properly led."[1]

After Stonewall Jackson's death at Chancellorsville, Lee reorganized his army into three infantry corps led by James Longstreet, Richard S. Ewell, and Ambrose P. Hill. During the first week in June, Lee launched his invasion through the Shenandoah Valley by capturing the Union garrison at Winchester, Virginia, and then crossed the Potomac River. By mid-June, the Confederate Army was marching through central Pennsylvania, seizing supplies and wrecking Union war machinery.

The 100,000 Union troops, under the command of Joseph Hooker, had crossed the Potomac and marched north to stay between Lee and Washington. But Hooker, who believed he had not received proper support from the Lincoln administration, asked to be relieved of his command. On June 28, the president accepted his offer and named George Gordon Meade as commander of the Army of the Potomac. When Meade took over the army, it was concentrated near Frederick, Maryland. Lee's army was scattered around Chambersburg, York, and Carlisle, Pennsylvania. When Lee learned that Federal troops had crossed the Potomac, he ordered his troops to reunite near the small town of Gettysburg.

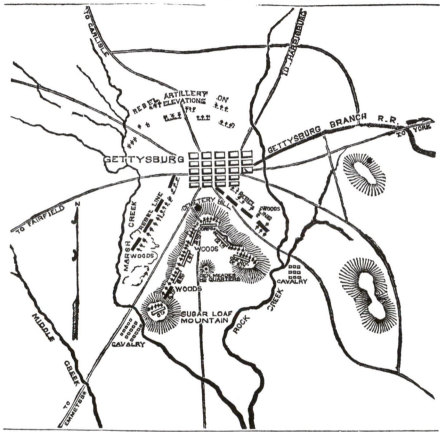

THE BATTLE-FIELD AROUND GETTYSBURG.

The above sketch of the battlefield at Gettysburg was made by one of our correspondents, who care- | *as topographical engineers, and is, therefore, in all essential points, absolutely correct. The wood in front of the left wing is where I* | *very short lines in reinforcing the point of attack. The enemy was compelled to march his infantry in* | *assigned and substantially maintained. The el tion occupied by the Rebel artillery was n lower than that on which the National troops w*

Battlefield at Gettysburg. *The battlefield at Gettysburg is shown in this map that appeared in the* New-York Tribune *(July 7, 1863). The casualty figures during the three-day battle were staggering and the highest of the war up to that point. The Union victory also was a turning point in the war, as the Confederacy never again marched so far into the North.*

In the meantime, Hill had learned that there was a large supply of shoes at Gettysburg, and he sent a division ahead to seize the shoes. But Union cavalry, commanded by Brigadier General John Buford, had arrived in Gettysburg the day before. Buford had recognized the strategic importance of

Gettysburg, which was flanked by ridges and hills. When Hill's division marched into Gettysburg on July 1, Buford's dismounted cavalry was ready and held off the much larger force. As the horsemen were about to give way, a division arrived and drove back the Rebel troops. By afternoon, Confederate reinforcements made their way to Gettysburg and when Lee arrived, he ordered an attack. The Rebel troops swept through the Union lines sending them retreating through the town to nearby Cemetery Hill. Lee wanted his men to continue the fight, but Ewell thought the enemy's position was too strong. By evening, more Union divisions arrived and set up a formidable position that resembled a fishhook. Anchored by Culp's Hill, the line extended west to Cemetery Hill, then south along Cemetery Ridge to a hill called Little Round Top.

Surveying the Union line the next morning, Longstreet believed it was too strong and advised a flanking movement. However, Lee believed his battle-tested men could defeat the Federals and he ordered Longstreet to attack. For various reasons, the attack did not begin until 4 P.M. In the meantime, Union commander Dan Sickles was concerned about the terrain north of Little Round Top. He moved his troops to higher ground, and there they held a salient with its apex in a peach orchard and one side anchored in a group of boulders called Devil's Den below Little Round Top. Although the new position gave Sickles higher ground to defend, it isolated his men from the rest of the Union troops. During the next few hours, some of the war's deadliest fighting took place at Devil's Den, in the peach orchard, in a wheat field, and on Little Round Top. The Rebels broke through Sickles's line, but the Federals rushed in reinforcements. The Confederates almost seized Little Round Top, but Mead's chief of engineers recognized the problem and galloped off to find reinforcements who arrived just in time. One of the heroes at Little Round Top was Colonel Joshua L. Chamberlain. His men had run out of ammunition in beating off repeated Rebel assaults on the hill. So Chamberlain ordered his men to fix their bayonets on the rifles and charge. The assault surprised the Confederates, and Little Round Top remained in Union hands. By the time the fighting ended on July 2, both sides had suffered large casualties, but the Union line remained largely intact.

Lee was determined to achieve victory in Pennsylvania, and he still believed his troops could accomplish it. He felt the Union center was vulnerable because troops had been moved to protect the two flanks attacked by the Rebels. Shortly after 1 P.M. on July 3, Confederate artillery began the largest Southern bombardment of the war. Union guns fired back, and for two hours the two sides dueled. Then at approximately 3 P.M., 14,000 Confederate troops under the command of Major General George Pickett moved against the Union center across a mile of open fields. Federal artillery blasted the Rebels, while Yankee infantry behind stonewalls poured more gunfire into them. The Confederate assault collapsed under the deadly firing, although several hundred troops managed to seize some cannons before being driven off. Pickett's Charge, as it would later become known, had lasted approximately 90 minutes. Of the 14,000 Rebel attackers, half had been killed or wounded.

Meade did not counterattack, despite the pleas of some of his men. "We have done well enough," he told one officer.[2] On the other side, Lee was devastated by the defeat. "It's all my fault," the beloved general said as he rode among his men.[3] Lee began his retreat on July 4 as a wagon train estimated to be 19 miles long carried thousands of wounded men south. The Confederate army had lost 28,000 men killed, wounded, or missing. The Union suffered 23,000 casualties. It was the largest single-battle toll of the war thus far. Moreover, Gettysburg proved to be the turning point of the war. As historian James M. McPherson has written, "Lee and his men would go on to earn further laurels. But they never again possessed the power and reputation they carried into Pennsylvania those palmy midsummer days of 1863."[4]

Four months later, 17 acres of the Gettysburg battlefield were dedicated for a cemetery where Union soldiers who had fallen in the battle would be buried. President Lincoln was invited to contribute "a few appropriate remarks" at the ceremony on November 19. Lincoln decided to use the event for a public statement on the meaning and the significance of the war. Contrary to popular myth, the president did not write the speech on the back of an envelope during the train ride to Gettysburg. He started the speech weeks earlier, but finished it only after arriving in Gettysburg. After an eloquent two-hour speech by orator Edward Everett, the president was introduced to the 15,000 people in attendance. Lincoln began his speech with the words: "Four score and seven years ago our fathers brought forth, upon this continent, a new nation, conceived in liberty, and dedicated to the proposition that all men are created equal." The president's address lasted only two minutes, and its brevity surprised the people in attendance who had heard Everett's lengthy speech. But the Gettysburg Address has become revered because Lincoln articulated the reason the Union was fighting the war—to preserve a nation in which all men are created equal.

This chapter begins with editorials on the Confederacy's invasion of the North in June 1863. The *New-York Tribune* argued that the invasion would bolster the war effort in the North. Lee urged his troops not to pillage Northern property, a plea that the Richmond *Daily Dispatch* found laughable given what the paper said the Union army had done to the South. After the battle, Northern newspapers exalted in the Union victory at Gettysburg, while Southern newspapers downplayed the devastating loss. The ceremony dedicating a national cemetery at Gettysburg also prompted numerous editorials. The *New York Herald* said the cemetery would be a new monument to freedom. On the other hand, the *Richmond Examiner* ridiculed the cemetery dedication at Gettysburg. The *Springfield Republican* called Lincoln's now-famous address a "perfect gem."

INVASION OF NORTH

The New-York Tribune *claimed that the South's invasion would actually aid the war effort in the North.*

New-York Tribune, 1 July 1863

An Anonymous Writer: "The Rebel Strategy"

We view the advance of the Rebels into Pennsylvania in no spirit of overweening confidence. War is largely a game of chance, and its results often defy all antecedent calculation. But, while we indulge in no boastful anticipation, we heartily thank to the Rebel chiefs for transferring the seat of war from their own wasted fields to the rich valleys and teeming hillsides of the Free States.

They did not need to do this for the sake of fighting. Our army of the Potomac lay directly in their front, ready for the battle at an hour's notice. They chose to evade it by a flank movement, and come North.

If they deemed the line of the Rappahannock too strong to enforced, they might have had a battle a few miles westward of Washington. They declined this also, being evidently anxious to eat before they fought. It was well, and their movement is doing a world of good. Having already fairly earned the praise of doing more to upset Slavery than all the Abolitionists ever lived, they now lend a hand to secure the downfall of the Rebellion.

Mind that we are not predicting Union victories at hand. We may have these and may not have. But in either or any case, we are indebted to Lee's advance for these:

I. "Peace Movement," Ewell, Longstreet, Early, J.E.B. Stuart, &c., have rather taken the wind out of the sails of Fernando Wood, Vallandigham, Rynders & Co. It is plain that Peace for this distracted country lies behind smart fighting, and a good deal of it.

II. We bear less and less of the wickedness of "invading the South," and the expediency of ceasing to afflict "our Southern Brethren." People who have tried not to see it begin to realize that we are involved in a bloody, desolating war, and that "Abe Lincoln" cannot terminate it if he would.

They discover that, if we are to have any country at all, we must fight for it....

IV. There will be no more borrowing trouble about enforcing the draft, at least so long as a Rebel regiment remains on this side of the Potomac. If there is a married Copperhead who thinks of skulking, just speak to his wife about it; if a young bachelor, notify his mother. Don't tell the girls of his pusillanimity, unless the case should be an exceedingly hard one. It can't be necessary.

V. Nor can there be any further objection to negroes fighting so soon and so much as they choose.... Forty negro regiments might march through the Sixth Ward to-morrow and hardly elicit a brickbat. Those who *will* fight for our country are not afraid of having too many to fight with them; those who *won't* fight have at least the grace to be ashamed of preventing others. If every Black in the Free States were to volunteer to-morrow, a fading hiss from the principal Copperhead dons will be the only note of dissatisfaction.

Patriots! lovers of the starry flag, especially when it symbolizes Universal Freedom! the clouds may be dark for the moment, but they have a silver lining; this sickness is not unto death, but forebodes renovation; though tried as by fire, the Union shall emerge triumphant and glorious, from this stern ordeal. Long live the Republic!

General Lee forbade his army from pillaging private property in Pennsylvania to show that Confederate troops were superior to Union soldiers who had devastated the South. But the Daily Dispatch *argued that the South had every right to retaliate against the North. (Some Confederate troops ignored Lee's order and pillaged property in their march through Pennsylvania.)*

Daily Dispatch (Richmond), 24 June 1863

An Anonymous Writer: "More about Retaliation"

While our troops in Pennsylvania are "respecting private property," the Yankees in Mississippi are burning Panola and Batesville. Such is the return we receive for that amazing magnanimity which sacrifices our friends out of consideration for our enemies. The latter, it seems, are the only fit subjects for Confederate mercy. Our own people are not worthy to taste its benefits. How long is this state of things to continue? How long are we to submit to Yankee outrages without even attempting to retaliate? How long are we expected, when smitten on one cheek, to turn the other? In a little time we shall have no towns and villages left to destroy, and then, we suppose, we may expect Yankee rage to subside, but not before.

We hear it said that if we retaliate it will only induce farther outrage on the part of the enemy. Such reasoning is too pusillanimous to command the attention of a brave people. If we are afraid to strike lest we be struck in return, we had better never entered upon this war. It would be better, even now, to give it up, and ask pardon of the Yankees for all the defeats our brave armies have inflicted upon them. But it is false reasoning. If we had retaliated sternly in the beginning we should have put an end to the system of outrages adopted by the Yankees at once. If we had hung a dozen Yankee officers when the Yankee Government refused to surrender the villain Mc-Neil, we should have had no more military murders. The scoundrel, Burnside, who has shown his incapacity to fight, would never have dared to murder officers in cold blood, for recruiting in Kentucky, our own territory. If, whenever the Yankee citizens murdered our citizens, taken in the act of defending their property against their armed marauders, five of their officers had been executed for every murdered citizen, an end would long since have been put to that atrocious system. War cannot be made upon the principles inculcated by the Peace Society.

The Yankees invade our country with the avowed purpose of starving us out and reducing us to ruin. They steal all our negroes—they kill all the cattle, hogs, sheep and horses, that they cannot carry away—they burn the crops in the barns and in the field—they shoot or hand our people if they attempt to defend their homes—and they do all this with perfect impunity. They know they will never be called to a reckoning. They believe we are afraid to retaliate, for thus they interpret the Christian meekness of our Government. That meekness, far from softening their wrath, tends only to inflame it to the highest pitch. They look upon our country as a game preserve, which they may enter and plunder whenever they may feel disposed to do so, without the slightest risk of prevention or punishment. Our submission is a standing invitation to them, and they fail not to take advantage of it.

In what respect could we be worsted by retaliation? The enemy could not treat us worse than is treating us now! He burns and pillages whatever he chooses, and he hands and shoots whomsoever he pleases. He could but do the same if we retaliated, and he could not well do worse. But he would not do worse. He does what he is now doing because he fears not retribution. His own country has heretofore, with the exception of a small portion of it last year, been secure from invasion. He has had no fear for his home and his fireside, his family, and his property. He knows not, practically, what war is. He has no conception of its horrors, no idea of the losses it entails. It is of the last importance to give him a lesson in these particulars, because without such lesson he will never incline to peace.

BATTLE OF GETTYSBURG

The Harrisburg Telegraph *claimed the Confederate invasion of the North destroyed any claims that the South was fighting merely to maintain its constitutional rights.*

Harrisburg (Pa.) Telegraph, 7 July 1863

An Anonymous Writer: "Passing the Rubicon"

[W]hen Lee crossed the Potomac, he and his ragged followers passed the Rubicon, and from the moment the feet of the slave driver touched free soil, his fate was sealed. Hereafter the Democratic twaddle concerning the constitutional rights of the South will be rejected. The campaign of Pennsylvania has unveiled the true scheme of the invader. His own confession, that he came with fire and sword to devastate and destroy the property and lives of the people of the North, fixes the standard of Southern "constitutional rights," and presents the objects of the rebellion in their true aspect.

The New-York Times *said the Army of the Potomac, which had been repeatedly defeated by Lee, had redeemed itself with the victory at Gettysburg. (Note that the* Times *misspelled Gettysburg, putting an "h" at the end.)*

New-York Times, 7 July 1863

An Anonymous Writer: "The Unheralded Heroes of Battle"

The Army of the Potomac has not only won a great battle, and delivered the nation from the gravest peril of the war, but it has triumphantly vindicated its claim to be classed with the veteran and heroic armies that history delights to honor. In all the details that reach us of the Titanic conflict that raged during three days about Gettysburgh, no fact shines out more conspicuously and cheeringly than the fortitude and unflinching valor of our men. They were equal to every crisis in the varying fortunes of the fight. Was it needed to stand firm and unswerving in line of battle, while the air was darkened by the missiles of a hundred guns parked by the rebels to clear the way for an infantry assault?—there was not a corps in the Union Army that was not equal to the duty; and at least half of the corps composing the army at some time during the battle, were called on to endure this fearful, fiery trial. Was it needed after standing for hours before this withering blast of concentrated artillery fire, to receive the shock of the rebel army, massed and thrown forward in columns, in those impetuous charges that have so often before proven successful—the veteran soldiers of Meade's army were ready for the fierce onsets, and met them, steel to steel, as only the brave can meet a foe. Was it needed to fall back before overwhelming odds, yet not to fly; but to give blow for blow in falling back, and watch for the opportune moment to change retreat into victory and win back the lost ground? This, too, the army of the Potomac was capable of, as it again and again illustrated in the three days' battles around Gettysburgh. The annals of warfare are searched in vain for instances of more universal and better sustained valor than characterized our army during the recent combat.

In all the accounts that have reached the public from a score of different observers who watched the battle from different standpoints, there is entire harmony in this particular. In no single instance is there a mention of alarm or flight on the part of any, the most insignificant, column of Union soldiers. Twice or thrice, during the three days' conflict, when the enemy massed his whole army against particular parts of our line to break it, our men were borne back by the mere weight of numbers. It was mechanical pressure, nothing else, the veterans of the Potomac gave way to. But they retired slowly, and in order, with their faces to the foe, lessening his dense ranks at every step by the terrible musketry fire, and still more fearful dashes of iron hail from deluging artillery, until the pressure of numbers fairly cease, and changed to their own side; and then with resurgent shout they turned back the tide of the battle, and in turn drove the enemy far beyond the line of his advance. Wounded and slain, the prisoners by thousands, were the trophies that remained in their hands after each fierce onset of the enemy.

Fortune has dealt hardly by the Army of the Potomac. It has been led to battle oft; to victory but seldom. It has borne a part in many of the most sanguinary struggles that have marked modern war. And there has been a singular and painful gradation in the steps by which it reached disasters. This first battle of Bull Run was more than doubled, in its casualties by the more honorable but indecisive battle of Fair Oaks. The second bloody struggle was wholly eclipsed by the terrors and carnage of the Seven Days' retreat from before Richmond. The retreat from Richmond was exceeded in disheartening influence upon the country by the retreat upon Washington after Pope's defeat in the second and most bloody battles of Manassas Plains. The battle of Antietam was only an arrest of the succession of reverses. It gave ground of confidence and hope as to what the Army of the Potomac could do. But the reign of hope was brief. For soon came the unredeemed slaughter of Fredericksburgh [*sic*]; and still later, the unaccountable catastrophe of Chancellorsville. This last was the climax of disaster.

After such a history of misfortune, disappointments and defeats, it is not amazing that any soul or spirit was left in the hearts of the men of the Army of the Potomac? What other army of which we have record, has ever lived through such shocking misguidance, such weakening of its country's confidence and such loss of the world's praise, and yet come out of it all with escutcheon clear, with courage unquestioned, with patriotism exalted, and crowned with all the honors and rewards of victory? But the Army of the Potomac has done this thing. It has leaped at once from the depths of its disappointment and gloom to the height of glory and success.

When we remember the past, we must admit that of a truth the patient and long-suffering, the faithful but unappreciated heroes of the Army of the Potomac have wrested their laurels from the hands of reluctant Fortune. They have, in one last great effort, vindicated their own manhood, won the undying gratitude of their country, and extorted the admiration of the world. Leaders may do much for an army, but they can do nothing without courage and tenacity in soldiers. These qualities in the humble rank and file make heroes, found empires, establish great principles, and mould the destiny of nations and races. And so far-reaching, we believe, will be the deeds wrought by our glorious soldiers at Gettysburgh.

There are tens of thousands of bereaved homes in the North, whose weeds and whose woes are connected for the rest of this mortal life with the battles and marches of the Army of the Potomac. But immedicable grief has its halo at last in the honorable fame that is laid up for all who can lay any claim to the glory its heroes have won. History will tell that the battle of Gettysburgh did not win a victory only, but inspired a nation with confidence in its citizen soldiers, and gave to the world a knowledge of martial prowess, worth a hundred battles and victories, in securing from attack the great principles that underlie the fabric of American Free Government.

After the news of Gettysburg reached the South, many newspapers tried to preserve morale. The Charleston Courier *said it was time for the Confederacy "to show the kind of stuff we are made of."*

Charleston Courier, 14 July 1863

An Anonymous Writer: "The Duty of the Hour"

The crisis demands coolness, courage, firmness, patience. We were happy and hopeful ten days ago; we should not yield to despondency now. This is the time for us to show the kind of stuff we are made of....

Is this a time to yield to despondency and gloom? Is this a time to stand trembling with white faces and quaking hearts? We have beaten the enemy. He has suffered heavy loss in every discomfiture. We shall smite him again and defeat him utterly.

The Chronicle & Sentinel *compared the defeat at Gettysburg to losses the American revolutionaries faced.*

Chronicle & Sentinel (Augusta, Ga.), 15 July 1863

An Anonymous Writer: "The Varying Fortunes of War"

People struggling as we are, must expect disaster. What nation ever achieved its independence without it? In the early history of the Revolutionary war, Washington suffered an overwhelming defeat at New York and Brooklyn. He retreated through New Jersey, hotly pressed by the enemy, and when he landed in Pennsylvania after his perilous flight, the grand army was reduced to some three or four thousand half starved, half naked, and half mutinous troops.

On the same day that the disastrous rout was experienced in New York and New Jersey, the State of Rhode Island fell into the hands of the enemy. Many were ready to give up the contest. To offer further resistance was, in their view, positive madness. There has been no point in our experience yet reached, at all comparable in gloom to that which was suffered by the patriots of '76. If we have not made up our minds to submit to sacrifice and hardship we have not yet imbibed the spirit which animated their bosoms, and we cannot, like them, hope to come forth victorious from the struggle.

GETTYSBURG ADDRESS

The New York Herald *said that with the national cemetery at Gettysburg, the United States had a new monument dedicated to freedom.*

New York Herald, 20 November 1863

An Anonymous Writer: "Consecration of the National Sepulchre at Gettysburg"

Yesterday a portion of the battlefield of Gettysburg was consecrated as a national cemetery for the interment of the gallant men who fell in battle there, and who had been buried, as is usual in such cases, nearly where they fell, over the whole extended scene of the fight. Disinterred and gathered into the consecrated place, their bones will, in themselves, be a monument of the consideration in which brave men are held by a free people, and will in future constitute one of the grand pilgrim shrines of our history.

Bunker Hill Monument has until now stood alone as a great national memento erected on the spot to commemorate a struggle for American freedom. But now there is another, different in character and with a deeper interest for us all. Bunker Hill reminds us how hard it is for a people to win their freedom, and Gettysburg how much harder it may be to keep it.

The Richmond Examiner *ridiculed the cemetery dedication at Gettysburg, saying that it was nothing more than an overblown theatrical display.*

Richmond Examiner, 28 November 1863

An Anonymous Writer: "Glittering Foil"

The dramatic exhibition of Gettysburg is in thorough keeping with the Yankee character, and its minor incidents admirably suited to their present condition and to the usual dignity of their chosen chief. There was the wonted Yankee line of theatrical display—the substitution of glittering foil and worthless paste for real brilliants and pure gold. Stage play, studied attitudes, and effective points were carefully elaborated and presented to world as the honest outpourings of a nation's heart. In spite of shoddy contracts, of universal corruption, and cruel thirst for Southern blood, these people have ideas of the great virtues and lofty qualities which ennoble a nation....

The Springfield Republican *called Lincoln's address at Gettysburg a "perfect gem" that should be studied as a model speech.*

Springfield (Mass.) Republican, 21 November 1863

An Anonymous Writer: A Perfect Gem

Surpassingly fine as Mr. Everett's oration was in the Gettysburg consecration, the rhetorical honors [of] the occasion were won by President Lincoln. His little speech is a perfect gem; deep in feeling, compact in thoughts and expression, and tasteful and elegant in every word and comma.... Turn back and read it over—it will well repay study as a model speech.

QUESTIONS

1. Do you agree with the *New-York Tribune*'s argument that the Confederate invasion benefited the North? Why or why not?
2. Why did Southern newspapers such as the *Chronicle & Sentinel* constantly draw comparisons to the patriots during the American Revolution?
3. What do you think of the *New York Herald*'s statement that Gettysburg served as a reminder to Americans about how hard it is to maintain their freedom? Explain.

NOTES

1. James M. McPherson, *Battle Cry of Freedom: The Civil War Era* (New York: Oxford University Press, 1988), 647.

2. Shelby Foote, *The Civil War: A Narrative, Fredericksburg to Meridian* (New York: Random House, 1974), 575.

3. Ibid., 567–68.

4. McPherson, *Battle Cry of Freedom*, 665.

CHAPTER 17

Military Draft, 1862–64

At the outset of the Civil War, both the North and the South depended on men volunteering to meet the manpower needs of the two armies. Although there were plenty of men when the war began, it became clear after the first year that new measures were needed to keep the military adequately staffed. Military service required enormous personal sacrifices if a man had a family or owned a business. Moreover, in the North, wartime industries often paid better than a soldier's wages. For the first time in American history, the Union and Confederate governments were forced to use drafts.

The Confederate Congress approved the first of three conscription acts on April 16, 1862. It required all white males between the ages of 18 and 35 to serve in the military for three years or until the end of the war. Men in certain occupations deemed essential to the Confederacy, including government workers, politicians, teachers, ministers, contractors, shoemakers, blacksmiths, millers, and newspaper employees, were exempted from service. A drafted man also could hire a substitute to take his place. The conscription law took responsibility for recruiting and organizing military units away from the states and placed it with the Confederate government. President Jefferson Davis argued that conscription was the only fair means of distributing the burden of military service equally and consolidating control of Southern troops.[1]

The exemption provisions were always among the most controversial aspects of the Confederate conscription laws. The laws exempted newspaper editors and their essential employees, but in 1864, Davis asked the Congress to rescind the exemption. Hundreds of newspapers employees, including some editors, had joined the Rebel army. Many editors saw the president's proposal as an attempt to silence opposition newspapers by putting their editors in the army.

Staunch defenders of states' rights in the South, including governors Joseph E. Brown of Georgia and Zebulon B. Vance of North Carolina, criticized the draft and fought it in the courts. The exemption and substitution clauses also were highly controversial. Critics charged that those wealthy or politically connected escaped the draft. The criticism increased when the Confederate Congress added another unpopular provision that exempted owners of 20 or more slaves from the draft. Some Southerners used conscription as an excuse for deserting or failing to appear for service. Bands of deserters and men who refused to be enlisted regularly fought conscription agents and troops sent in to enforce the draft laws. By the fall of 1864, increased violence by the deserter gangs, Southern military defeats, and public opposition to the war led to a general breakdown in conscription. Confederate officials began debating what had once been unthinkable: enlisting the South's large number of slaves.

By the end of 1862, the North likewise was facing a sharp decline in the number of military volunteers. On March 3, 1863, President Abraham Lincoln signed the Enrollment Act requiring males in various age groups, beginning with those ages 20 to 45, to serve in the military. The act provided for exemptions from the service, including men with physical and mental disabilities, and those who had sole responsibility for the care of aged parents or young children. Drafted men who had the financial means could either pay a $300 exemption fee or hire a substitute. The country was divided into 185 congressional districts, and each district was required to secure a certain number of men for service. If the proper number of men volunteered in a district, no draft was needed. This meant that government authorities in each district actively recruited men to keep the draft from affecting people in their area.

As in the South, groups opposed the draft in various ways, and sometimes the protest turned violent. By far the worst violence took place in New York City during five days in June 1863. Many working-class New Yorkers, especially Irish Catholics, believed that Protestants were forcing the war on them for the freedom of blacks. They were also concerned that blacks would take their jobs at lower wages. On June 11, draft officers in New York began drawing the names of men to be enlisted. No disturbances took place the first day, but when the draft resumed, hundreds of angry men attacked the draft office and nearly beat the superintendent to death. Mobs looted the homes of prominent citizens, burned Protestant churches, and attacked well-dressed men on the street with shouts of, "There goes a 300 dollar man." The rioters also directed their violence at the city's blacks, lynching a half-dozen residents and burning black establishments, including the Colored Orphan Asylum, while the children escaped out the back.

New York police tried to disperse the mob but had only limited success until July 15 when army regiments from Pennsylvania reached the city. The troops, many of whom had fought at Gettysburg, battled the rioters for two days, inflicting severe casualties. In all, an estimated 1,000 people were killed in the rioting, including ten policemen and soldiers. Rioters set fires that destroyed more than 50 buildings in the city. The draft resumed in August with thousand of new troops posted in New York to enforce it.[2]

The conscription acts were controversial in that the Federal and Confederate governments replaced the states as the primary agencies for mobilizing military personnel. Moreover, provisions in the drafts that allowed for exemptions and hiring substitutes led to charges that it was "a rich man's war and a poor man's fight." Although conscription did little to ensure popular support for the war in either the North or South, they ensured that both sides had adequate armies to fight.

The drafts in the North and South prompted a great deal of editorial debate. The Confederacy's conscription act was debated on the pages of the Atlanta *Southern Confederacy* with a soldier claiming that the poor were shouldering too great a burden, and the newspaper arguing that the controversial exemption for slaveholders was necessary. The attempt by President Davis to remove the exemption for newspapers employees prompted sharp attacks from virtually all the South's editors. In the North, newspapers that supported the Lincoln administration generally approved of the draft, while opposition papers often were highly critical of it. The *Chicago Tribune* maintained the draft was a military necessity, while the *Cleveland Plain Dealer* said conscription would simply produce more opposition to the war.

Newspapers editorialized heavily about the draft riots in New York City. Democratic papers such as the *New York World* blamed the Lincoln administration for the riot, while Republican papers such as the *New-York Times* urged the strongest measures possible against the rioters. Confederate newspapers, such as the *Richmond Examiner,* found great satisfaction in the riots, claiming that it showed the North was tired of fighting.

CONFEDERATE CONSCRIPTION LAW DEBATED

In a letter to the Atlanta Southern Confederacy *a Georgia soldier criticized the draft exemption given to slaveholders. He said the poor were being asked to shoulder too great a burden in fighting the war.*

Southern Confederacy (Atlanta, Ga.), 30 October 1862

A Georgia Soldier: "Are We Whipped? Must We Give Up?"

Messrs Editors:

I notice in your issue, of the 25th inst., an editorial with the above cap-
tion, which contained many good suggestions and some wise counsel.
It is but too true that many are skulking and hiding, hatching excuses
to avoid conscription. I will admit for the sake of argument that their
reason is as you assign it a fear to contend on the field of battle. But as
to the justice of the clause of the Exemption Bill to which you refer, I
must say that your ideas of justice and equity are quite different from
mine. I cannot for my life see how it is, that because the institution of
slavery elevates the social position of the poor man, that therefore the
poor should fight the battles of our country, while the rich are allowed
to remain at home. I grant it. But is it just that each conscript, who happens to own ten negroes of certain age should be exempt from military
duty?—Why sir, what say you to the poor white man who has *ten children* all dependant [*sic*]upon him for succor and support? Shall he be
exempt? No, you answer, "go fight for the negroes of your neighbor,
because it elevates you in society." You say that the negroes must work
to support our army. Why sir, have you not learned that of all men left
at home, the man who owns ten negroes or more is the last to help either the soldier or his family.

It is but too true. I tell you that the worst enemy our young republic has is the spirit that pervades our land to an alarming extent of extorting from the poor and needy to build up the rich and powerful.
Our army is composed of poor men—men who listened to that old cry,
"*We* pay the taxes, *we* are the bone and sinew of the country. *Our* business is too large and complicated to leave. *You* go; you have nothing to
leave but your family and they will be taken care of."

It is easy to be a soldier, to leave home and its endearments, *on
paper*. But when the reality is tested it is something different. I have
seen the soldier in the heat of battle and in the monotony of camp. I
have seen him in pleasure and in melancholy; in prosperity and in ad-
versity, but the source of most trouble and anxiety to his mind, is the
ill treatment of his family by the very men who are, by the clause referred to, exempt from duty. The soldier can meet the enemy of his
country in dreadful battle, but the thought that his family are [*sic*] suf-

fering at the hands of the rich for whom he is fighting, unnerves the strongest arm and sickens the stoutest heart. The men of wealth are erecting new mills, tan-yards, shoe-shops, &c., and are filling them with their sons. This will be done and other means will be resorted to until the army will be composed of poor men exclusively. Their families will be left to the scanty charities of Extortion and Speculation. Then, sir, you may well ask, "Shall we be whipped?" The answer then would not be difficult. Sir, I have already heard it argued that the *poor* man could not be injured by Lincoln's proclamation. Say they, "it is true, we might lose our negro or two, but what is that to life, to continued exposure, to prolonged absence from wife and children." If poor men must fight, the rich ought to pay the expenses of the fight. The poor men who are now in the army are patriots. They deem no sacrifice too great to be made; no privation too severe to be borne for liberty. They leave home and friends for *country's* sake. Let the appeal be made to their patriotism, to the justice of our cause, but for God's sake don't tell the poor soldier who now shivers in a Northern wind while you snooze in a feather bed, that it is *just* and *right* that the men, whom Congress has exempted, should enjoy ease at home, amassing untold riches, while *he* must fight, bleed, and even die, for their ten negroes. If we are ever whipped, it will be by violations of our own constitution, infringements of justice and right. When burdens are borne equally, *dangers* must be also. People's eyes may be closed by glaring newspaper pleas of *necessity* and *right*, but they will at some time be opened. Then if ever, *we will be whipped.*

A Soldier.
Jonesboro, Georgia.

The Southern Confederacy *responded to the soldier's letter in the same issue. The paper defended the exemption for slaveholders with traditional racial arguments that the South would be in grave danger if blacks were left without anyone supervising them.*

Southern Confederacy (Atlanta, Ga.), 30 October 1862

An Anonymous Writer: "The Negroes and the Poor"

We cheerfully lay before our readers today, the communication of "A Soldier," in opposition to our views upon that section of the Exemption Bill which exempts a white man to take care of plantations having a certain number of negroes. "A Soldier" has made the best of his case. His pleadings are plausible. His language is pretty strong, but he is entirely courteous and respectful...

We regret to find that he misapprehends one of our positions.... We were contending for the wisdom and justice of that provision of the law which exempts *somebody* to take care of and control the negroes and make them work. We don't advocate the exemption of the rich and conscription of the poor, because they happen to be rich or poor, but that the negroes must have some white person to remain with and care for them and cause them to make bread. That's all.

And we will here remark that the law does not exempt the owner specially. It says, "To secure *the proper police* of the country *one person,* either as agent, owner or overseer" shall be kept on each plantation of 20 negroes or any number which State laws require one white man to be kept with, provided there is no white male adult on the place, not liable to do military duty. A rich man can't keep an overseer and stay at home too. A rich man fifty, sixty or seventy years old with half a dozen sons over 18 must send them all to the war and oversee his own plantation.

The poor of the country would be very unsafe in their property and to some extent in their persons, if the negroes were left without any one to keep them at work and regulate their conduct.

But, "A Soldier" inquires if a rich man with ten negroes is exempt, why not a poor man with ten children? Simply because ten white children are not negroes. The "proper police of country" don't require a white man to stay at home to control his children.

The negro has intelligence and brutality combined, enough to make him very troublesome, and even very dangerous, if left without proper control; but he has not enough of intelligence with high moral development, to leave him among us without absolute control. The poor man can leave his ten children with his wife. She can keep them at work and control them—if not as well as the husband and father, at least enough to prevent their being a pest—a terror to the country—lazy, thieving, vicious, brutal—to say nothing more. But a man's negroes can't be thus left. They must have a man to control and take care of them. This "A Soldier," we have no doubt, will admit. It is one of the *accidents* of that provision of the law that it exempts a rich man occasionally while it does not a poor man. That is not the *design.* It is intended to have the negroes looked after. *It must be done;* hence, this is a wise provision of the law. It may be the misfortune of the poor man to be conscribed while a few rich men are not, but the law does not make that distinction or contemplate any such gross injustice or inequality, in its operation.

The accidents or misfortunes of any provisions of law, or any man upon which it operates, must not be used to condemn the law....The enacting of laws that will mete out equal and exact justice to all persons in all cases and under all circumstances, is impossible. Laws must be enacted for the *whole* people and must be framed so as to secure "the greatest good to the greatest number."...

"A Soldier," and all who think as he does, must recollect that there are thousands of rich men in our army who have gone voluntarily into the ranks and are daily performing the labors of the camp; and fight the battles of freedom, whenever the Yankees are met. He is too sweeping in his criticisms. He will find this out by looking round among his own neighbors; and his remark that the rich at home will not do anything for the families of the soldiers is also, we are very sure too broad. There may be, and doubtless are some hoggish rich men who refuse to do their duty in this respect. It would be strange if there were not, for the world has bad and selfish men in every community—both rich and poor. We have no doubt the rich in all communities are more liberal towards the poor than our correspondent seems to suppose.

Another controversial exemption in the Confederate draft law excused newspapers editors from military service. When President Davis proposed ending the exemption, many newspapers such as the Richmond Enquirer *howled in protest.*

Richmond Enquirer, 3 November 1864

An Anonymous Writer: "The Need for Exemption"

Exemption by law gave an honorable position to the Press, secured its independence, and left no rod suspended over its head, but such as the people raised by their support or rejection. But an editor emerging from that cesspool of corruption, the detail system, would be an object of offence to the virtuous people of these States, and the paper he conducted ceases to be an organ of public opinion, and becomes the miserable conduit of those to whose favor he owned his exemption from the ranks.

States' rights newspapers in the South, such as the Atlanta *Daily Intelligencer* argued that the conscription law took power away from the states and put in the hands of the Confederate government.*

Daily Intelligencer (Atlanta, Ga.), 15 March 1864

An Anonymous Writer: "Don't Surrender Rights"

The way to "whip the Yankees," is not by a surrender of your personal rights, nor the sovereignty of your State to the Central power at Richmond. Whenever this is done we shall virtually surrender what we have demanded from the old Union, and to maintain which so much blood has already been shed.

UNION CONSCRIPTION LAW DEBATED

Union newspapers that supported conscription, such as the Chicago Tribune, *maintained that it was a military necessity and that patriotic men should be proud to serve their country.*

Chicago Tribune, 16 May 1863

An Anonymous Writer: "What of the Conscript Law"

There is only one way of dealing with the great question of raising men for the army—and that is, we repeat it, by enforcing the Conscription law. There is surely nothing unfair, either in provisions, or requirements. It is not to be levied upon any particular class in the community, but upon all the members of it—rich and poor alike; and whoever is drafted must find a substitute, or go himself. If, as the old Latin proverb has it—"It is sweet and beautiful to die for one's country"—and tens of thousands of our best and bravest American citizens have found it so—every man of us ought to be equally willing to prove its beatitude by rendering a cheerful obedience to the law which summons him to become a hero as well as a patriot.

But Democratic publications in the North argued that the federal government was exceeding its authority in holding a draft. The Cleveland Plain Dealer *claimed conscription would merely produce more opposition to the war.*

Cleveland Plain Dealer, 19 February 1863

An Anonymous Writer: "The Conscription Bill—A Friendly Warning"

Now, that the exigencies of this great civil war, have after battles on sea and land, sieges, drafts, confiscations, assessments, abolitions, and proclamations, resulted at last in a Conscription *en masse*, we propose to offer a few reflections which seem pertinent....

It is useless, it is downright *criminal*, to disguise the fact, that the fruits of this amazing war have so disappointed the people, and the manner in which it has been waged, have so alienated the people from the present Administration, that a broad, settled, and almost hostile, discontent is rife in the land....

The people are not willing to be defrauded in the contest they have made with their public agents. They have given sons, husbands, fathers, for the war; they have given unexampled supplies of money; they have given more still—their moral support. They ask in return to give them assurances of an end to legislation hostile to the spirit of American freedom. They ask that the Executive confine himself to his Constitutional authority under our system of laws. They ask that the "Chicago Platform" be made subordinate to the Constitution of our fathers. They ask that this insane negro business be utterly stopped....They ask that the East fill up it[s] quota under the draft before more Western men are taken from their families and homes. They ask that this great struggle be of truth a contest for our Government and laws, and not a speculation for contractors, an engine for party, a mere crusade for black men, *or a lever for the construction of a new and strange system of government* on this continent.

The New York Evening Post *fended one of the most controversial provisions of the conscription act, the substitution provision.*

Evening Post (New York), 19 December 1863

An Anonymous Writer: "The Enrollment Law"

Concerning the three hundred dollar exemption clause there is much difference of opinion; we still hold the belief, after considerable inquiry, that it should be retained. There is no doubt that it is a boon to the large middle class of industrious mechanics and farmers, who, just beginning life, with families of young children dependent upon them, cannot, in many cases, serve under arms without serious distress to those whom they leave unprovided for at home. Almost every one of this class whose presence at home is really necessary to his family, can raise a sum of three hundred dollars to secure his exemption. But repeal this clause, and force every man to go or procure a substitute, and these men become at once the prey of sharpers and brokers, or are compelled, at every sacrifice, to serve in person. No this class, which mainly carries on the varied industry of the free states and creates their prosperity, deserves the most careful consideration at the hands of legislators.

The question to be settled is, whether the government shall engage, for a stated sum, to procure substitutes, or whether it shall throw this burden upon those who are drafted. Now if it were difficult or impossible for the government to procure men for the sums it receives under the exemption clause, then it might be urged that this should be done by those persons upon whom the draft falls. But it so happens that there is little or no trouble upon this point. We suggested, some time ago, that some of the states which find it hard to fill their quotas should apply to the general government for permission to recruit among the freedmen in the southern states. It is amongst these that the Provost Marshal General can easily get substitutes for those who pay the exemption fee. We speak now of the blacks in the states over which the Proclamation extends...

Moreover, experience has shown that the characters who offer themselves in the North as substitutes are the lowest and vilest of the population. They cheat those who engage in them; cheat the government by running away when they can; and are vicious element, not fit to form a part of our armies.

For these reasons we hold that the three hundred dollar exemption clause should be retained in the law.

DRAFT RIOT IN NEW YORK

The New York World, *the chief Democratic paper in the city, blamed President Lincoln and the Republican Party for the riots.*

New York World, 14 July 1863

An Anonymous Writer: "A Burning Sense of Wrong"

New-York yesterday saw the saddest sight that she has ever seen since her first foundation stone was laid....Crowds all day marched hither and thither along the streets, reckless, unguided, with a burning sense of wrong toward the government which has undertaken to choose at random from among them the compulsory soldiers of a misconducted war—with a sense of wrong, we say, but wreaking their wrath cowardly and meanly on defenceless, inoffensive negroes, blindly on property-owners whose buildings chanced to be hired by government officials, senselessly on the policemen whose discipline and power day by day insure them that security and order which guards their labor and lives. The law-abiding citizen hangs his head with shame that a government can so mismanage a struggle for the life of the nation, so wantonly put itself out of harmony and sympathy with the people, so deny itself the support of those whom it represents and serves, as that...here, in the chief city and very heart of the nation, such scenes as those of yesterday can shock the sight....

Will the insensate men at Washington now at length listen to our voice? Will they now give ear to our warnings and adjurations? Will they now believe that Defiance of Law in the rulers breeds Defiance of Law in the people?...Will they continue to stop their ears and shut their eyes to the voice and will of a loyal people, which for three long years has told them by every act and every word that this war must be nothing but a war for the Union and the Constitution?

Does Mr. Lincoln now perceive what alienation he has put between himself and the men who three years ago thundered out with one voice in Union square—"The Union, it must and shall be preserved"?...Does any man wonder that poor men refuse to be forced into a war mismanaged almost into hopelessness, perverted almost into partisanship? Did the President and his cabinet imagine that their lawlessness could conquer, or their folly seduce, a free people?

The New-York Times *condemned the rioters and called for the use of force to restore order. The term* grape *used in the last line refers to artillery shells used by the armed forces.*

New-York Times, 15 July 1864

An Anonymous Writer: "The Raging Riot"

The mob in our City is still rampant. Though the increasing display of armed force has done something to check its more flagrant outrages, it is yet wild with fury, and panting for fresh havoc. The very fact of its being withstood seems only to give it, for the time, new malignity; just as the wild beast never heaves with darker rage than when he begins to see that his way is barred. The monster grows more dangerous as he grows desperate. More than ever, everything depends on the energy and vigilance of the authorities, and the sustaining cooperation of all true men. Official duty and public spirit should supremely rule the hour. The man in public place, or in private place, who falters in this dread crisis should stand accursed.

We trust that Gov. Seymour does not mean to falter. We believe that in his heart he really intends to vindicate the majesty of the law, according to his sworn obligations. But, in the name of the dignity of Government and public safety, we protest against any further indulgence in the sort of speech with which he yesterday sought to propitiate the mob. Entreaties and promises are not what the day calls for. No official, however high his position, can make them, without bringing public authority into contempt. This monster is to be met with a sword, and that only. He is not to be placated with a sop; and if he were, it would only be to make him all the more insatiate hereafter. In the name of all that is sacred in law and all that is precious in society, let there be no more of this. There is force enough at the command of Gov. Seymour to maintain civil authority. He will do it. He cannot but do it. He is a ruined man if he fails to do it. This mob is not our master. It is not to be compounded with by playing blackmail. It is not to be supplicated and sued to stay its hand. It is to be defied, confronted, grappled with, prostrated, crushed. The Government of the State of New-York is its master, not its slave; its ruler, and not its minion.

It is too true that there are public journals who try to dignify this mob by some respectable appellation. The *Herald* characterizes it as the people, and the *World* as the laboring men of the City. These are libels that ought to have paralyzed the fingers that penned them....

This mob is not the people, nor does it belong to the people. It is for the most part made up of the very vilest elements of the City....It has not even the poor merit of being what mobs usually are—the product of mere ignorance and passion. They talk, or rather did talk at first, of the oppressiveness of the Conscription law; but three-fourths of those who have been actively engaged in violence have been boys and young men under twenty years of age, and not at all subject to the Conscription. Were the Conscription law to be abrogated tomorrow, the controlling inspiration of the mob would remain all the same. It comes from sources quite independent of that law, or any other—from malignant hate toward those in better circumstances, from craving for plunder, from a love of commotion, from a barbarous spite against a different race, from a disposition to bolster up the failing fortunes of the Southern rebels. All of these influences operate in greater or less measure upon any person engaged in this general defiance of law; and all combined have generated a composite monster more hellish than the triple-headed Cerberus.

It doubtless is true that the Conscription, or rather its preliminary process, furnished the occasion for the outbreak. This was so, simply because it was the most plausible pretext for commencing open defiance. But it will be a fatal mistake to assume that this pretext has but to be removed to restore quiet and contentment. Even if it be allowed that this might have been true at the outset, it is completely false now. A mob, even though it may start on a single incentive, never sustains itself for any time whatever on any one stimulant...

You may as well reason with the wolves of the forest as with these men in their present mood. It is quixotic and suicidal to attempt it. The duties of the executive officers of this State and City are not to debate, or negotiate, or supplicate, but to *execute the laws*. To execute means to enforce by authority. This is their only official business. Let it be promptly and sternly entered upon with all the means now available, and it cannot fail of being carried through to an overwhelming triumph of public order. It may cost blood—much of it perhaps; but it will be a lesson to the public enemies, whom we always have and must have in our midst, that will last for a generation. Justice and mercy, this time, unite in the same behest: *Give them grape, and a plenty of it.*

The rioters attacked the New-York Tribune *for its support of emancipation. The paper claimed that Confederate sympathizers organized the violence against blacks and other targets.*

New-York Tribune, 14 July 1863

An Anonymous Writer: "The Riot"

Resistance to Draft was merely the occasion of the outbreak; absolutely disloyalty and hatred to the Negro were the moving cause. It was not simply a riot but the commencement of a revolution, organized by the sympathizers in the North with the Southern Rebellion....

The city must protect itself. There are loyal citizens enough to do so, if they understand this crisis in our affairs. Let them not be deceived by the belief that this is a mere outbreak against the Draft. It has a deeper meaning, and is literally a removal of the seat of war to the banks of the Hudson. These howling mobs are hounded on by thoughtful and designing men who are at work in the interest of the Southern rebellion.

The Dubuque Herald, *a staunchly Democratic newspaper, said it was only right that the* Tribune *was attacked by the mob because of the way the newspaper had "sneered" at the nation's laws.*

Dubuque (Iowa) Herald, 15 July 1863

An Anonymous Writer: "They Who Sowed the Wind Are Reaping the Whirlwind"

The telegraph announces that the exasperated people of New York have destroyed the office of the *Tribune* newspaper, the organ par excellence of the party which has thrown away the Constitution of the United States, sneered at the laws, and proclaimed it to be the right of the mob to rule. The mob, acting upon the principles inculcated by the Abolition and Republican leaders, has taken the reins of Government into its hands in New York, and catching the inspiration of fanaticism from the New York *Tribune*, it breaks through the restraints of law, and subjects to its excited passions as one of the first victims of its rage, the *Tribune* itself. This is but natural. For many years past the *Tribune* newspaper has been the foremost, the most ingenious and the ablest of all the newspapers in bringing the people of these United States to the belief that neither Constitutions nor law should stand in the way of the attainment of a desirable object, be that object even the destruction of property. It was the *Tribune* when taught the doctrine of disobedience to the Constitution and laws, and which declared it to be a virtue in the people to resist the execution of such laws as did not accord with their sentiments.

The Richmond Examiner *was one of many Southern newspapers that reveled in the news of the draft riot. The newspaper claimed the riot proved the North was tired of the war.*

Richmond Examiner, 18 July 1863

Anonymous Writer: "A Revolution"

This affair is a revolution. We here get a glimpse of what is slumbering under the shoddy. What would have happened had Lee won the last day of Gettysburg? No one can doubt that the war would have ended in a month.— Whatever contractors and office holders pretend, the people of the North are tired of the war and will no longer furnish army after army to be slaughtered, for the fruitless purpose of destroying the Southern States and driving its population into exile.

QUESTIONS

1. Do you think the Georgia soldier makes a convincing argument against the draft exemption for slaveholders? Do you think the *Southern Confederacy* makes a convincing argument on behalf of the exemption? Why or why not?

2. Why would newspapers concerned about the war infringing on personal freedoms be critical of the draft?
3. Do you believe Confederate editors had a valid argument in condemning attempts to draft newspaper employees? Explain.
4. Do you find it surprising that *New-York Times* and *New-York Tribune* were targets of the rioters? Explain.

NOTES

1. Emory M. Thomas, *The Confederate Nation, 1861–1865* (New York: Harper & Row, 1979), 152–54.

2. Adrian Cook, *The Armies of the Streets: The New York City Draft Riots of 1863* (Lexington: University Press of Kentucky, 1974), 193–94.

CHAPTER 18

Georgia Campaign, 1864

After a series of bitter defeats in 1863, the Confederacy appeared to be reeling as the new year began. In March, President Abraham Lincoln promoted Ulysses S. Grant to lieutenant general and commander of all Union armies. Grant wanted to seize the opportunity in 1864 to break the South's back before the pivotal presidential election in November. He decided on coordinated campaigns on several fronts to keep the Confederate armies from reinforcing one another. Grant appointed William T. Sherman as commander of the western armies, the largest of which was known as the Army of the Tennessee. Following its impressive victory at the battle of Chattanooga, the Army of the Tennessee had spent the winter of 1864 outside the city awaiting orders for its next move. Just across the state line, Confederate forces under the command of Joseph E. Johnston protected Georgia from what was expected to be the Union's first major campaign against the state.

Grant instructed Sherman "to move against Johnston's army, to break it up, and to get into the interior of the enemy's country as far as you can, inflicting all the damage you can against their war resources."[1] Sherman' invasion force consisted of three armies totaling nearly 100,000 men. Johnston had only 50,000 troops, but maintained a strong position behind Rocky Face Ridge near Dalton, Georgia. The Georgia campaign began on May 7 when Federal skirmishers tested the ridge and a larger army marched around through mountain gaps to cut the Confederate army off from its railroad line. Alerted to this threat, Johnston pulled his army back to the small town of Resaca. The battle of Resaca took place May 13–15 with Union troops making repeated advances on the Southern lines. Confederate soldiers turned back the attacks and then advanced on the Federals.

Once again, the Union army swung around Johnston's army and crossed a key river threatening the railroad. To protect his supply line, Johnston evacuated again to Cassville where he hoped to trap Sherman. But his two chief commanders bungled the plan and with their line untenable, the Confederates retreated again to Allatoona on May 20. In just two weeks, Sherman had marched his army more than halfway to Atlanta and suffered only 3,000 casualties.

While Northern newspapers cheered the early success of Sherman's campaign, some Confederate editors tried to put the best face on the situation. They rarely used the word "retreat" in editorials about Johnston's backward march, using popular euphemisms such as "retrograde movement." But other Southern newspapers were critical of Johnston's defensive strategy. Sharp fighting took place at New Hope Church, but neither side gained a distinct advantage, and Sherman resumed his flanking movement east to cut off the railroad. By mid-June, both sides were just north of Marietta with the Confederate army occupying a formidable position along Kennesaw Mountain and its spurs. Tired of his inability to meet Johnston head-on, Sherman decided to launch an all-out attack against the Confederate lines. But Rebel troops beat back repeated assaults, inflicting the worst casualties of the campaign so far. Sherman moved his army east again and to defend himself, Johnston retreated across the Chattahoochee River, just outside Atlanta on July 9.

Tired of his general's defensive strategy, President Jefferson Davis replaced Johnston with John Bell Hood, who had advocated offensive action. Given his opportunity, the aggressive Hood attacked the Federal Army at the battles of Peachtree Creek and Atlanta. At both, the Confederates were beaten back and suffered heavy casualties. Sherman then decided to lay siege to Atlanta and worked his way around the city to cut off its last railroad line. Trying to prevent being encircled, Hood attacked the Federals at Jonesboro but was repulsed again. To prevent losing his entire army, Hood evacuated Atlanta on September 1 after destroying everything of military value. The next day a victorious Union Army marched into the city and raised the stars and stripes over city hall. Sherman telegraphed President Lincoln with the message: "Atlanta is ours, and fairly won."[2]

The fall of Atlanta set off celebrations in the North and many editors reveled in the news. Some Confederate newspapers downplayed the loss of the "Gate City," but most acknowledged it was a major setback for the South. Sherman was not finished with Georgia, however. He proposed to march his army through the heart of Georgia to the coast, wrecking everything in its path. Although he would have no supply line and only about twenty days of rations, the general believed his army could live off the countryside. Sherman argued that the effect of such a campaign would be devastating and might end the war more quickly.[3]

Sherman divided his army into two columns and they left Atlanta on November 16 taking different paths to confuse the Confederates. Hood and his army had moved north hoping to draw the Federals into Tennessee, so there was only a small Rebel force to battle Sherman. With little opposition, the "March to the Sea," as it came to be known, covered about 15 miles a day. As Federal troops made their way through the state, groups of foraging soldiers, soon called "bummers," plundered the countryside, taking food and property and destroying anything that might be of use to the Confederacy. Many slaves who had escaped from their masters followed the army or cheered troops as they marched by.

After marching more than 250 miles, Sherman's army reached the outskirts of Savannah in mid-December. A Confederate force commanded by William J. Hardee was defending the port city, and the Federals laid siege. However, when it became apparent Savannah was doomed, Hardee's troops escaped into nearby South Carolina. Sherman telegraphed President Lincoln on December 22 with the message: "I beg to present you, as a Christmas gift, the city of Savannah, with 150 heavy guns and...about 25,000 bales of cotton."[4]

This chapter traces editorial reaction to the Georgia campaign. It begins with editorials on what appeared to be the Union army's seemingly effortless march to Atlanta. While Northern editors trumpeted the march, many Southern papers, especially ones in Georgia such as Atlanta's *Daily Intelligencer,* seemed to downplay the seriousness of the threat. The next group of editorials exemplifies the reaction to the capture of Atlanta. Northern papers exalted in the news. Southern editors acknowledged that Atlanta's fall was a blow to the Confederacy but urged readers not to give up hope.

Sherman's famous "March to the Sea" prompted less editorial comment, in part, because the general kept his plans secret for a long time. Confederate papers not surprisingly expressed great outrage over the Union's army's tactics, as the editorial from the *Confederate Union* shows. The fall of Savannah prompted some soul-searching by Confederate papers. Northern papers, such as the *New-York Tribune,* expressed surprise at how easily the Union had captured the state's largest city.

RESPONSE TO CONFEDERATE RETREAT

Northern newspapers delighted in the Union army's seemingly easy march to Atlanta. When Sherman's troops reached the outskirts of the city, the Philadelphia Inquirer *termed the march irresistible.*

Philadelphia Inquirer, 5 July 1864

An Anonymous Writer: "Sherman's Irresistible Advance"

On the 3d of July General Sherman had his head-quarters at Marietta, a town of some importance on the Western and Atlantic Railroad, one hundred and eighteen miles south of Chattanooga and just twenty miles north of Atlanta.... Our army has thus made another forward step in its grand and wonderful march from Chattanooga to Atlanta. Its leader moves on as if he know no such word as fail....

[T]he capture of Atlanta, and the destruction of the railways, foundries, factories, and depots there, will be a *material* victory of the most valuable character.

In an editorial, the Atlanta Daily Intelligencer *responded to readers who accused the paper of downplaying Johnston's retreat and the threat to the city. The paper quoted people who regularly asked the editor, "Why do you publish such flattering opinions about the situation?"*

Daily Intelligencer (Atlanta, Ga.), 19 May 1864

An Anonymous Writer: "Long Faces"

We are stopped daily on the street almost at every step, by people who anxiously enquire the news. A large number...wear the longest faces they can put on and their dark or pallid looks would lead one unacquainted with them to suppose they had lost their dearest and best friend or perhaps a whole family of friends. They croak in our ears a most dismal, raven cry. Some of them say to us, "Why do you publish such flattering opinions about the situation? You know as well as I do that Johnston is falling back, and that Atlanta is threatened, you are misleading the people by holding out to them hopes which will be dashed to the ground. It looks mighty black for us up there. Johnston's been outgeneraled, and we are losing ground that we never will get back."

Such men want us to write doleful news, and make them, as well as every other of our readers, uncomfortable. We will write an article which, we hope, may suit them, and over which the buoyant and cheerful reader may enjoy his laugh....

Yes! General Johnston is falling back.

Yes! the enemy; the Yankees; the terrible, great big, bugaboo Yankees; the fellows with cerulean abdomens or *azure corporations,* as some of our compeers name them are thundering at our gates. Don't you hear them? Why, even whilst I write, the reverberations of their knocks are shaking the ground. Their cannon shots are echoing amongst the hills to the Northward; their shells are screaming through the air. See the baleful fires they are lighting up in the North of Georgia. The lurid flames light the way in their victorious march to the very heart of the South. Don't you hear their shouts? Their yells, exultant and full of the vindictive fire and pride of successful soldiers? There! your home is on fire and the shots and leaden hail and the thunderbolts of hideous war are crashing about our desolate and abandoned hearth-stones. Your wives and children have fallen into the hands of a ruthless and savage foe. Volumes of smoke slowly float into heaven, and do you see it there? There is only a pile of ashes where once stood your home. Mine went that way, long ago. Dear me! how sad a thing it is to be a martyr. And look over yonder. Why as sure as you live, there is blood and somebody has been hurt. That is dreadful. Why you look so pale.

Mr. Despair, and all the rest of your lowering brood, does this picture please you? We hope so. We do not intend it for sensible, and reasonable people who have a proper abiding faith in the certainty of our victory.

Atlanta Captured

With the capture of Atlanta, the North had a new hero in General Sherman. The Baltimore American *said the general would go down in history not only for his army's capture of the city, but his concise telegraph message describing it.*

Baltimore American, 8 September 1864

An Anonymous Writer: "Fairly Won"

"Atlanta is ours, and fairly won," says General Sherman, in his modest dispatch. He has unconsciously uttered words of pith and conciseness, that have already become historic, and that have taken their place among the immortal brevities of famous commanders....

The military importance of Atlanta and its environs is incalculable. It was at once the machine shop, the granary, the storehouse, and the armory of the Confederacy....

But General Sherman has fairly won a double victory. He has made a moral conquest at the same time that he has gained a military advantage. The effect of his campaign upon the remnants of Hood's army will be dispiriting in the extreme. No more effective fighting can be obtained from his broken and disheartened ranks. They are engaged in a cause which has no further inducement to present, and nothing but hopelessness to offer. The moral effect upon the peace Copperheads of the North is no less striking. It has already disarmed them of their principal weapon. It has made them ridiculous in the eyes of the world, and despicable in the eyes of their loyal fellow citizens.

The Columbus Times *would have nothing to do with any despondency over the fall of Atlanta and downplayed the loss.*

Columbus (Ga.) Times, 9 September 1864

An Anonymous Writer: "No Fuss"

Who ever heard of such a fuss being made over the fall of a twenty year old town, three hundred miles in the interior of a State, as we and the Yankees are making over the *evacuation* of Atlanta?

The Daily Intelligencer, *which had been forced to flee from Atlanta to Macon, Georgia, displayed grudging respect for Sherman's success in the campaign.*

Daily Intelligencer (Atlanta, Ga.), 8 September 1864

An Anonymous Writer: "The Position"

Sherman prosecutes war deliberately, like a business or laboring man works. The most extraordinary inventive genius and the most superhuman labor of men, have been applied to the machinery of his advance....

The Richmond Daily Dispatch *admitted that the fall of Atlanta could give confidence to the war effort in the North. But it downplayed the military significance of the city's capture.*

Daily Dispatch (**Richmond**), 5 September 1864

An Anonymous Writer: "No Misfortune"

We regard the evacuation of Atlanta by our troops as a misfortune only in so far as it will have the effect of consolidating all parties in the North in favor of a continued prosecution of the war. In itself it is no misfortune whatever. The Yankee papers have been telling us for many weeks past that Sherman could enter and take possession any day he pleased. But he regarded the mere possession as an empty triumph, which it was not worth the cost of life to obtain. He cared not about taking it unless he could take Hood and his whole army along with it. That he was expecting and preparing to do, to that end all his movements were directed, and for that purpose he made the recent change in his line, concentrating upon his right and cutting off the West Point railroad. He expected, no doubt, to throw his army around Atlanta to the south of the city, and, holding all the passages of the Chattanooga to the north of it, in that way compel a surrender. General Hood, to prevent such a catastrophe, and to prolong the tenure of Atlanta, which he saw it would soon be necessary to abandon, ordered the attack of Hardee upon the enemy on the West Point railroad. This battle—one of the most severely contested of the war—resulted in driving the enemy, with immense slaughter, from his entrenchments. But there was an interval of seven miles between Hardee's corps and the main body, and into this gap Sherman thrust a heavy column. Hardee being thus cut off and exposed to an attack in flank and rear, was compelled to retreat after having inflicted on the enemy much more damage than he received. Hood made a corresponding movement, and the whole army is safe at Lovejoy's station.

We do not regard these operations as by any means decisive of any question whatever. Hood's army still exists, and its spirit is still unbroken. Every step that Sherman takes in advance increases the difficulty of retreat in case of disaster, and that disaster will eventually come is among the probabilities, at least, of the future. His line is already enormously long, and Wheeler is operating upon it, cutting off his supplies, capturing his small garrisons and tearing up the railroads. Should a retreat once begin, there will be no end to this disaster.

MARCH TO THE SEA

Sherman kept his famous "March to the Sea" secret for weeks. When Northern newspapers such as the St. Paul Pioneer-Press *finally learned what his army was doing, many expressed delight.*

St. Paul (Minn.) Pioneer-Press, 24 November 1864

An Anonymous Writer: "Sherman's Seaward March"

The public mind has become so familiar with great events, and so sated with sensations, that it has almost lost the capacity for surprise.... But Sherman has introduced us to a new acquaintance in the world of wonders. His present enterprise surpasses all former achievements of the war in boldness of conception in comprehensiveness of its contemplated results. There is no longer any doubt that he began, a week ago, that grand movement which has formed the subject of so many mysterious paragraphs in the newspapers.

In an editorial after Savannah was captured, the New-York Times *said the little resistance that Federal troops encountered on the march showed that Southern citizens had given up hope of winning the war.*

New-York Times, 14 February 1865

An Anonymous Writer: "Confidence No Longer Exists"

In Georgia, on the contrary, it appears well ascertained that the great majority of the inhabitants stayed quietly at home, and awaited the invader's approach in respectable quiet. So far from destroying their property in order to deprive him of the means of subsistence, they did not even drive off their mules, horses or cattle, though this would have been one of the easiest and most obvious modes of damaging him. In fact, it is hard to see that any Georgian farmer, except those who joined the militia, made the smallest personal sacrifice in aid of the Confederacy, at the most important juncture in its history, and when they were most earnestly and solemnly entreated to make every sacrifice, by the men who are supposed to have, and who ought to have, if the concern were a sound one, their fullest confidence.

There is only one interpretation that can be put on this extraordinary apathy, and that is, that confidence in the success of the rebellion no longer exists anywhere outside of the official class and the army, if it exist there. The Governors of States who write the flaming appeals whenever our raiders make their appearance, are, of course, as members of the oligarchy, closely allied in sentiment, as well as in interest, with the Confederate leaders; but it appears, of late, plain that the farmers who have so far escaped the net of the conscription, either have grown tired of the contest or despair of success, and that their great aim now is not to serve the rebellion, but to avoid sharing its fortunes.

One target of Sherman's march was Georgia's capital, Milledgeville. After capturing the town, Union troops proceeded to wreck large parts of it, especially government property. The Confederate Union *expressed outrage at what the soldiers did.*

Confederate Union (Milledgeville, Ga.), 6 December 1864

An Anonymous Writer: "Sherman's Army in Milledgeville"

Robbery of every kind and in every degree was the order of the day.... [W]e were told that every Southern man should feel that it was very expensive to be a rebel. Indeed, they seemed to think that every thing we had belonged to them; and that it was a very great crime to hide any thing from them, and hiding did very little good, for they are the most experienced and adroit thieves that we ever heard of, and knew exactly where to look for hidden treasure. A full detail of all the enormities practiced upon the inhabitants of this place and the vicinity would fill a volume, and some of them would be too bad to publish. In short if an army of Devils, just let loose from the bottomless pit, were to invade the country they could not be much worse than Sherman's army.

CAPTURE OF SAVANNAH

The Richmond Examiner *said Sherman's successful campaign in Georgia should serve as a wake-up call for the Davis administration.*

Richmond Examiner, 27 December 1864

An Anonymous Writer: "No Army"

Sherman now believes he can live on the country anywhere and with thirty-five or forty thousand men, march whither he will. So he can, if he marches through a country in which there are neither armies, nor extensive fortifications. There was no army in Georgia when he left Atlanta, and it was no great fear for him to walk down to Savannah, plundering and oppressing old men and the women and children who occupied the farm-houses by the way. He has burnt and destroyed many quiet cottages, he has ruined and murdered many defenceless persons, but he has done nothing that a band of escaped galley-slaves could not have done as well as an army. No doubt but that he can come on through the Carolinas to Richmond exactly as he came to Savannah, if the Confederate forces are not in the way; but perhaps Mr. Davis is now convinced of the necessity of employing armies against the progress of an enemy in the interiour of the country.

The New-York Tribune *reveled in the capture of Savannah, while mocking Southern papers that had claimed Sherman's march was a "retreat" or "escape" through Georgia.*

New-York Tribune, 26 December 1864

An Anonymous Writer: "Savannah"

Savannah is fallen like a ripe apple into Sherman's lap. His magnificent march from Atlanta to the Atlantic concludes in the streets of the first commercial city of the Empire State of the South. The "retreat" through Georgia is consummated, and the "escape" of Sherman seems to be at this moment tolerably well secured. That General lies now at the mouth of a river which divides the great States of Georgia and South Carolina, and which is navigable almost to the northern boundary of either. He is in possession of that point on the seaboard which, more than Charleston and more than Mobile, insures the control of the vast system of inter-communication between the States of the Confederacy on which depends its military strength and its political existence. This city, important in a hundred ways to the Rebellion, falls at last without an effort at defense, and passes into the possession of Gen. Sherman rather as if it obeyed a national law than as if it fell a victim to the chance of conflict. The garrison fled silently away, and the citizens, instead of resenting, appear to have welcomed the arrival of a conqueror.... They are not so much subjugated by a hostile power as released by the interposition of a friendly

Victory at Savannah is victory everywhere in the South—and since Hood is flying from Tennessee with a beaten and demoralized army, utterly incapable to withstand the advance of Thomas, there is in fact no army remaining to the Rebellion but that army which, under command of Lee, now forms the garrison of Richmond. And to that army the question must soon be presented, whether will abandon the capital of the Confederacy, or

whether it will surrender the Rebellion itself. Not less than this is the meaning, and is sure to be the result, of the great success of Sherman.

QUESTIONS

1. Why did Southern newspapers downplay the threat that General Sherman posed to Atlanta, and do you think that helped the Southern cause?
2. What do think of the *Baltimore American*'s claim that the capture of Atlanta had stripped the Copperheads of the in chief criticism? Explain.
3. Do you think the *New-York Times* was correct in that the seeming ease of
   Sherman's march showed that the South had given up hope of winning?
   Why or why not?
4. How hard do you think it was for Confederate editors to express admiration for the Union Army's campaign against Georgia?

NOTES

1. *War of the Rebellion: A Compilation of the Official Records of the Union and Confederate Armies, Series* I (Washington, D.C.: Government Printing Office, 1891),
32(3): 246.

2. James Lee McDonough and James Pickett Jones, *War So Terrible: Sherman and
Atlanta* (New York: Norton, 1987), 194–313.

3. *War of the Rebellion,* Series I, 29(3): 660.

4. *War of the Rebellion,* Series I, 44: 783.

CHAPTER 19

Presidential Election, 1864

As the year 1864 began, President Abraham Lincoln faced the real danger that he would not be reelected or even renominated. The Republican Party was largely a collection of political factions, and a powerful group of radicals had emerged. From the start, the Radical Republicans had been critical of Lincoln's conduct of the war. They also believed the president had not moved fast enough in ending slavery. By 1864, the radicals wanted a new party nominee, and they had precedent on their side. No American president since Andrew Jackson in 1832 had won a second term.

Several Republicans were interested in securing the nomination, including Secretary of Treasury Salmon P. Chase and 1856 party nominee John S. Frémont. Chase formed an election committee, but his efforts ended following charges of corruption in the Treasury Department. Frémont, a disgruntled Union general, meanwhile forged a group of abolitionists and other radicals, including some Democrats, into a third party. The Radical Democratic Party, as it became known, endorsed a one-term presidency, abolition of the electoral college, a constitutional amendment abolishing slavery, and equality before the law regardless of race or sex. Leading radicals such as Wendell Phillips and Frederick Douglass endorsed Frémont.[1]

When the Republicans met at the party's convention in Baltimore, they sought to rally around their president. Appealing to Democrats who supported the war and other conservatives, the gathering called itself the National Union convention. To symbolize a Union party image, delegates nominated Democrat Andrew Johnson of Tennessee as vice president to replace Hannibal Hamlin, an outspoken radical. The party platform endorsed an unrelenting war to force the "unconditional surrender" of the South. In an effort to appeal to radicals, the party blamed slavery for causing the war, praised the Emancipation Proclamation, and called for a constitutional amendment to abolish slavery.[2]

The Democratic Party also was divided between members who favored strong prosecution of the war and those who favored increased efforts at securing peace. During the Democratic convention in Chicago, the factions sought a compromise. They nominated for president former General George B. McClellan to appease war Democrats and as his running mate, Congressman George Pendleton, a supporter of the peace movement. The party platform declared the war a failure and called for an armistice, followed by a peace convention, which it claimed would lead to reunion between the North and South. In his letter of acceptance, McClellan expressed the opinion that peace could not be permanent without reunion. Critics charged that McClellan had repudiated the party platform.[3]

Both parties recognized that the course of the war could play a major role in the outcome of the election. Although the Federal army had won major victories in 1863, as the election season began, the Confederacy was far from beaten. General Ulysses S. Grant's army had suffered major casualties during its campaign in Virginia. Union troops had been unable to break the Confederate lines outside Petersburg and then suffered a disaster at the battle of the Crater. In July, Confederate General Jubal Early raided Maryland and threatened Washington, D.C., before being turned back. Meanwhile, Confederate leaders sought to help the Democrats by suggesting that the South might be willing to enter into peace talks. Confederate agents traveled to Niagara Falls in July to meet with a group of Union officials that included *New-York Tribune* editor Horace Greeley. But the talks fell apart when the South insisted on its independence.

Then the president's re-election hopes received a big boost with three key Federal victories. First, Admiral David Farragut's Union fleet captured the Confederate port of Mobile. That was followed by the news that Atlanta had fallen to General William T. Sherman's army after a four-month campaign. Finally, General Phillip T. Sheridan drove Early's troops out of the Shenandoah Valley, removing the threat to Washington.[4] Frémont soon withdrew his candidacy, and all but the most radical of Lincoln's critics united behind the president. In the months leading up to the election, Republicans charged Democrats with disloyalty and treason, pointing to the party's peace platform. Democrats countered by claiming that Lincoln repeatedly violated Constitutional principles and argued that emancipation would incite a race war. The debate was fueled by editorials from newspapers representing both candidates.

Balloting for the election began in September to allow absentee votes to be counted. By 1864, nineteen states had passed laws allowing soldiers in the field to vote. Union troops voted in overwhelming numbers for their commander-in-chief. When all the ballots were counted in November, Lincoln won all but three states (Delaware, Kentucky, and New Jersey) and 55 percent of the popular vote. The Republican Party also was a big winner in congressional races. The new Congress would have a Republican majority of three-fourths.

President's Lincoln's victory ensured that the costly war would go on. At the swearing-in ceremony for his second term, President Lincoln gave one of the shortest but one of the most eloquent inaugural addresses in American history. He did not use the address to place blame for the war or claim success for his administration. Instead, he offered words of understanding and inspiration. He concluded his address with the memorable lines, "With malice toward none; with charity for all; with firmness in the right, as God gives us the right, let us strive on to finish the work we are in; to bind up the nation's wounds; to care for him who shall have borne the battle, and for his widow, and his orphan—to do all which may achieve and cherish a just, and a lasting peace, among ourselves, and with all nations."[5]

The election of 1864 produced one of the greatest outpourings of editorial debate during the war. The chapter begins with editorials on the nominations of Lincoln and McClellan. The Confederacy clearly had a stake in the outcome of the presidential race, and Southern newspapers used the election to bolster morale. In the months between the party conventions and the election, newspapers used their editorial pages to bolster the candidate they supported and disparage their opponents. After Lincoln was reelected, many Northern newspapers proclaimed the election to be a momentous democratic event. Southern newspapers recognized that the president's reelection meant the war would continue. Editors also voiced their views on Lincoln's second inaugural address. The *Chicago Times* called the address "slip shod" and "puerile," but the *National Intelligencer* said the now-famous concluding passage deserved to be "printed in gold."

CANDIDATES NOMINATED

The Philadelphia Inquirer *argued that Republican leaders were out of step with the public regarding popular opinion of President Lincoln whom the newspaper claimed had "a powerful hold on the popular heart."*

Philadelphia Inquirer, 9 June 1864

An Anonymous Writer: "The National Union Nominee"

Mr. Lincoln's re-nomination is clearly the work of the people of his party. The politicians *may* have been for him; if they were they *followed,* instead of

Long Abraham Lincoln a Little Longer.

Lincoln Reelected. *Following his reelection as president in 1864, a tall Abraham Lincoln stood even taller, as portrayed in this cartoon from the magazine* Harper's Weekly *(November 26, 1864). With Lincoln in office "a little longer," many in the North were confident the Union would soon defeat the Confederacy.*

leading, the people. Whatever may be the differences of opinion as to his policy or his administrative ability, it is clear that he has a powerful hold on the popular heart; in his integrity and patriotism, and the absolute singleness of purpose with which he has striven for three long years to restore the Union.

Democratic newspapers like the Cleveland Plain Dealer *hailed the nomination of McClellan, or "Little Mac" as he was often known. The* Plain Dealer *said the general had been an outstanding military leader but was treated unfairly by the administration.*

Cleveland Plain Dealer, 8 September 1864

An Anonymous Writer: "Our Noble Standard Bearer"

The nomination of General McClellan for the Presidency by the National Union Democratic Party has given intense joy to all classes and conditions of the people. His exalted purity of character, splendid talents, and bright statesmanship all indicate qualifications for the high position he will be called upon to fill by his countrymen.... From the inception of the war he fully comprehended the magnitude and gigantic character it would assume and all his efforts were bestowed to meet with adequate and complete power the means and material necessary for a "short, sharp and decisive campaign." But the shrieking minions of the Administration bent upon Disunion and Annihilation resolved he should be forced to take the field, whether prepared or not, and from that day they have hounded him like bloodhounds and thrown every impediment in his way, every obstacle in his path, in order to secure his downfall.

Lincoln, then saw how the rising fame, prestige, glory and virtues of Little Mac would make him a formidable rival for the Presidency. By at once putting him out of the way of the people—preventing him from achieving any more splendid victories...he hoped to sink him into forgetfulness. But an outraged people did not so easily forget, *they remember!*

CONFEDERATE VIEWS OF ELECTION

The Augusta Chronicle & Sentinel *said Lincoln's reelection would mean the war would continue until the South was subjugated. But if McClellan was elected, Southerners could expect peace negotiations to begin.*

Chronicle & Sentinel **(Augusta, Ga.), 18 September 1864**

An Anonymous Writer: "The Presidential Canvass in the United States"

The great object to be obtained is the defeat of Lincoln. His re-election means war: relentless, exterminating war. The emancipation of the slave; the subjugation of the people of the South; the confiscation of property; the obliteration of all political rights. The shield held up to our view as he makes war upon us, is the head of Medusa.

On the other hand if Gen. McClellan should be elected, a cessation of hostilities will follow. The war will be suspended. The star of hope will rise above the surging billows. That result once attained, hostilities will never be resumed. Negotiations will be seriously entered upon. The trifling, irresponsible style of treating the great questions at present carried on at home and abroad, will come to an end; and a settlement will be reached which will restore the States to their pristine glory.

As Republicans and Democrats engaged in a war of words over the presidential candidates, Southern newspapers like the Mobile Register & Advertiser *took great joy in the split it was causing in the North.*

Mobile Register & Advertiser, **11 March 1864**

An Anonymous Writer: "The Prospect"

The war is on the turn, and for the first time an equilibrium of forces is coming to be established between the belligerents. While the Confederacy grows strong in a regenerated Government, credit and currency; in an invigorated popular faith and confidence; in swelling armies in accumulated wrongs, to be avenged, and in the whispering hopes of coming victories—our enemies are foundering in a sea of complicated troubles, personal, political, civil and military. Faction is lifting its head to distract the counsels of the Administration party, and a powerful opposition lies crouching and ready to spring at the throats of the political monsters who have covered with blood and mourning and desolation our fairest country, the most prosperous people, and the freest institutions, the sun has ever shined upon. In the confusion and discord at home, the North has managed by its bigotry, its ferocity and its insolence, to raise up hosts of enemies abroad. Verily, the way of the transgressor is hard, and the robber nation is destined to reap the harvest of a terrible retribution.

CANDIDATES DEBATED

The Cleveland Plain Dealer, *an outspoken Democratic newspaper, took a novel approach in pointing out what it claimed were the differences between Lincoln and McClellan.*

Cleveland Plain Dealer, 5 November 1864

An Anonymous Writer: "What Do You Want?"

Do you want high taxes?
Vote for Lincoln.
Do you want four years more of war?
Vote for Lincoln.
Do you want the Constitution utterly destroyed?
Vote for Lincoln.
...
Do you want the degraded Negroes made your social and political equals?
Vote for Lincoln.
Do you want the Union of your fathers forever destroyed?
Vote for Lincoln.
Do you want to be arrested and confined in loathsome dungeons without process of law and without hope of release?
Vote for Lincoln.
...
Do you want conscription?
Vote for Lincoln.
...
Do you want peace and Union?
Vote for McClellan.
Do you want a Constitution re-established?
Vote for McClellan.
Do you want a government of law?
Vote for McClellan.
...
Do you want the writ of *habeas corpus* restored to you?
Vote for McClellan.
...

Do you want that terrible corruption which now prevails in the Government checked?
Vote for McClellan.
Do you want all the blessings which must flow upon the land when the peace and Union are established?
Vote for McClellan.
Do you want a man for President of spotless purity, of distinguished patriotism, a ripe scholar, of exalted talent, of glorious repute, of solid understanding, and of dignified demeanor?
Vote for George B. McClellan.

The Baltimore American, *a Republican supporter, was sharply critical of McClellan's leadership of the army claiming that he had a great opportunity to prove his leadership but failed.*

Baltimore American, 17 September 1864

An Anonymous Writer: "McClellan's Career"

The Democratic press of the North is making itself ridiculous by its adulation of McClellan. We can set down much to a spirit of partisanship; we can not only forgive, but participate in a certain amount of hero-worship when we find a genuine impersonation of heroism.... The great characteristics of generalship or of statesmanship are not exhibited in every generation. It is the peculiar pride and boast of America that it has evolved a larger amount of brain force, of strong intellectual power, of *vis nervosa,* within the past century than any other nation during the same period. It is no less remarkable that during the present war, under circumstances adapted to call out and develop the highest degree of intellectual activity, there has been a perfect dearth of first class ability. No man in the history of the world ever had presented to him such a magnificent opportunity for establishing pre-eminence over his fellows as McClellan. Great men not only control events and circumstances, but generate them. But in this case circumstances were ready made. Events destined to leave an extraordinary mark on the historic page were rapidly crowding upon one another. The lurid flames of war had already lighted up a focus for the concentrated gaze of the world. The saddle was ready, and all that the young chieftain had to do was to vault into it. The crown of immortality was already prepared to encircle his brow.... The country was in extremity, the people were frantic, and they wanted a "guide, philosopher and friend." They wanted a leader like Moses or Washington to cling to, to look up to confidingly, to idolize, if we must say so. We hailed the "Young Napoleon" as the ideal of our waking visions. We looked up to him as the "coming man," as the rising star of destiny. We regarded him with affectionate admiration and greeted him with enthusiasm. But months wore on and our Oracle gave no sign. Murmurs of impatience were drowned in the notes of preparation. We looked for the grand and majestic, but only found in the ordinary and the commonplace. We sought the flash of the meteor, but only discerned the flare of the rocket.... We saw him refusing or neglecting to obey the peremptory order of the President to move, after seven months of inaction, or rather of pompous parades and grand reviews. We saw him refusing to report to the constitutional head of the War Office, and going directly over that Department to the President, leaving it in ignorance of his operations. And when at length he reluctantly moved, compelled by superior authority, his movements were so slow, dilatory and ill-timed, that we were well nigh disgusted.

MEANING OF THE ELECTION

The Springfield Republican *said the fact that the United States held an election during a devastating civil war was a triumph for democracy.*

Springfield (Ill.) Republican, 10 November 1864

An Anonymous Writer: "The Result—The Triumph"

There is a magnificent completeness in the triumph of the government on Tuesday through the re-election of President Lincoln. Its grand, tidal success, and the quiet and order with which it was achieved, in the midst of the greatest war of history, and while the deepest interest and passions were involved and aroused in the result, make it all one of the glorious events of the world's life; give to the republican institutions new strength and added luster; and hold consequences, the most important and the most valuable to the people of this and all other nations.

Harper's Weekly *expressed similar sentiments and said the South could learn a lesson by the North's obedience to the Constitution.*

Harper's Weekly, 19 November 1864

An Anonymous Writer: "The Election"

Abraham Lincoln and Andrew Johnson have been elected, by enormous and universal majorities in almost all of the States, President and Vice-President of the United States for the next four years. This result is the proclamation of the American people that they are not conquered; that the rebellion is not successful; and that, deeply as they deplore war and its inevitable suffering and loss, yet they have no choice between war and national ruin, and must therefore fight on....

The moral effect of the election both at home and abroad will be of the most impressive character. It shows our foreign enemies that they have nothing to hope from the divisions of this country, while the rebels will see in it the withering and invincible purpose of their loyal fellow-citizens, who ask of them nothing but obedience to the Constitution of the United States, and the laws and acts made in pursuance of it. Whenever they shall choose to overthrow the military despotism that holds them fast—whenever they shall see that no great section of this country can, under equal and respected laws, have any permanent and profound interest different from all the rest—then they will find that the loyal men of the country are longing to throw down their arms and cement a Union that shall be eternal.

But the lesson of the election is, that every constitutional act and law must be absolutely respected. There must be no threats, no revolts, and no hope of extorting terms by arms. The Constitution is the sole condition of the Government; and if citizens differ as to what is constitutional, that difference must be peacefully and constitutionally settled. This is what the people have declared by four years of war, and this is what they confirm by the re-election of Mr. Lincoln. In himself, notwithstanding his unwearied patience, perfect fidelity, and remarkable sagacity, he is unimportant; but as the representative of the feeling and purpose of the American people he is the most important fact in the world.

One other of the most significant lessons of the election is, that the people are conscious of the power and force of their own Government. They expect the utmost vigor in the prosecution of the war by every legitimate method, and they naturally require that the authority of the Government, which is to be established by the continuance of the war, shall not be endangered by its end. When the authority of any Government is openly and forcibly defied it must be maintained unconditionally by arms. When that authority is established and unquestioned, every wise Government will be friendly, patient, conciliatory but firm and just.

Yet the grandest lesson of the result is its vindication of the American system of free popular government. No system in history was ever exposed to such a strain directly along the fibre as that which ours has endured in the war and the political campaign, and no other could possibly have endured it successfully.... Thank God and the people, we are a nation which comprehends its priceless importance to human progress and civilization, and which recognizes that law is the indispensable condition of Liberty.

The Richmond Daily Dispatch, on the other hand, claimed the presidential election was not in fact free and that Lincoln would do anything in his power to hold onto office.

Daily Dispatch (Richmond), 9 November 1864

An Anonymous Writer: "Long Remembered"

Yesterday will be long remembered in the annals of mankind. On yesterday, twenty millions of human beings, but four years ago esteemed the freest population on earth, met at various points of assemblage for the purpose of making a formal surrender of their liberties—not to a great military conquerer; not to a renowned statesman; not to a fell-citizen who has done the State services that cannot be estimated in worldly wealth; not to one who has preserved the State from foreign tyranny, or increased its glory and its greatness at home; not to a Caesar or a Napoleon, the glory of whose achievements might be pleaded as an apology for the abject submission of the multitude; but to a vulgar tyrant, who has never seen a shot fired in anger; who has no more idea of statesmanship than as a means of making money; whose career has been one of unlimited and unmitigated disaster; whose personal qualities are those of a low buffoon, and whose most noteworthy conversation is a medley of profane jests and obscene anecdote—a creature who has squandered the lives of millions without remorse and without event the decency of pretending to feel for their misfortunes; who still cries for blood and for money in the pursuit of his atrocious designs. To such a man, yesterday, the people of the so-called United States surrendered their lives, their liberties, their persons, and their purses, to have and to hold the same for at least four years, and for so much longer as he shall choose. For it is plain that, if he so will it, he may hold on for his natural life, and transmit the sceptre to his descendants. There is nothing in the world to prevent him, should he feel so disposed, and there is no reason to think that thus disposed he will not be....

We are prone to believe that every nation enjoys the exact proportion of freedom to which it is entitled. If the Yankees have lost their liberties, therefore, we think it self-evident that it is because they never deserved to have them. If they are slaves, it is because they are fit for the situation. Slaves they have been for years to all the base passions that are indicative of a profligate and degenerate race; and when nations advance to that point, the transition to material bondage costs but a single step.

The Richmond Examiner *said Lincoln's reelection ensured that the war would continue. The paper claimed that the North was bent on the South's annihilation.*

Richmond Examiner, 11 November, 1864

An Anonymous Writer: "The Situation"

What we are certain of, the real, present, inevitable fact is, that the whole of the material resources, the army, the navy, the arsenals, the treasury, of the Federal States all are now firmly grasped and wielded by the hands of those who have vowed to destroy us, to seize our lands and houses, to beggar our children, and brand our names for even as the names of felons and traitors. This is the "situation." This is what we have now to deal with; and on the way in which we meet it depends the whole future of our race and nation. If we shrink from the conflict, better were it for us and ours that we had never been born. Fortunately there is no middle course for us. We must be victors, or we must be annihilated; and it is better so.

PRESIDENT LINCOLN SWORN IN FOR SECOND TERM

The president's second inaugural address prompted varied editorial reaction. Not surprisingly, the Chicago Times, *one of Lincoln's biggest critics, ridiculed the address.*

Chicago Times, 6 March 1865

An Anonymous Writer: "The Inaugural Address"

The inaugural addresses of the past presidents of the United States are among the best of our state papers. Profound in their comprehension of the principles of the government; exalted in their aspirations; magnificent in their patriotism; broad, liberal, catholic in their nationality; elevated in their literary style—they will stand forever as the grandest monuments of American statesmanship. They were consonant with the national character. They were the natural product of the glorious years in which the republic grew from its revolutionary birth to be the most powerful nation on the face of the earth.

Contrast with these the inaugural address of Abraham Lincoln, delivered in the city of Washington on Saturday, and printed in these columns this morning!...Was ever a nation, once great, so belittled? Is such another descent of record in the history of any people?

We had looked for something thoroughly Lincolnian, but we did foresee a thing so much more Lincolnian than anything that has gone before it. We did not conceive it possible that even Mr. Lincoln could produce a paper so slip shod, so loose-joined, so puerile, not alone in literary construction, but in its ideas, its sentiments, its grasp. He has outdone himself....

Let us trust in Heaven that it is not typical of our national degeneracy. Great indeed, is our fall if the distance be so far as this performance of yesterday is beneath the statesmanship of former times.

On the other hand, the National Intelligencer *in Washington, D.C., gushed over the inaugural address and said the concluding remarks should be "printed in gold."*

National Intelligencer (Washington, D.C.), 6 March 1865

An Anonymous Writer: "The Inaugural Address"

[W]e desire no better words from the President for our platform than compose the concluding paragraph of his Inaugural Address. They are equally distinguished for patriotism, statesmanship, and benevolence, and deserve to be printed in gold:

> With malice towards none; with CHARITY for all; with firmness in the right, as God gives us to see the right, let us strive on to finish the work we are in; to BIND UP THE NATION'S WOUNDS; to care for him who shall have borne the battle, and for his widow and his orphan—to do ALL which may achieve and CHERISH a just and lasting PEACE, among ourselves, and with all nations.

By the time Lincoln was sworn in for a second term, many of his once-sharpest critics had nothing but praise for the president. One was the New York Herald, *which just a year earlier had called Lincoln a "joke."*

New York Herald, 4 March 1865

An Anonymous Writer: "President Lincoln's Second Term"

He is most remarkable man. He may seem to be the most credulous, docile and pliable of the backwoodsmen, and yet when he "puts his foot down he puts it down firmly," and cannot be budged. He has proved himself, in his quiet way, the keenest of politicians, and more than a match for his wiliest antagonists in the arts of diplomacy. He upsets, without an effort, the most formidable obstacles of caucuses and congresses, and seems to enjoy as a huge joke the astonishment of his friends and enemies. Plain common sense, a kingly disposition, a straightforward purpose, and a shrewd perception of the ins and outs of poor weak human nature, have enabled him to master difficulties which would have swamped almost any other man. Thus to-day, with the most cheering prospects before him, this extraordinary railsplitter enters upon his second term the unquestioned master of the situation in reference to American affairs, at home and abroad.

The Harrisburg Telegraph *contrasted Lincoln's second inauguration with his first.*

Harrisburg (Pa.) Telegraph, 4 March 1865

An Anonymous Writer: "The Inauguration"

The brilliant and imposing ceremonies which attended the inauguration on to-day contrast wonderfully with the scene witnessed on the 4th day of March, 1861. Then, Gen. Scott had cavalry, and infantry, and artillery ranged around the President whom the American people had chosen, to prevent a mob from attempting violence. It was a strange and mournful spectacle, and men's hearts sank within them for the future of a country, which in its vigorous youth began to exhibit the worst excesses of the semi-barbarous nations of the east.

When we consider to-day, the progress we have made by arms and civil management in overwhelming treason, we cannot question that Abraham Lincoln has kept well the pledge he made to "put his foot down firmly." He has taken back nearly every stolen fort and arsenal, re-captured whole States, and banished rebel Governors, reduced the rebellion to two armies, and given the system of human bondage its final death blow. In accomplishing this arduous work, he has kept the peace in the North, fused our people into one sentiment of unalterable resolve that the Union shall stand, and preserved us from collision with foreign powers. It has required an immense amount of prudence, sagacity and firmness to compass these things, and the fact that so much has been done, and so well done too, is the strongest guarantee that there will be no relaxation until the whole business is ended, and treason is buried at the cross-roads with a stake driven through its breast.

The nation enters upon a new lease of life to-day. It says to all the world, through the man whom it will install as its first officer, "Ere this cycle roll around, the ability of a Republican Government to maintain itself, will be taken out of the sphere of vexed questions; all mankind will see and own, that the virtue and courage of a free people are strong enough to sustain shocks which would resolve aristocracies or monarchies into their original elements."

QUESTIONS

1. What was different about the *Cleveland Plain Dealer*'s editorial? Do you think it was effective?
2. How is the writing style different from the editorial in the *Mobile Register & Advertiser* and the *Cleveland Plain Dealer?*
3. What do you think of the statement that the fact the election was held was a triumph for democracy?
4. Was the *Harrisburg Telegraph* editorial effective in the way it contrasted the events surrounding Lincoln's first inaugural with that of his second? Why or why not?

NOTES

1. William Frank Zornow, *Lincoln and the Party Divided* (Norman: University of Oklahoma Press, 1954), 72–86.

2. Ibid., 87–104.

3. Ibid., 129–40.

4. John C. Waugh, *Reelecting Lincoln: The Battle for the 1864 Presidency* (New York: Crown, 1997).

5. Roy P. Basler, ed., *Abraham Lincoln: His Speeches and Writings* (Cleveland: World Publishing, 1946), 792–93.

CHAPTER 20

Arming the Slaves, 1861–65

More than one-third of the Confederacy's population was African Americans. Approximately 97 percent of these 3.5 million blacks were slaves, and from the beginning of the fighting they were used in a variety of ways to support the South's war effort. Many slaves, of course, worked on farms and plantations growing the crops and cotton needed by the Confederacy. But thousands of blacks also worked in war-related industries such as manufacturing and transportation. They also did much of the drudgery work for the Confederate armed forces: digging trenches, erecting barricades, driving wagons, washing uniforms, and cooking food. Using black workers to handle these tasks meant that more white men in the South could be available for combat duty.[1]

As early as 1861, some state leaders in the Confederacy displayed a readiness to use free black men in the state militia. The "Native Guards," a regiment of free blacks in Louisiana, was mustered into state service, and the Tennessee legislature authorized the recruitment of former slaves. During the early years of the war, however, few Southerners seriously considered using slaves to serve as soldiers in the regular army. But after the Union began enlisting African American troops in 1863, some Southern leaders began discussing the idea publicly. The Alabama legislature recommended to Richmond that slaves be enlisted, and several newspaper editors backed the plan.

Then in a meeting of officers in January 1864, General Patrick Cleburne proposed that the Confederacy immediately begin training a reserve of slaves to serve as soldiers. Cleburne knew that his plan would be controversial in the South, but he argued that military, economic, and moral reasons required it. Although 12 commanders in the general's division endorsed the idea, others officers vehemently disagreed. The talk also was preposterous to President Jefferson Davis, who had described the Emancipation Proclamation as "the most execrable measure recorded in the history of guilty man." He ordered Cleburne and his commanders to stop any further discussion of the matter. The proposal was not made public until after the war.[2]

However, as battlefield losses mounted for the Confederacy during 1864, talk of enlisting slaves intensified. Thousands of black troops were fighting for the Union by this point, proving that African Americans could make good soldiers. A group of Southern governors endorsed the impressment of blacks "for the public service as may be required." Then in November, Davis urged the Confederate Congress to purchase 40,000 slaves to work as laborers with the promise of eventual freedom. Congress did not act on the proposal, but the issue of how to use blacks in the army continued to be debated. By early 1865, Davis had come to believe what was once unimaginable: the South must arm its black men. "We are reduced to choosing whether the Negroes shall fight for us or against us," the president declared.[3]

The president's proposal to enlist black troops prompted the most intensive debate in the South since the secession crisis. Supporters argued that military necessity required the Confederacy to tap its last source of military manpower. It was far better for the South to lose its slaves, they reasoned, than to lose its freedom. Opponents claimed that acknowledging blacks could be soldiers disproved the Southern notion that African Americans could be anything other than slaves. Enlisting African Americans would end the institution of slavery, they argued, and thereby the Southern way of life. As Civil War historian Emory M. Thomas has written, "The debate over arming the slaves was a debate over the South's entire racial attitude."[4]

Robert E. Lee, the Confederacy's most beloved general, had remained silent on the issue, although there had been rumors that he supported arming slaves. Then in February, he wrote a letter to a congressional supporter of a black enlistment bill, saying the plan was "not only expedient but necessary. The Negroes, under proper circumstances, will make efficient soldiers.... Those who are employed should be freed. It would be neither just nor wise...to require them to serve as slaves."[5]

Even with Lee's support, the Confederate Congress delayed taking any action to recruit black soldiers. Not until March 13 did Congress pass a law arming the slaves, but the measure did not provide for their emancipation. In the meantime, at Lee's encouragement, the Virginia legislature passed its own law enlisting black soldiers without any promise of freedom. No other Confederate state followed Virginia's lead. Two African American regiments from Virginia were quickly organized and began drilling in Richmond. The move was too late, however. The Confederate capital fell to the Union army before the troops could be mustered into service.

The debate over arming slaves produced a tremendous amount of editorial reaction, especially in the South. The chapter begins with newspaper editorials on the initial idea of the South using slaves, a plan first discussed by the Alabama legislature and supported by several newspapers. General Cleburne's controversial plan to enlist blacks was quashed by the Davis administration before it could become public, so there was no editorial discussion of the idea.

But there was plenty of newspaper reaction once the topic was revived and aired publicly in the fall of 1864. Response to the idea from editors ranged from fervent opposition to equally fervent support. The same was true when President Davis announced plans for using blacks in the army and when the subject was debated in the Confederate Congress. All the while, editors in the North watched with amusement as the plans for enlisting slaves were discussed. They reveled in the prospect that a government committed to the institution of slavery now was being forced to consider using blacks to fight. Finally, the *Daily Dispatch* admitted that blacks could indeed make good soldiers.

INITIAL PLAN FOR ENLISTING SLAVES

The idea of the Confederacy using slaves had been quietly discussed in some circles since early in the war. But the idea did not spark public debate until several newspapers published editorials in support. One of those was the Jackson *Mississippian.*

Mississippian (Jackson) [As reprinted in *Montgomery (Ala.) Weekly Mail*], 9 September 1863

An Anonymous Writer: "Employment of Negroes in the Army"

We must either employ the negroes ourselves, or the enemy will employ them against us. While the enemy retains so much of our territory, they are, in their present avocation and status, a dangerous element, a source of weakness. They are no longer negative characters, but subjects of volition as other people. They must be taught to know that this is peculiarly the country of the black men—that in no other is the climate and soil so well adapted to his nature and capacity. He must further be taught that it is his duty, as well as the white man's, to defend his home with arms, if need be.

We are aware that there are persons who shudder at the idea of placing arms in the hands of negroes, and who are not willing to trust them under any circumstances. The negro, however, is proverbial for his faithfulness under kind treatment. He is an affectionate, grateful being, and we are persuaded that the fears of such persons are groundless.

There are in the slaveholding States four millions of negroes, and out of this number at least six hundred thousand able-bodied men capable of bearing arms can be found. Lincoln proposes to free and arm them against us. There are already fifty thousand of them in the Federal ranks. Lincoln's scheme has worked well so far, and if no[t] checkmated, will most assuredly be carried out. The Confederate Government must adopt a counter policy. It must thwart the enemy in this gigantic scheme, at all hazards, and if nothing else will do it—if the negroes cannot be made effective and trustworthy to the Southern cause in no other way, we solemnly believe it is the duty of this Government to forestall Lincoln and proceed at once to take steps for the emancipation or liberation of the negroes itself. Let them be declared free, placed in the ranks, and told to fight for their homes and country.

We are fully sensible of the grave importance of the question, but the inexorable logic of events has forced it upon us. We must deal with it, then, not with fear and trembling—not as timid, time-serving men—but with a boldness, a promptness and a determination which the exigency requires, and which should ever characterize the action of a people resolved to sacrifice everything for liberty. It is true, that such a step would revolutionize our whole industrial system—that it would, to a great extent, impoverish the country and be a dire calamity to both the negro and the white race of this and the Old World; but better this than the loss of the negroes, the country and liberty.

If Lincoln succeeds in arming our slaves against us, he will succeed in making them our masters. He will reverse the social order of things at the South. Whereas, if he is checkmated in time, our liberties will remain intact; the land will be ours, and the industrial system of the country still controlled by Southern men.

Such action on the part of our Government would place our people in a purer and better light before the world. It would disabuse the European mind of a grave error in regard to the cause of our separation. It would prove to them that there were higher and holier motives which actuated our people than the mere love of property. It would show that, although slavery is one of the principles that we started to fight for, yet it falls far short of being the chief one; that, for the sake of our liberty, we are capable of any personal sacrifice; that we regard the emancipation of slaves, and the consequent loss of property as an evil infinitely less than the subjugation and en-slavement of ourselves; that it is not a war exclusively for the privilege of holding negroes in bondage. It would probe to our soldiers, three-fourths of whom never owned a negro, that it is not "the rich man's war and the poor man's fight," but a war for the most sacred of all principles, for the dearest of all rights—the right to govern ourselves. It would show them that the rich man who owned slaves was not willing to jeopardize the precious liberty of the country by his eagerness to hold on to his slaves, but that he was ready to give them up and sacrifice his interest in them whenever the cause de-manded it. It would at once remove all the odium which attached to us on account of slavery, and bring us speedy recognition, and, if necessary, inter-vention.

We sincerely trust that the Southern people will be found willing to make any and every sacrifice which the establishment of our independence may require. Let it never be said that to preserve slavery we were willing to wear the chains of bondage ourselves—that the very avarice which prompted us to hold on to the negro for the sake of the money invested in him, riveted upon us shackles more galling and bitter than ever a people yet endured. Let not slavery prove a barrier to our independence. If it is found in the way—if it proves an insurmountable obstacle to the achievement of our liberty and separate nationality, away with it! Let it perish. We must make up our minds to one solemn duty, the first duty of the patriot, and that is, to save ourselves from the rapacious North, WHATEVER THE COST.

DEBATE OVER USING SLAVES BEGINS

During the fall of 1864, various Southern leaders began calling for greater use of blacks in the military. The Richmond Enquirer, *one of the most widely read newspapers in the Confederacy, floated a trial balloon that received widespread attention in the South and North.*

Richmond Enquirer, 6 October 1864

An Anonymous Writer: "Fight Blacks to the Last Man"

We should be glad to see the Confederate Congress provide for the pur-chase of two hundred and fifty thousand negroes, present them with their freedom and the privilege of remaining in the States, and arm, equip, drill and fight them. We believe that the negroes, identified with us by interest, and fighting for their freedom here, would be faithful and reliable soldiers, and under officers who would drill them, could be depended on for much of the hardest fighting. It is not necessary now to discuss this matter, and may never become so, but neither negroes nor slavery will be permitted to stand in the way of the success of our cause. This war is for national independence on our side, and for the subjugation of white[s] and the emancipation of negroes on the side of the enemy. If we fail the negroes are nominally free and their masters really slaves. We must, therefore, succeed. Other States may decide for themselves, but Virginia, after exhausting her whites, will fight her blacks through to the last man. She will be free at all costs.

The idea of enlisting blacks was too much for many newspapers to stand. The North Carolina Standard *spoke for many Southern newspapers in expressing outrage at the idea.*

North Carolina Standard (Raleigh), 18 October 1864

An Anonymous Writer: "Do We Dream"

Do we dream, or is this sad reality? Do we indeed live in a Gospel land, under the sun of the nineteenth century? What people is this? Are these the descendants of Washington, and Jefferson, and Gaston, and Lowndes, and Moultrie, and Prentiss, and Jackson, and Polk, and Harrison, and Clay? The people—no, the government of the North—with a refinement of cruelty to which language can give no adequate expression, has armed hundreds of thousands of these poor creatures, huddled them in camps, and hurled their bodies against our breastworks and through storms of grape, and canister, and minnie balls, and thus sent them to their death in their efforts to overcome us; and now it is proposed that we should do the same thing—should "lay aside our scruples," and commit this great sin against our slaves, against ourselves, against humanity, and against God. Is our government going to do it? If it does, it will proclaim by such an act that the white men of the Confederate States are not able to achieve their own liberties, and will thus in reality give up a contest which it will seek to prolong by the cowardly sacrifice of an unwarlike and comparatively innocent race.

The proposition is to free two or three hundred thousand slaves, and then order them to fight for us. Will they do it? Would they not, with arms in their hands, either desert to the enemy or turn their weapons against us? And what would our soldiers say to a proposition which would place negro troops on the same footing with themselves?

We have a right to speak freely, and we intend to do so, so far as the Conservatives of this State are concerned. They, the Conservatives, have done more than their duty in this war. There are fewer deserters among them, and there are fewer of them at home than the original secessionists. They are willing to continue the war by white men, and between white men, as long as there is ground to hope that the South can succeed, provided every honorable effort is made meanwhile to obtain peace; but they are not willing to remain in the ranks and fight side by [side] with the negroes, against negroes and abolitionists, while originals are skulking from service, or making the employment of negroes as soldiers a pretext for not going to the war themselves. The abolitionists of the North are thrusting the poor negro between themselves and danger; and now the secessionists of the South are suggesting the same thing, and proposing to arm our slaves, in the hope that some of them may escape the bullets they ought long since to have dared on the field of battle.

This proposition to arm our slaves is not only inexpressibly wrong in itself, but it is calculated to demoralize our slave population, and thus increase the chances that the institution will be destroyed by the war. Every intelligent slaveholder and non-slaveholder, and every citizen who has a spark of Conservatism or humanity in his bosom, should set his face against it like a flint. The prayer which, in the very nature of things, would be put up for the success in battle of *our* share of these poor creatures, as against the share or interest in similar creatures on the federal side with which they would contend, would cause the blood to run cold and the hair to stand on end. Our secession readers may imagine such a prayer, but we must be spared the effort to conceive it and commit it to paper....

The New-York Times *no doubt spoke for many in the North when the paper said it was surprised by the Confederacy's idea of using slaves in the military.*

New-York Times, 21 October 1864

An Anonymous Writer: "Desperation of Rebel Fortunes"

We confess that this development takes us by surprise. Few who knew the South in her old days of pride and chivalry—few who knew the unutterable contempt entertained by the dominant race for the humanity of the negro, could believe that anything whatever could ever reduce her to the adoption of such a policy as this, or even to its discussion.

Of all the signs of the fearful straights of the Southern Confederacy, of all the proofs of the desperation of rebel fortunes, this is by far the most striking and conclusive.

Moreover, it furnishes ground of justification of our own Government in its policy of using, militarily, the negro element of the South, as an aid in operating upon the rebellion. When our Government first proposed to use the negroes as soldiers, it was furiously denounced, on several grave grounds, both by the rebels and Copperheads. It was said to be atrociously cruel to arm an inferior against a superior race, as the former would indulge in general massacre, rape and arson. It was said to be against the law of nations, placed on the same level with well-poisoning and we were challenged to produce a precedent for it; and though last, not least, it was pronounced a "mean Yankee trick." No brave people, they declared, with a particle of self-respect, would consent to owe anything, not even the preservation of its Government, to a race which, from time immemorial, had been hewers of wood and drawers of water, for anybody who chose to catch and flog them.

DAVIS PROPOSES EMANCIPATION

President Jefferson Davis took center stage in the debate when he urged the Confederate Congress to purchase 40,000 slaves to work as laborers with the promise of eventual freedom. Although Davis said he was not yet ready to support the enlistment of blacks in the army, he said that option should be preserved. Such talk was too much for the Richmond Examiner.

Richmond Examiner, 8 November 1864

An Anonymous Writer: "First Step to Universal Abolition"

[T]he existence of a negro soldier is totally inconsistent with our political aim and with our social as well as political system. We surrender our position whenever we introduce the negro to arms. If a negro is fit for free labour—fit to live and to be useful under the competitive system of labour—then the whole race is fit for it. The employment of negroes in our armies, either with or without prospective emancipation, would be the first step, but a step which would involve all the rest, to universal abolition. It would be so understood and regarded by all the world. Our enemy would perceive that he had succeeded in his design to the point of moral subjugation, and would not doubt that our absolute submission was far removed. To our own hearts it would be a confession, not only of weakness, but of absolute inability to secure the object for which we undertook the world, incompatible with that independence of action for which the South arrives.

But the objections to this project are so manifest that it is unnecessary at present even to suggest them. The President opposed the introduction of negroes into the army as soldiers, but desires a corps of forty thousand to be used in labour on fortifications as engineers, as teamsters and as sappers and miners. To a proposition of that sort, no one could have the least objection, if he had not concluded with an obscure passage, which, if it means anything, means that the forty thousand slaves so employed shall be set free at the end of the war as a reward for their service. Here, while refusing to employ the slaves under arms, he adopts the fatal principle of the original proposition to its fullest extent and puts forth an idea which, if admitted by the Southern people as a truth, renders their position on the matter of slavery utterly untenable. We hold that the negro is in his proper situation—that is to say, in the condition which is the best for him; where he reaches his highest moral, intellectual and physical development and can enjoy the full sum of his natural happiness; in a word, that while living with the white man in the relation of slave he is in a state superior and better for him than that of freedom. But the negro's freedom is to be given him as a reward for his service to the country; his freedom, therefore, is a boon—it is a better state— a natural good of which our laws deprive him and keep him from. Now, that is the whole theory of the abolitionist, and we have the sorrow to think that if one portion of this Presidential message means anything it means that...

The Macon (Ga.) Telegraph *took a more measured approach to the proposal. In an editorial, the paper argued that blacks could be rewarded for their service to the Confederacy, but that the government should not go so far as to give them their freedom.*

Macon (Ga.) Telegraph, 14 November 1864

An Anonymous Writer: "Rewards but no Freedom"

Negroes can be used to advantage in the army and hospitals, but there is no reason why they cannot successfully be employed and liberally rewarded—not by freedom, which would prove a curse to them and a danger to us; but by such wise enactments as might improve their condition, without changing their status. As slaves they should be used and as slaves returned to their masters. If it be necessary to secure their services for the Government, to purchase the negroes required for the army, let them be bought, and at the expiration of their term of service, let them, as a reward for duties faithfully done, be permitted to select the State in which they will reside and the master whom they will serve. The negro, like the child, is little influenced by promises of reward in the future, and while our enemies would soon find means to make him distrust our promise of freeing him, he could easily be induced to believe that for faithful service rendered, he would be permitted to choose his own home and master....

The Richmond Enquirer, *a supporter of President Davis on many issues, endorsed his plan to use slaves as laborers and then reward them with freedom.*

Richmond Enquirer, 11 November 1864

An Anonymous Writer: "Slavery Not Object of War"

If the necessity exists, then, we say not forty thousand only, but any number that the necessity may require; for negro slavery was the mere occasion, and is not the object or end of this war. We would show to the world the lesson that, for national independence and freedom from Yankee domination, in addition to sacrifices already made, the people of these States are ready and willing, when the necessity arises, to sacrifice any number or all of the slaves to the cause of national freedom. And we would teach the enemy that "emancipation" has but merely brought to our attention the fighting resources of four millions of slaves, and that the Spring campaign shall open with an army of a quarter of million of negroes, besides our noble veterans, and that the scene of operations shall be the country of the enemy. We would respond to General Grant's "cradle and grave" assertion with the battle shout of an army of half a million.

Not surprisingly, many Northern editors took great delight in the debate under way in the Confederacy. The Philadelphia Inquirer *said it was poetic justice for leaders that had fomented rebellion.*

Philadelphia Inquirer, 11 November 1864

An Anonymous Writer: "Davis's Message—The Rebel President Turned Abolitionist"

[T]he leaders of the Rebellion are now beginning to experience for the first time the dire troubles of wide and violent political divisions within their little household. Heretofore they have had a fair approach to unanimity, that is, all have been of one mind who dare express an opinion at all. Now that they propose to lay hands on the heretofore inviolable "nigger," there is a wide spread revolt. They are now to experience the bitter fruits, within their own lines, of that agitation for "abolition" on the one side and fire-eating resistance on the other, with which, for a quarter of a century, they made the politics of the United States one unceasing round of horrible discord.

REACTION TO PLAN

The Charleston Mercury *wanted nothing to do with President Davis's proposal. "We want no Confederate Government without our institutions," the paper argued.*

Charleston Mercury, 13 January 1865

An Anonymous Writer: "No Government without our Institutions"

By the compact we made with Virginia and the other States of this Confederacy, South Carolina will stand to the bitter end of destruction. By that compact she intends to stand or to fall. Neither Congress, nor certain makeshift men in Virginia, can force upon her their mad schemes of weakness and surrender. She stands upon her institutions—and there she will fall in their defence. *We want no Confederate Government without our institutions.* And we will have none. Sink or swim, live or die, we stand by them, and are fighting for them this day. That is the ground of our fight—it is well that all should understand it at once. Thousands and tens of thousands of the bravest men, and the best blood of this State, fighting in the ranks, have left their bones whitening on the bleak hills of Virginia in this cause. We are fighting for our system of civilization—not for buncomb, or for Jeff Davis. We intend to fight for that, or nothing. We expect Virginia to stand beside us in that fight, as of old, as we have stood beside her in this war up to this time. But such talk coming from such a source is destructive to the cause. Let it cease at once, in God's name, and in behalf of our common cause! It is paralizing [*sic*] to every man here to hear it. It throws a pall over the hearts of the soldiers from this State to hear it. The soldiers of South Carolina will not fight beside a nigger—to talk of emancipation is to disband our army. We are free men, and we chose to fight for ourselves—we want no slaves to fight for us. Skulkers, money lenders, money makers, and blood-suckers, alone will tolerate the idea. It is the man who won[']t fight himself, who wants his nigger to fight for him, and to take his place in the ranks. Put that man in the ranks. And do it at once. Control your armies—put men of capacity in command, re-establish confidence—enforce thorough discipline—and there will be found men enough, and brave men enough, to defeat a dozen Sherman's. Falter and hack at the root of the Confederacy—our institutions—our civilization—and you kill the cause as dead as a boiled crab.

The Richmond Examiner *did not like the idea of enlisting slaves, but said if the alternative meant losing the war, it would support the president's plan.*

Richmond Examiner, 25 February 1865

An Anonymous Writer: "Is Slavery Necessary?"

The principle of slavery is a sound one; but is it so dear to us that rather than give it up we would be slaves ourselves? Slavery, like the Sabbath, was made for man; not man for slavery. On this point also, as well as all the others, the only practical question now ought to be: Is it necessary, in order to defend our country successfully, to use negroes as soldiers—not abandoning any principle, but reserving for quieter times the definitive arrangements which may thus become needful?—If it is necessary, as General Lee has said—that is, if the alternative is submission to the enemy—then no good Southern man will hesitate. It may be under protest that we yield to this imperious necessity; but still we yield.

The Galveston News *argued that Southern blacks would gladly fight against a country that had mistreated them.*

Galveston (Tex.) News, 31 March 1865

An Anonymous Writer: "The Negro Question"

[T]hose of our negroes who have had an opportunity of experiencing something of the freedom that the Yankees give them will not only be willing, but glad of the opportunity, to fight them, as the worst enemies of their race....

The New-York Tribune *noted sarcastically that the Confederacy now wanted to reward blacks for their service to the army with freedom. It should be noted that the term "Sambo" was used widely to refer to African Americans, even among people who supported their advancement. The term did not have the derogatory connotation that it does today.*

New-York Tribune, 15 February 1865

An Anonymous Writer: "Dixie for Sambo"

That Slavery is the best possible condition for the negro, is the first article in the Rebel creed. That the negro loves his master above all men, takes pride in his service, and would by no means accept freedom if it were offered to him, used to be the second. The stress of circumstances has somewhat modified this cannon; no one talks for arming negroes who does not admit or insist that, to arm them to any purpose, they must be promised freedom....

The New York Herald *ridiculed the president's plan to enlist slaves, saying, "the chief abolitionist turns out to be Jeff. Davis himself."*

New York Herald, 1 March 1865

An Anonymous Writer: "The New Plan for Abolishing Slavery"

Jeff. Davis is going to free the slaves and bestow upon them the title deeds of the seceded states in order to achieve Southern independence. He feels that the sacrifice is great; but he is prepared to make it for the Southern confederacy. This is a highly novel and original plan and Jeff. Davis ought to take out a patent for it immediately. It is cutting off a man's head to save his life. It is pulling out the cornerstone to keep the edifice standing.... The seceded States flounced out of the Union because they were afraid that Lincoln would interfere with slavery. They put themselves under the lead of Jeff. Davis, who promised to protect slavery against the attacks of the Yankee vandals. They have been fighting for four years to prevent us from bringing them back into the Union, where the awful abolitionists might get another chance at slavery. Now, after the elapse of all this time, and after the shedding of all this blood, presto! the chief abolitionist turns out to be Jeff. Davis himself.

By the end of March 1865, two black Confederate regiments had been organized and began drilling in Richmond. The Daily Dispatch *noted that the men appeared to make outstanding soldiers.*

Daily Dispatch (Richmond), 25 March 1865

An Anonymous Writer: "The Cause Progressing"

The cause progressing—Daily accessions are made to Major Turner's negro troops, now being drilled and organized at Smith's factory, on the corner of Twenty-first and Cary streets, by Lieutenant Virginius Bossieux. At 5 o'clock yesterday afternoon we witnessed a drill at their barracks, and have no hesitation in saying that, for the time they have been at it, as much aptness and proficiency was displayed as is usually shown by any white troops we have ever seen....

QUESTIONS

1. How can you explain President Davis's initial opposition to using slaves in the military and his later idea to enlist them in the army?
2. Why did the proposal to enlist slaves prompt such heated debate by Southern newspapers?
3. Why would Northern papers take great satisfaction in the idea of the Confederacy enlisting slaves?

NOTES

1. Bell Irvin Wiley, *Southern Negroes, 1861–1865* (New Haven, Conn.: Yale University Press, 1938).

2. James M. McPherson, *Battle Cry of Freedom: The Civil War Era* (New York: Oxford University Press, 1988), 831–33.

3. *War of the Rebellion: A Compilation of the Official Records of the Union and Confederate Armies,* Series IV (Washington, D.C.: Government Printing Office, 1900), 3:1110.

4. Emory M. Thomas, *The Confederate Nation, 1861–1865* (New York: Harper & Row, 1979), p. 292.

5. *War of the Rebellion,* series IV, 3:1012–13.

CHAPTER 21

Hampton Roads Peace Conference, 1865

O
ne final attempt at negotiating an end to the Civil War took place at what became known as the Hampton Roads Peace Conference. The conference was the brainchild of Horace Greeley, editor of the influential *New-York Tribune*. Greeley, who had organized a failed peace mission at Niagara Falls in 1864, had followed news reports of the burgeoning peace movement in the South. He wrote to Francis Preston Blair, the patriarch of a powerful Maryland family and advisor to U.S. presidents since Andrew Jackson, telling him that the right man could persuade Confederate officials to open peace negotiations. Blair convinced President Abraham Lincoln to let him travel to the South and meet with the president of the Confederacy.

On January 12, 1865, Blair proposed a plan to Jefferson Davis in which the two sides would agree to a cease-fire and then join together to oust the French-supported regime in nearby Mexico, which had been threatening to become involved in the war. Blair argued that the scheme would bring the North and South together and provide the foundation for a lasting peace. Davis had little hope for success at the conference, but he believed that its inevitable failure would blunt the peace movement in the Confederacy. The president gave Blair a letter saying he said he was ready to hold a conference with the objective of "securing peace to the two countries." Although Lincoln showed no interest in the plan for Mexico, the president replied that he would meet with Confederate officials "with the view of securing peace to the people of our one common country."[1]

Davis appointed three commissioners to attend the conference: Vice-President Alexander H. Stephens, Confederate Senate President pro tem Robert M.T. Hunter, and Assistant Secretary of War John A. Campbell. Lincoln sent Secretary of State William H. Seward. The meeting at Hampton

Roads, Virginia, almost was called off because of differences between the agendas of the two sides. But General Ulysses S. Grant, who had high hopes for the conference, personally intervened. At the last moment, Lincoln decided to attend the meeting. As the three Southern commissioners traveled between the Confederate and Union lines near Hampton Roads, soldiers on both sides shouted, "Peace! Peace!"

The meeting took place February 3 on the Union steamboat *River Queen* off Fort Monroe. Stephens proposed an armistice to end the fighting, but Lincoln said the Confederate states must first agree to return to the Union. The Confederate commissioners suggested that the Mexican scheme would provide a foundation for peace. The Confederate vice president suggested that the two governments could secretly negotiate a treaty to end the fighting and consolidate the troops in designated locations. The Union and Confederate armies would attack in concert to drive the French out of Mexico. Lincoln said the United States Congress alone possessed the power to declare war and make treaties. Moreover, agreeing to any plan to oust the French from Mexico was tantamount to official United States recognition of the Confederacy.

On the question of slavery, Lincoln suggested the possibility of compensating Southern owners for the loss of their slaves. He also said the Emancipation Proclamation was a wartime measure that would be terminated after peace had been achieved. But the president insisted that no slaves freed would be re-enslaved. Seward reminded the commissioners that the House of Representatives had just approved the Thirteenth Amendment ending slavery in the United States, and its ratification would make all questions about slavery in the future moot. The commissioners asked what would happen if the Southern states returned to Union and helped defeat the amendment. Seward said that such an event would be addressed at the time.

An exasperated Hunter told Lincoln and Seward that they had offered the Confederacy little beyond unconditional surrender. Seward said that neither he nor the president had used those terms. He also assured the commissioners that the South would receive all the safeguards of the Constitution against confiscating property. Lincoln said the North shared in the responsibility for slavery in the United States and that he would support compensation to slave owners for the loss of their property. The president then urged the Confederates to lay down their arms and return to the Union. It was clear that the two sides remained far apart. The South still demanded its independence while the North insisted on reunion. After four hours, the peace conference ended with no tangible results.[2]

The North's demand for surrender and reunion inspired a surge of patriotism by many in the South. Mass meetings in support of the war were held in Richmond, Mobile, Lynchburg, and other cities. In a defiant speech before the Confederate Congress three days later, Davis said the South would never submit to the "disgrace of surrender." He called Lincoln "His Majesty Abraham the First" and predicted that Confederate forces would "compel the Yankees, in less than twelve months, to petition us for peace on our own terms."3

This chapter follows editorial reaction to the Hampton Roads Peace Conference. It begins with newspaper editorials during the weeks leading up the conference. Not surprisingly, the *New-York Tribune* encouraged a peace conference. But the *Tribune*'s New York rivals ridiculed the idea. After the conference ended unsuccessfully, newspapers had various reactions. The *Tribune*, not surprisingly, held out hope that peace could still be achieved. But the *Harrisburg Telegraph* claimed that Davis had made sure the peace conference failed so that he could use it as a propaganda tool. At the same time, the *Daily Dispatch* argued that the conference would rekindle Confederate patriotism. An angry *Richmond Examiner* said the North had insulted the South by demanding its unconditional surrender.

PEACE CONFERENCE PLANNED

Not surprisingly, given Horace Greeley's role in planning the conference, the New-York Tribune *urged the North and South to enter into peace talks.*

New-York Tribune, 7 December 1864

Horace Greeley: "No Possible Harm"

We do not know, and have at no time felt confident, that the Rebels are yet prepared to agree to any terms of pacification that our Government either would, or should deem acceptable; but we can imagine no possible harm that could result from ascertaining precisely what they *are* ready to do. The recognized object of war, at least among civilized and Christian nations, is an honorable and satisfactory Peace; and how are we to know when this end has been rendered attainable unless we take some means to ascertain?

The New-York Times *argued against peace talks and said the Union should accept nothing less than the unconditional surrender of the South.*

New-York Times, 5 January 1865

An Anonymous Writer: "The Attempted Blair Mission"

There has been no time when the loyal people of the North were less inclined than now to abate one iota from the claim to an unconditional submission of the rebels to the Constitution and the laws. While the intrinsic
right remains the same as ever, the power to enforce that right has been
made doubly certain—first, by the proof afforded by the recent Presidential
election that faction cannot divide the North—and second, by the fact that
the "Confederacy" has now no army, worthy of the name, left, save that
which Gen. Grant keeps cribbed in Richmond. It is the universal belief of all
loyal people that the war, though it may linger for months, is in its last stage,
and that the blood and treasure which have yet to be expended bear but a
small proportion to the sacrifices already made. It is but natural that the very
magnitude of their past sacrifices shall deepen their determination not to
barter away the glorious results, after having suffered so much. They would
consider it the height of folly to purchase exemption from the few trials that
are left, by any concession. The fortunes of war have given us a new claim to
the absolute submission to the law of the land which we originally demanded as a matter of right, and now less than ever will we take anything
short of that.

It is probably that most Southern people egregiously mistake the designs of the North. They sincerely believe that we are bent on subjugating
and degrading them. They do not comprehend at all that we are fighting
only for the same constitutional authority over them that we recognize as
equally binding upon ourselves. This misunderstanding is deplorable, but
we are not responsible for it, nor can we remove it. President Lincoln has,
from the beginning, officially certified in his Messages that this war had no
other object than the maintenance of the Constitution and that the rebels
could have peace at any time by submission thereto. The Southern people
have preferred to put faith in the falsehoods of their own leaders. There has
been no misrepresentation too gross for them to credit, and their minds are
filled with the most perverted ideas concerning the temper and purposes of
our Government. But no mission to Richmond, either public or private, can
correct this. Such a mission could only have communication with the rebel
authorities, and these have always known the real truth. They have falsified,
both because they did not know better, but because they could live only by
deception. A mission to Richmond, dealing only with the rebel authorities,
could do nothing toward undeceiving the people. That can be done only by

actual contact with people, when no longer subject to Confederate control. Our armies are the only effective propagators of the truth.

Savannah now presents a capital illustration of what our armies can accomplish in this line. Within one week after Gen. Sherman's occupation of the city, a public meeting called by the Mayor and a large number of influential citizens, including many members of the city government, unanimously passed resolutions declaring their readiness to submit to the national authority under the Constitution, and to claim the privileges and immunities contained in the Proclamation and Message of the President of the United States. A few days of personal intercourse with Gen. Sherman, his officers and soldiers, have wrought a wonderful change of feeling. Dread and abhorrence have given way to a generous trust; and there is now even prospect that Savannah will soon become a thoroughly loyal city. As Gen. Sherman turns northward toward Richmond, the same popular enlightenment will go with him. Every day's march will tell more in the interests of peace than all the peace plans or peace missions that ever have or ever will be projected.

The Columbus Times *dismissed any move toward peace, saying, "We would sooner go to the devil."*

Columbus (Ga.) Times, 2 January 1865

An Anonymous Writer: "Selling Out"

There is no conceivable fate on this earth that we would not accept in preference to a re-union with the Yankee people. We would sooner go to the devil, if he were on top of the ground, and had dominion only over our temporal interests. If, therefore, in the vicissitudes of this war it should become necessary to barter away our liberties, our property, everything, to save ourselves from Lincoln's yoke, we announce, in advance, that we shall be ready for the trade. Nothing akin to this necessity, however, is now upon us, nor, by the blessing of God, will it ever be, if we are true to ourselves and discharge the duties which patriotism imposes. Not while we have an untouched reserve of 300,000 fighting men, can we entertain, with the least degree of patience, the proposition to discontinue the contest for independence. Faith, courage, perseverance will bring us the boon, if we but struggle on. This people cannot be conquered without their consent.

Northern Reaction to Failure of Conference

The New-York Tribune *held out hope that peace could be reached even after the failure of the Hampton Roads conference. The* Tribune *suggested peace negotiations be held with individual Confederate states.*

New-York Tribune, 11 February 1865

Horace Greeley: "Rival Accounts of the Peace Conference"

It is settled, we presume, that we can have no peace with the Confederacy; but it does not follow that none can be made with the States composing it. On the contrary, we believe that a majority of the people of those States are today ready for a pacification whereof the Union shall be the corner stone, with Liberty for All inscribed proudly and truly over its porch. And so, avoiding the ferocity, the frenzy and the bad states, of our Richmond contemporaries, we shall work on for such a Peace, even though it be attainable only through further War, trusting that its blessed event cannot be far off.

The Harrisburg Telegraph *accused President Davis of making sure the peace conference failed so that he could use it as a propaganda tool and re-unite the South against the Union.*

Harrisburg (Pa.) Telegraph, 11 February 1865

An Anonymous Writer: "Jeff Davis as a Traitor and a Trickster"

If there is a sharp knave beneath the canopy of heaven, Jeff. Davis is the individual best entitled to the name. As a traitor and a knave, he will live as long in history as will Cain as a murderer, Arnold as a traitor, and Ananias as a liar. His last trick crowns the infamy of Davis. Feeling that power was departing from his clutches—that he was losing prestige among the mass of traitors and influence with their leaders, Davis devised the peace mission composed of Stevens, Hunter and Campbell, with the deliberate purpose of rendering it a failure, that he might be able to revive the drooping spirits of his followers, and re-kindle the flame which burned with such fury in the South in 1861. Already, with Davis' engineering, mass meetings have been held in Richmond, at which it was resolved that the "imperious ultimatums of the Lincoln dynasty impel and constrain every true hearted son of the South to arm with resolute determination to force either a recognition of their independence, or compel their brutal enemies to achieve their extermination." By this means Jeff. Davis hopes to re-unite the people of the South in his favor. His toadies, those who have been living in office at Richmond, are laboring arduously to create in his behalf something of the old frenzy with which his accession to power was hailed; and night after night the officeholders, who will suffer most by a cessation of hostilities and return to the Union, are holding meetings to assure the poor devils who have been doing the bloody work of treason, that "President" Davis is in favor of war, opposed to peace, and ready to sacrifice every man in the South rather than submit to the Constitution and Union. All this is a trick of the arch-traitor. He knew when he sent his peace commissioners to consult with Mr. Lincoln, that all effort to effect a cessation of hostilities short of a recognition of the Federal power and re-entrance into the Union, would fail and now out of this failure Davis is laboring to extract the influences to "fire the Southern heart." But the scamp in this, as in all his dealings, has overreached himself. A year ago, Davis triumphantly assured his blind followers that it was only necessary for the South to "hold on;" the people of the North would themselves become weary of the war, and soon yield not only a recognition of the Confederacy, but implore to become its ally. The rebels have "held on," and to the first proposition of peace short of a full recognition of the Federal authority, they have received a decided and deliberate negative answer. The authorities and the people loyal to the Union, are determined to prosecute the war to the bitter end, yielding nor accepting any terms of peace but those of unconditional surrender. In this dilemma Davis proposes peace on impossible terms. Here again he has overreached himself, as the mass of the rebels will soon discover the folly of waging an unequal war against the Government, with that Government determined on its prosecution until it has enforced peace and submission to all its authorities.

SOUTHERN REACTION TO FAILURE OF CONFERENCE

The Richmond Daily Dispatch argued that the peace conference was not a failure because it showed the willingness of the South to end the war. Moreover, the unreasonable terms of the North would rekindle Confederate patriotism, the newspaper claimed.

Daily Dispatch (Richmond), 8 February 1865

An Anonymous Writer: "The Olive Branch of Peace"

The Confederate People will have no reason to regret that a Commission, composed of eminent public functionaries, has formally held out the Olive Branch of Peace to the United States. This step has at once made known to the people of both countries, and of the world, the readiness and solicitude of this Government to terminate a long and bloody struggle, and it has had the result of inducing our enemies, in a moment of unguarded triumph, to disclose their real designs and purposes. There can hereafter be no sort of misconstruction of their object. They have not left a peg to hang a doubt on....

If our public spirit has, in some measure, declined, the reply of Lincoln to our Peace Commissioners will kindle again in a broad and irresistible flame the fervid and self-sacrificing patriotism of 1861. The absentees from our army will return, the land will rise as one man, and every soldier will have the strength of two men in his arm. Our cause is just, and if we are true to ourselves, we may look forward, with trust in God, to the most brilliant and successful campaign in the whole war.

The Richmond Examiner *said the Confederacy should be insulted that the Union would insist on an unconditional surrender by the South.*

Richmond Examiner, 6 February 1865

An Anonymous Writer: "Unconditional Surrender"

Did it ever before befall, in the history of mankind, that a Power which had in the field three unconquered armies such as ours, with a Government firmly seated in its metropolitan city, and a territory scarcely yet touched by an enemy four times as great as that of some first rate European kingdoms, was asked for an unconditional surrender of its armies, its Government, and the lives, liberties and fortunes of all its inhabitants—men, women and children—to the absolute discretion of an invading enemy, with the certainty besides that this discretion would be exercised for the extirpation of its present race of inhabitants and the re-settlement of the country by strangers? There is no record of such demand; and the very monstrousness of it in the present case indicates that our enemy has purposely made his demands so incredibly preposterous in order to shake all forms of reconstruction or reconciliation impossible, and has made up his mind to go for conquest and the rights of conquest. Be it so. This is indeed throwing away the scabbard. There is at least a stern satisfaction in knowing that parley is at an end, and that the fate and fortune of ourselves, our country and our children lies in the edge of the sword.

QUESTIONS

1. Why would Lincoln and Davis agree to a peace conference when the two sides were so far apart?
2. Why was the South so angry at the North's demand for surrender and reunion?
3. Does it surprise you that the peace conference was the idea of Horace Greeley given what you know about the editor? Explain.

NOTES

1. Roy P. Basler, ed., *The Collected Works of Abraham Lincoln*, vol. 8 (New Brunswick, N.J.: Rutgers University Press, 1952–1955), 275–76.

2. Edward Chase Kirkland, *The Peacemakers of 1864* (New York: Macmillan, 1927), 197–251.

3. James M. McPherson, *Battle Cry of Freedom: The Civil War Era* (New York: Oxford University Press, 1988), 824.

Confederacy Surrenders, 1865

S ince the summer of 1864, the major fighting in Virginia had become centered around the city of Petersburg. Located just 25 miles south of Richmond, Petersburg was a major transportation center, and all but one of the railroads that connected the Confederate capital to the army passed through the city. Both sides recognized that if Petersburg fell to the Union army, it would force the evacuation of Richmond and likely shorten the war. General Robert E. Lee's Rebel army dug in around Petersburg, and Federal troops made repeated attempts during the summer to dislodge Lee.

The most famous attempt took place when Union troops tunneled 511 feet to the Confederate line and packed 8,000 pounds of gunpowder under enemy troops. Early in the morning of July 30, a spectacular explosion blasted a giant hole in the Rebel line. With Confederate troops in disarray, 15,000 troops rushed into the crater left by the explosion. But a Southern counterattack drove out Federal troops and slaughtered those trapped in the crater. The Union army lost an estimated 4,000 men compared with just 1,500 for the Confederacy. After the fiasco, General Ulysses S. Grant resigned himself to maintaining a siege on Petersburg that would exhaust Rebel resources.[1]

By the end of 1864, the well-supplied Union army totaled about 110,000 men, while Lee had only 66,000 poorly equipped troops. Over the winter, Federal forces cut the last road into Petersburg and were threatening the only remaining railroad line. "I mean to end the business here," Grant told one of his commanders. By March 1865, Lee recognized that his army was soon to be encircled, so he planned a surprise offensive on the enemy position at Fort Steadman. The predawn attack was successful initially, but Union troops rallied and recaptured the fort, trapping many of the rebels. Sensing he could finally achieve victory at Petersburg, Grant ordered a final assault on the city. At the Battle of Five Forks on April 1, Grant's army smashed the right side of the Confederate force. Lee knew that he would have to evacuate Petersburg and that Richmond, too, would soon fall.

President Jefferson Davis was worshipping at St. Paul's Church on Sunday, April 2 when he received a telegram from Lee saying that Richmond must be abandoned. Lee told the president he would hold Petersburg until nightfall to allow the capital to be evacuated. Davis and other Confederate officials quickly boarded trains south for Danville, Virginia, with all the important documents they could carry, and they established a temporary capital there. The remaining government documents were burned, as was anything else of military and industrial value in the city. By evening, the Confederate army began its retreat south, and the following day, Federal forces occupied Richmond. One of their first tasks was to raise the United States flag over the state capitol. President Abraham Lincoln toured Richmond the next day, accompanied by cheering throngs of newly freed blacks.[2]

Lee hoped to move out of Virginia and join General Joseph Johnston's army in North Carolina. However, Lee had the more immediate problem of feeding his hungry men, and so he marched west to the small town of Amelia Courthouse where he expected to find a trainload of rations. But because of a mix-up, ammunition instead of food had been sent there. The confusion cost the Confederate army its small lead on the pursuing Federal troops. As Lee's army continued fleeing west toward Appomattox Station, Union forces attacked. At Sayler's Creek, Federal troops captured 6,000 exhausted Confederate soldiers and a large portion of their wagon train. Believing that Lee was beaten, Grant sent his foe a note on April 7 requesting the surrender of the Confederate army. Lee's men were hungry and exhausted, and the general seriously considered surrendering. But on April 9 he decided to try to break through Federal troops blocking the road near Appomattox Courthouse. Although the rebel army initially drove back Union cavalry, they were quickly met by infantry reinforcements. Lee recognized that he had nowhere else to go, and sent a note through the lines offering to surrender.

Grant and Lee met that day at the home of Wilmer McLean. When the war began, McLean was living near Manassas, and his home served as a Confederate headquarters during the battle of First Bull Run. He had moved his family to Appomattox Courthouse in 1863 trying to escape the fighting. Now in McLean's parlor, the war was coming to an end. Grant's terms for Lee were generous: soldiers who surrendered could go home and would not be disturbed by U.S. authorities as long as they observed their parole. In effect, Grant was guaranteeing that Confederate soldiers would be immune from prosecution as traitors to the United States government.

Lee agreed to the terms and the two generals signed the surrender papers. They talked briefly, saluted, and returned to their separate camps. Grant later sent three days' rations to the hungry Confederate troops.[3]

The lack of rancor was also evident three days later when Confederate troops marched to Appomattox to stack their arms and surrender their battle flags. As Confederate soldiers marched between the two lines of Federal troops, Union commander Joshua L. Chamberlain ordered his men to carry arms, the salute of honor. Touched by the act, Confederate General John B. Gordon ordered his troops to salute in kind. In the terms of surrender and the formal ceremony at Appomattox, the once bitter enemies had shown deep respect for one another. The same was true when the two other main Confederate armies—one commanded by Johnston and the other by General Kirby Smith—later surrendered to Union forces. Many on both sides hoped that would set the tone for the days to follow.

This chapter surveys editorial reaction in the days leading up to the surrender at Appomattox—as well as reaction to the surrender. The chapter begins with editorials on the capture of Richmond. No sooner had the news of Richmond's fall sunk in, than came word of Lee's surrender to Grant at Appomattox Courthouse. Not surprisingly, many Northern newspapers used their editorial space to express thanks to the men who had waged war with the South. Most of the editorials in these first three sections come from Northern papers for two reasons. First, few newspapers still were publishing in the South and, second, news of Richmond's surrender and capture took a week or more to get to most Southern cities. Finally, editorial writers in the North and South used their pages to express ideas about what to do now that the bitter war was over.

FALL OF RICHMOND

Among the first troops to enter Richmond following its capture were units from the all-black 25th Corps. In an editorial, the Boston Advertiser *noted the significance of the act for black Americans.*

Boston Advertiser, 4 May 1865

An Anonymous Writer: Historical Justice

[I]t is...historical justice...that the troops who were first to enter Richmond were, at least in part, of that despised race whose wrongs have entered so largely into the merits of this struggle. It was fitting that negro troops should first occupy the capital of a confederacy, of which, in the days of its hope, African slavery was pronounced by the highest authority to be even the corner-stone.

Northern editors reveled in the news of Richmond's surrender and the fact that Confederate leaders had been forced to flee from the capital. The New York Herald *called them "fugitives from justice."*

New York Herald, 5 April 1865

An Anonymous Writer: "The News from Virginia"

There is no longer any power besides the United States in the limits of the old Union that can set up even the flimsiest pretence to nationality. At this hour the rebellion is "without civil or military organization," and "without the emblems or the semblance of nationality." This is the admission of the Richmond Examiner—which no one will accuse of prejudice in our favor.... [T]he rebellion as an organized power is dead and...it gave up the ghost in the hour when it was forced to leave the first and last of its strongholds.... [B]y its capture the rebellion is put down, and that they who may be still in arms are mere vagabonds and fugitives, without cause or purpose or power....

So long as they could, with some appearance of justice, claim a nationality; so long as they had cities, a capital, and established means of intercourse with nations, their position before the world was respectable. But now all that is done with. They are a mere group of fugitives from justice; and while but yesterday they had the noble ambition to change the fate of nations, to-day they only hope to escape from the consequences of their own acts.

SURRENDER AT APPOMATTOX COURTHOUSE

Like newspapers all over the North, the New-York Times *celebrated the surrender news. It hailed the thousands of men who had died to restore the Union and bring freedom to all Americans.*

New-York Times, 10 April 1865

An Anonymous Writer: "Peace!"

The great struggle is over. Gen. Robert E. Lee and the Army of Northern Virginia surrendered yesterday to Lieut. Gen. U. S. Grant and the Army of the Potomac.

The thrilling word PEACE—the glorious fact of PEACE—are now once again to be realized by the American people.

The profound joy of the nation in this auspicious result cannot be expressed in effervescent enthusiasm and noisy huzzahs, but will appear in the form in which it is so fitly and opportunely proclaimed by the Secretary of War—ascriptions of Praise to Almighty God and offering of honor to the great leader of our armies, whom he has used as his instrument to save the nation....

We have achieved, too, that for which the war was begun—that for which our soldiers have so long and grandly fought, and that for which so many thousands of brave men have laid down their lives. We have achieved the great triumph, and we get with it the glorious Union. We get it with it our country—a country now and forever rejoicing in Universal Freedom. The national courage and endurance have their full reward.

Ceremonies celebrating the end of the fighting took place all over the North. As an editorial in the Baltimore American *noted, one of the most symbolic took place at Fort Sumter where the war had begun.*

Baltimore American, 14 April 1865

An Anonymous Writer: "The Old Flag on Fort Sumter"

There will be a solemn and impressive scene in Charleston harbor this day. The flag that waved above the ramparts of Sumter amid the smoke and roar of the Rebel cannonade will be elevated to its former position. The flag whose staff was shot away the ninth time after it had been struck by the iron hail which kept pouring upon the fortress hour after hour, will again wave over a scene alike of desolation and of triumph. The flag that was taken up by Lieutenant Hall after its fall, nailed to the staff because the halliards had become useless, and planted upon the ramparts amid flying shot and shell, will be raised again in a serener atmosphere and under happier auspices. The flag which, by the terms of surrender, the garrison was allowed to salute with fifty guns, and which Major Anderson bore with him on his departure, he will to-day, by direction of the Government, restore to its wonted place.

Some Southern newspapers remained defiant in the face of defeat. The Albany Patriot refused to attribute defeat to Northern superiority and instead placed its blamed on the apathy of the Southern people.

Albany (Ga.) Patriot, 27 April 1865

An Anonymous Writer: "The News"

We are yet unconquered, and until the sword of the enemy is at our throats, we upbraid our fellow citizens for their recent nefarious conduct. God help our country.

PRAISE FOR ARMY AND ITS LEADERS

Many groups and individuals received editorial praise for their roles in the Union army's victory. The Harrisburg Telegraph *lauded the army's fighting men.*

Harrisburg (Pa.) Telegraph, 6 May 1865

An Anonymous Writer: "The Soldiers Are Coming Home!"

Happy news! How its announcement will cheer the heart of many a weary wife and mother who, at home, in tears and in prayers have waited for the return of their loved ones.... They are coming covered with the dust of the march—they are coming grim with the blackness of battle—they are coming from fields of immortal victory and invincible valor....To them belong the nation's blessing. The soldiers of the Republic are now its crown jewels, more glorious and richer than any which glisten in the diadem of a king.

The Chicago Tribune *hailed General Grant for his role in defeating Lee's fearsome army.*

Chicago Tribune, 5 April 1865

An Anonymous Writer: Praise for Gen. Grant

It is certain also that Gen. Grant took upon himself personally the severest task of the war—the task of overcoming Gen. Lee and capturing the rebel capital. Lee's army was incomparably the most formidable one that the enemy ever put in the field. It was led by a great captain. The judgment of the world has pronounced Gen. Lee on of the foremost military chieftains of ancient or modern times. If it was necessary that the rebellion should come—if it was ordained that civil war should desolate us, and that our sons and brothers should fall on a hundred battle fields—we may still entertain a respect for the genius and humanity of Robert E. Lee. We cannot admire the traitor to his country and flag, but we can nevertheless admit his consummate ability and the elevation of character he has often displayed in a bad cause. That he was a formidable antagonist is attested by the numerous fields on which he successively defeated us. McClellan, Pope, Burnside and Hooker measured weapons with him and were worsted. Ever since the seven days battles in front of Richmond he has been our most dreaded antagonist. The reputation of his army was equal to that of its general. It was a victorious, audacious, and arrogant army, strong in the belief that it was invincible. It had been repulsed at Gettysburg but not pursued. Its losses in that engagement had been made good, and it lay on the south bank of the Rapidan in the spring of 1864, confident of its ability to drive back or demolish any force that crossed that threshold. Gen. Grant placed himself at the head of the Army of the Potomac, and in the desperate campaign which followed he not only drove Lee to the entrenchments of Richmond but thoroughly humbled his army and took the conceit out of them from the highest officer down to the lowest private in the ranks. No such job has been successfully undertaken by any other American general. That it was costly we know, but the cost was far greater to the enemy than to ourselves, for it has resulted in the overthrow of their government and the establishment of ours.

WHAT TO DO NEXT

In the days that followed the surrender, editorial writers turned to the subject of what to do now that the fighting was over. Many papers, such as the

*National Intelligencer in Washington, D.C., called for Americans to re-
member all they had in common, including many national traditions.*

National Intelligencer (Washington, D.C.), 12 April 1865

An Anonymous Writer: "Let Us Be Brothers"

Our instant work is *to create an American sentiment.* And why not? Wherever the sin...be it our labor to look only to the redemption of the nation,
henceforward, until the old Union shall be in working order, fully manned
and fairly out at sea.

We should call back pleasant memories and proud traditions.... The
great AMERICAN names of the far past, which knew no North or South,
names we so revere, should speak to us now through all their channels of influence.... Whatever difference of opinion our system of Government has
given rise to among eminent men...these are now gone.... Let us henceforth
be humble; let us be wise; let us be brothers....

---

*The New-York Tribune, a bitter critic of slavery, nonetheless cautioned the
North about being vindictive toward the South.*

New-York Tribune, 11 April 1865

An Anonymous Writer: "Magnanimity in Triumph"

We plead against passions certain at this moment certain to be fierce and
intolerant; but on our side are the Ages and the voice of History. We plead
for a restoration of the Union, against a policy which would afford a mo-
mentary gratification at the cost of years of perilous hate and bitterness. We
have borne for a quarter of a century the unjust imputation of hating the
South, when we hated and fought to subvert only Slavery, the scourge alike
of South and North, and the sole cause of discord between them. We have
done what we could—of course, not always wisely—to baffle, to circum-
scribe, and ultimately to overthrow, the Slave Power. At length, through a
succession of events which no human being could have devised or foreseen,
the end which we sincerely hoped but hardly expected to see, is plainly before us. American Slavery is visibly in the agonies of dissolution; if we live a
year longer, we shall almost certainly see it laid in the grave; and, whenever
abolished here, its expulsion from the last rood of Christendom that it now
curses cannot be postponed five years. Let us take care that no vindictive
impulse shall be suffered to imperil this glorious consummation.

Most newspapers in the South encouraged citizens to accept defeat grace-fully. The Chronicle & Sentinel *in Augusta, Georgia, said readers could learn from the example set by General Lee.*

Chronicle & Sentinel (Augusta, Ga.), 29 April 1865

An Anonymous Writer: "The Present"

The example set us by Gen. Lee ought to be promptly followed. He saw that the hour had come for yielding up the struggle, and he had the magnanimity to acknowledge it. There was a blended dignity and wisdom in his course. It inspired respect, even in his enemies. It was doubtless one of the most painful duties of his life to ride up to Gen. Grant and tender that sword which so many victories had illuminated. But it was one of the noblest acts of his splendid career. He saw that to protract the struggle, was to sacrifice human life wantonly. He was too great and too good for that.

In a similar vein, the Southern Watchman *in Athens, Ga., encouraged its readers to put aside bitterness and follow the laws of the United States.*

Southern Watchman (Athens, Ga.), 17 May 1865

An Anonymous Writer: "Render unto Caesar's the Things Which Are Caesar's"

We again repeat in substance what we have said before. However just and righteous our people may have conceived the cause in which they were engaged, we have been overpowered—our Confederacy has ceased to exist as a political organization, and we are now subject to the Constitution of the United States. It is the duty of good citizens to yield obedience to "the powers that be." After the surrender of our armies and the dissolution of our Government, it is folly to talk now about further resistance. We look upon all attempts to prolong the contest by a system of guerilla warfare as not only sheer madness, but a great crime against society. There is not the slightest shadow of a hope of success in any such attempts, but a certainty of speedy destruction.

We are aware that it is very difficult for human nature to forgive and forget such wrongs as have been inflicted upon us during this cruel war—it requires time to forget such things. Let our people "possess their souls in patience" and studiously avoid saying or doing any thing which would tend to stir up feelings of resentment. Let all remember that it is far more manly to yield quiet obedience to the laws of the country in which they live than by factious opposition and needless denunciation stir afresh the resentment of those with whom we have so lately been at war. It is now our interest to cultivate sentiments of peace. The country needs repose. We are threatened with famine. Let us all go diligently to work, and strive to raise on farm, garden and orchard everything which will sustain animal life; and let all our industrial pursuits be resumed and vigorously prosecuted. Let us trust, in the meantime, to a returning sense of justice, on the part of our fellow countrymen with whom we have been at war; and, above all, let us implicitly rely upon Him who is able to do more for us than we can ask. Do this, and all may yet be well.

QUESTIONS

1. Why was it significant that black troops were among the first from the Union army to enter Richmond after the city was captured?
2. Why was General Grant singled out for special praise by the *Chicago Tribune?* Do you think it was warranted?
3. Are you surprised that editorials published after the surrender did not express anger and recrimination, given how bitterly the war had been fought? Explain.

NOTES

1. James M. McPherson, *Battle Cry of Freedom: The Civil War Era* (New York: Oxford University Press, 1988), 758–60.

2. Burke Davis, *To Appomattox: Nine April Days, 1865* (New York: Rinehart, 1959), 93–188.

3. Shelby Foote, *The Civil War, A Narrative: Red River to Appomattox* (New York: Random House, 1974), 300.

CHAPTER 23

President Lincoln Assassinated, 1865

President Abraham Lincoln had endured threats to his life since the early days of his presidency. En route to Washington, D.C., for his inauguration in 1861, he was warned of a plot to assassinate him as he traveled through pro-secessionist Baltimore. The president agreed to change his schedule, passing through the city at night. Afterward, opponents ridiculed him as a coward, and Lincoln told friends he always regretted that he had "sneaked" into Washington. Thereafter he never paid much attention to concerns for his safety and often traveled without a bodyguard.[1]

Lincoln and his wife enjoyed attending the theater. They made plans to attend a production of *Our American Cousin* at Ford's Theater on Good Friday, April 14, and they invited General Ulysses S. Grant and his wife to attend. At the last moment, the Grants had to cancel their plans in order to go out of town. So the Lincolns attended the performance with a young army officer, Henry R. Rathbone, and his fiancée. The Lincolns' attendance that night at the theater was known in advance, which gave John Wilkes Booth plenty of time to make his assassination plans.

Booth was one of the country's best-known actors and had performed in front of the president. He was also devoted to the Southern cause and was a staunch defender of slavery. He never took up arms for the Confederacy but did not hesitate to denounce Lincoln and the federal government. Booth grew increasingly bitter as it became apparent the South was going to lose the war. Late in 1864, he devised a plot to kidnap the president and exchange him for prisoners of war. His conspirators in the kidnapping plot included David E. Herold, George A. Atzerodt, Lewis Paine, and John Surratt. The group met regularly at the boarding house of Mary Surratt, John's mother.

On March 20, the conspirators planned to kidnap the president as he rode to a performance for wounded soldiers at a Washington hospital. The plot failed when the president attended another function. Then General Robert E. Lee surrendered to Grant at Appomattox Courthouse on April 9, and an enraged Booth abandoned his original plan. Two days later, Booth listened to a victory speech by Lincoln in which the president said he favored limited suffrage for blacks. An enraged Booth vowed he would kill the president. Booth and his co-conspirators concocted a plan that called for Booth to assassinate the president, Atzerodt to kill Vice President Andrew Johnson, and Paine to murder Secretary of State William H. Seward.

Booth scouted Ford's Theater early on April 14 and returned to the theater about 10 o'clock that evening. He slipped into the president's box and shot Lincoln once in the back of the head with a .44-caliber muzzle-loading derringer. Booth then stabbed Rathbone with a large knife and leaped twelve feet from the president's box to the stage, breaking his right leg when he landed. Waving his dagger, he reportedly shouted, "Sic semper tyrannis!" a Latin phrase meaning, "Thus always to tyrants!" Hobbling on his broken leg Booth then fled out a rear door of the theater and used a waiting horse to escape. At about the same time, Paine broke into Seward's home and attacked the secretary, stabbing him in the neck with a knife. Seward was bedridden from a carriage accident and a neck collar he was wearing at the time probably saved his life. The third would-be assassin, Atzerodt, lost his nerve and never made an attempt on Johnson's life.

The mortally wounded president was rushed to a home across the street from the theater. Lincoln was placed in a room on the first floor, but he was so tall that he had to be laid diagonally across the bed. Three doctors attending the performance tried to save the president, but he never regained consciousness and died at 7:22 the following morning. Standing at Lincoln's bedside, Secretary of War Edwin M. Stanton said, "Now he belongs to the ages."[2] At 11 A.M., Chief Justice Salmon P. Chase administered the presidential oath to Vice President Johnson. The country had a new leader, and the business of government continued.

Funeral services for President Lincoln were held in the White House on April 19. The following day, his casket was placed in the rotunda of the Capitol where thousands of admirers viewed the body. On April 21, a funeral train took Lincoln's remains on the 1,700-mile journey back to Illinois. The train traveled through Philadelphia, New York, Buffalo, Cleveland, Indianapolis, Chicago, and dozens of small towns, attracting enormous crowds of bereaved onlookers. The 16th president of the United States was laid to rest on May 4 at Oak Ridge Cemetery in his hometown of Springfield, Illinois.

By dawn on April 15, a massive manhunt was under way for Booth and his accomplices. Paine, Atzerodt, and other conspirators soon were arrested. After fleeing the theater, Booth and Herold traveled to the home of Dr. Samuel Mudd, who set Booth's broken leg. The pair hid near Bel Alton, Maryland, for several days and then used a rowboat to cross the Potomac River into Virginia. They hid in a tobacco barn near Port Royal until April 26 when they were discovered by Federal cavalry. The soldiers ordered the pair to surrender. Herold promptly gave himself up, but Booth refused and was shot. A week later, a military tribunal was convened to try Atzerodt, Herold, Paine, Mudd, Mary Surratt, and four others on charges of conspiracy to assassinate the president. All were convicted. On July 7, Atzerodt, Herold, Paine, and Surratt were hanged. The four other conspirators received jail sentences ranging from six years to life. (John Surratt evaded capture for two years and was released when his trial ended in a hung jury.)

This chapter begins with editorial reaction to President Lincoln's assassination. Newspapers throughout the North and South expressed shock over the president's death. Most papers, including those in the South, expressed outrage over the event. But a few, such as the *Galveston News,* took some satisfaction in the killing. Many editors were quick to blame the South for Booth's action, and they applauded his death and the execution of his co-conspirators. In their editorial tributes, newspapers like the *New York Tribune* also sought to ensure that Lincoln's memory stayed alive.

REACTION TO ASSASSINATION

The shock of the president's assassination clearly was felt by the editor of the National Intelligencer *(Washington, D.C.), who found it difficult to put into words his reaction.*

National Intelligencer (Washington, D.C.), 15 April 1865

An Anonymous Writer: "We Have No Words"

Our heart stands almost still as we take our pen in hand to speak of the tragedy of last night. We have no words at command....

In lauding Lincoln, the Burlington Free Press *remarked on how "an unseen Providence" had protected the president until the war ended.*

Burlington (Vt.) Free Press, 15 April 1865

An Anonymous Writer: "The Assassination of the President"

How often has it occurred to the thoughts of all during the dreadful four years past, that while bloody treason was all around him, President Lincoln seemed to have a charmed life, as if an invisible host was his body-guard. He went about often entirely alone, often was in the midst of great throngs, visiting all places where his duty called him, and never so surrounded by protectors but what the stab or shot of an assassin could have reacted him. But an unseen Providence was his preserver till the power of the rebellion was broken to pieces. And now, by an assassin's hand, the blood of Abraham Lincoln, the strong and pure-minded, sagacious, inflexibly honest, kind-hearted, self-sacrificing Head of the Nation, has been given to swell the vast stream which has been poured out from the hearts of untold thousands of brave men of every rank in the army and every station in life, that this mighty people reaching from the Atlantic to the Pacific may have life and unity and liberty, in all its borders for ages and ages to come.

Surely this is a day of grief such as this nation never saw before.

The Galveston (Tex.) News, *a staunchly Confederate newspaper, did not mourn the president's death.*

Galveston (Tex.) News, 28 April 1865

An Anonymous Writer: "He Slowed the Wind and Has Reaped the Whirlwind"

In the plenitude of his power and arrogance he was struck down, and is so ushered into eternity, with innumerable crimes and sins to answer for.... He sowed the wind and has reaped the whirlwind.

The Cincinnati Enquirer *said the South would mourn the president's death because he wanted to readmit the states to the Union under generous terms.*

Cincinnati Enquirer, 17 April 1865

An Anonymous Writer: "A Great Calamity to the South"

The death of Mr. Lincoln we regard as one of great calamity to the people of the South. The assassin could not have done an act of greater injury to them than the taking of the life of the President. Mr. Lincoln was inaugurating measures that would have restored them to the Union on terms that had due consideration for their feelings, their persons and their property. He was a power, and could have carried out his plans of restoration, in defiance of the opposition of the radicals of the party. The Southern people should, therefore, be as anxious for the punishment of the assassin as the people of the North, for he has done them a very great injury.

Many Democratic newspapers such as the New York World, *which had been sharply critical of Lincoln, nonetheless grieved over the president's death.*

New York World (as reprinted in National Intelligencer [Washington, D.C.]), 17 April 1865

An Anonymous Writer: "The Terrible Shock"

Today every heart must suffer the terrible shock, and swell with overburdening grief at the calamity which has been permitted to befall us in the assassination of the Chief Magistrate. The splendor of our triumph is robbed of half its lustre. It is a deeper loss than if our first soldier had fallen by a hostile bullet...more than if any army had perished in shock of battle. For it is the Commander-in-chief of our armies and navies who has fallen; and he has fallen, not by the natural course of disease, nor in the accepted peril of war, but by the foul stroke of some unknown assassin. Our history has no parallel to this. Such grief as ours today is new to our nation's heart.

BLAME FOR ASSASSINATION

The Harrisburg Telegraph *was one of many Northern newspapers quick to blame the Confederacy for the president's death.*

Harrisburg (Pa.) Telegraph, 20 April 1865

An Anonymous Writer: "The Lesson of the Hour"

The death of the President must not merely be charged to the mad impulse of an infuriated assassin. Booth is not the only man with blood of his hands. The murderer does not stand alone in his great crime. Before God and High Heaven, those who have four years made it their boast to question and deride—to vituperate as an imbecile, denounce as a usurper, advertise as a tyrant, and charge on Abraham Lincoln all the crimes known to the calendar, have as large a share in the guilt of the President's death, as the monster who slew him.

The Richmond Whig *condemned the president's assassination and asked that the Confederacy not be held responsible for the event.*

Richmond Whig (as quoted in *National Intelligencer* [Washington, D.C.]), 19 April 1865

Anonymous Writer: "Assassination of President Lincoln"

The decease of the Chief Magistrate of the nation at any period is an event which profoundly affects the public mind, but the time, manner, and circumstances of President Lincoln's death render it the most momentous, the most appalling, the most deplorable calamity which has ever befallen the people of the United States.

The thoughtless and the vicious may affect to derive satisfaction from the sudden and tragic close of the President's career, but every reflecting person will deplore the awful event. Just as everything was happily conspiring to a restoration of tranquility, under the benignant and magnanimous policy of Mr. Lincoln, comes this terrible blow. God grant that it may not rekindle excitement or inflame passion again!

FATE OF CONSPIRATORS

The St. Paul Pioneer-Press *expressed disappointment that Booth was not forced to endure a public execution, but it derived some satisfaction that the actor died in an obscure place without an audience.*

St. Paul (Minn.) Pioneer-Press, 4 May 1865

An Anonymous Writer: "The Assassin Booth Killed"

There will be a general feeling of dissappointment [*sic*] that Booth was not taken alive in order that the vengence of the outraged law might be wreaked upon him under the awful solemnities of a judicial sentence and a public execution. But this dramatic *denouement* was probably just the sort of sensational finale to which the theatrical assassin aspired. We do not doubt that his obscure death in a barn in an out of the way corner of Virginia with no other spectators than his captors was the bitterest ending of his career which could have been devised.

The Philadelphia Inquirer *said the conspirators deserved the death penalty and applauded the decision to not make their execution a public ceremony.*

Philadelphia Inquirer, 7 July 1865

An Anonymous Writer: "Retribution"

President Johnson has approved the finding of the Military Commission convened in May to try the parties engaged in the late conspiracy against the Government. Payne [*sic*], Harold [*sic*], Atzerodt and Mrs. Surratt are sentenced to death, and to-day they will expiate their crime upon the scaffold, unless the Executive grants them a brief reprieve, which it is not probable he will do. Spangler is sentenced to imprisonment at hard labor for six years, while Mudd, Arnold and O'Laughlin are sentenced to imprisonment, at hard labor, for life.

The finding of the Court, and the approval of the President, together, with the prompt execution of the sentence, will meet the sanction of all loyal men. The horrible crime of which the condemned were guilty demands immediate retribution. The blood of our dead President cries from the ground for justice, and the attempt upon the life of Secretary Seward requires no less punishment, since Payne had the will to murder, though he failed.

It is proper that an example be made of these culprits. Hereafter it will serve as a warning to all evil-minded and traitorous persons. They will remember the fate of the men who were employed as assassins, to effect, or rather attempt, the overthrow of the Government which the leaders of Rebellion had vainly essayed to accomplish by force of arms.

We admire the course of the authorities in having the execution in the prison yard. It would be impolitic to make it a public one. The criminals are undeserving a public death, and the false sympathy which might be gotten up in such a case among the multitude, to say nothing of the "mock heroic" character which would surround them in the eyes of their Rebel friends, is avoided, and they will pass away and be remembered only as culprits who were destined to die as the vilest and lowest villain who murders his victim in an alley or on the highway.

TRIBUTES TO LINCOLN

In its tribute to the president, the Baltimore American *said Lincoln would remain in the country's memory forever.*

Baltimore American, 18 April 1865

An Anonymous Writer: "Crown of Immortality"

He has exchanged the laurel wreath of time for the crown of immortality.

The New-York Tribune *was prophetic in declaring that President Lincoln's grave would become a national shrine.*

New-York Tribune, 19 April 1865

An Anonymous Writer: "Sleep of the Honored"

[H]e sleeps the sleep of the honored and just, and there are few graves which will be more extensively, persistently visited or bedewed with the tears of a people's prouder, fonder affection, than that of Abraham Lincoln.

QUESTIONS

1. Can you sympathize with the editor of the *National Intelligencer* who found it hard to put into words the shock over the president's assassination?
2. How could a newspaper like the *Galveston News* justify condoning the killing of the president?
3. Do you find it surprising that Northern papers would assume the South was responsible for the president's assassination?

NOTES

1. William Hanchett, *The Lincoln Murder Conspiracies* (Urbana: University of Illinois Press, 1983), 37.

2. As quoted in David Herbert Donald, *Lincoln* (New York: Simon & Schuster, 1995), 599.

Selected Bibliography

Abbott, Richard H. *The Republican Party and the South, 1865–1877.* Chapel Hill: University of North Carolina Press.

Andrews, J. Cutler. *The North Reports the Civil War.* Pittsburgh, Pa.: University of Pittsburgh Press, 1955.

——. *The South Reports the Civil War.* Princeton, N.J.: Princeton University Press, 1970.

Ash, Stephen V. *When the Yankees Came: Conflict and Chaos in the Occupied South, 1861–1865.* Chapel Hill: University of North Carolina Press, 1995.

Barney, William. *The Road to Secession: A New Perspective on the Old South.* New York: Praeger, 1972.

Basler, Roy P., ed. *Abraham Lincoln: His Speeches and Writings.* Cleveland: World Publishing, 1946.

——. *The Collected Works of Abraham Lincoln.* Vol. 8. New Brunswick, N.J.: Rutgers University Press, 1952–1955.

"Bread and the Newspaper," *Atlantic Monthly,* 8 September 1861, 346–48.

Civil War Center. http://www.cwc.lsu.edu/

civilwar.com. http://www.civilwar.com/

Civil War Photographs. http://memory.loc.gov/ammem/cwphtml/cwphome.html

Clement, Frank L. *The Limits of Dissent: Clement L. Vallandigham & the Civil War.* Lexington: University Press of Kentucky, 1970.

Cook, Adrian. *The Armies of the Streets: The New York City Draft Riots of 1863.* Lexington: University Press of Kentucky, 1974.

Cornish, Dudley Taylor. *The Sable Army: Negro Troops in the Union Army, 1861–1865.* New York: Norton, 1966.

Coulter, E. Merton. *The Confederate States of America, 1861–1865.* Baton Rouge: Louisiana State University Press, 1950.

Craven, Avery. *The Growth of Southern Nationalism, 1848–1861.* Baton Rouge: Louisiana State University Press, 1953.

Crook, D.P. *The North, the South, and the Powers, 1861–1865.* New York: Wiley, 1974.

Current, Richard N. *Lincoln and the First Shot.* Philadelphia: Lippincott, 1963.

Curry, Richard Orr. *A House Divided: A Study of Statehood Politics and the Copperhead Movement in West Virginia.* Pittsburgh, Pa.: University of Pittsburgh Press, 1964.

Davis, Burke. *To Appomattox: Nine April Days, 1865.* New York: Rinehart, 1959.

Davis, William C. *Battle at Bull Run: A History of the First Major Campaign of the Civil War.* Garden City, N.Y.: Doubleday, 1977.

———. *Duel Between First Ironclads.* Garden City, N.Y.: Doubleday, 1975.

———. *Jefferson Davis: The Man and His Hour.* New York: HarperCollins, 1991.

Donald, David Herbert. *Lincoln.* New York: Simon & Schuster, 1995.

Dumond, Dwight L. *Southern Editorials on Secession.* New York: Century, 1931.

Durden, Robert. *The Gray and the Black: The Confederate Debate on Emancipation.* Baton Rouge: Louisiana State University Press, 1972.

Fahrney, Ralph Ray. *Horace Greeley and the Tribune in the Civil War.* Cedar Rapids, Iowa: Torch Press, 1936.

Ferris, Norman B. *Desperate Diplomacy: William H. Seward's Foreign Policy, 1861.* Knoxville: University of Tennessee Press, 1976.

———. *The* Trent *Affair: A Diplomatic Crisis.* Knoxville: University of Tennessee Press, 1977.

Foote, Shelby. *The Civil War: A Narrative,* 3 vols. New York: Random House, 1958–1974.

Fowler, William M., Jr. *Under Two Flags: The American Navy in the Civil War.* New York: Norton, 1990.

Franklin, John Hope. *The Emancipation Proclamation.* Garden City, N.Y.: Doubleday, 1963.

Futch, Ovid L. *History of Andersonville Prison.* Gainesville: University of Florida Press, 1968.

Gray, Wood. *The Hidden Civil War: The Story of the Copperheads.* New York: Viking Press, 1964.

Hanchett, William. *The Lincoln Murder Conspiracies.* Urbana: University of Illinois Press, 1983.

Harper, Robert S. *Lincoln and the Press.* New York: McGraw-Hill, 1951.

Harris, William C. *William Woods Holden: Firebrand of North Carolina Politics.* Baton Rouge: Louisiana State University Press, 1987.

Henry, Robert Selph. *"First with the Most" Forrest.* Indianapolis: Bobbs-Merrill, 1944.

Hesseltine, William B. *Civil War Prisons: A Study in War Psychology.* Columbus: Ohio State University Press, 1930.

Huntzicker, William E. *The Popular Press, 1833–1865.* Westport, Conn.: Greenwood Press, 1999.

Jones, Howard. *Union in Peril: The Crisis over British Intervention in the Civil War.* Chapel Hill: University of North Carolina Press, 1992.

Kennedy, Joseph C.G. *Preliminary Report on the Eighth Census, 1860.* Washington, D.C.: Government Printing Office, 1862.

Kirkland, Edward Chase. *The Peacemakers of 1864.* New York: Macmillan, 1927.

Klein, Maury. *Days of Defiance: Sumter, Secession, and the Coming of the Civil War.* New York: Knopf, 1997.

Klement, Frank L. *The Limits of Dissent: Clement L. Vallandigham and the Civil War.* Lexington: University of Kentucky Press, 1970.

Lee, Charles Robert, Jr. *The Confederate Constitutions.* Chapel Hill: University of North Carolina Press, 1963.

McDonough, James Lee, and James Pickett Jones. *War So Terrible: Sherman and Atlanta.* New York: Norton, 1987.

McPherson, James M. *Battle Cry of Freedom: The Civil War Era.* New York: Oxford University Press, 1988.

Mitgang, Herbert. *Lincoln As They Saw Him.* New York: Rinehart, 1956.

Moore, Albert B. *Conscript and Conflict in the Confederacy.* New York: Macmillan, 1924.

Murdock, Eugene C. *One Million Men: The Civil War Draft in the North.* Madison: University of Wisconsin Press, 1971.

Neely, Mark E., Jr. *The Fate of Liberty: Abraham Lincoln and Civil Liberties.* New York: Oxford University Press, 1991.

Nelson, Larry E. *Bullets, Bayonets, and Rhetoric: Confederate Policy for the United States Presidential Contest of 1864.* Tuscaloosa: University of Alabama Press, 1980.

Osthaus, Carl R. *Partisans of the Southern Press: Editorial Spokesmen of the Nineteenth Century.* Lexington: University Press of Kentucky, 1994.

Owsley, Frank L. *King Cotton Diplomacy: Foreign Relations of the Confederate States of America,* 2nd ed. Chicago: University of Chicago Press, 1959.

Parks, Joseph H. *Joseph E. Brown of Georgia.* Baton Rouge: Louisiana State University Press, 1977.

Potter, David M. *The Impending Crisis: 1848–1861,* completed and edited by Don E. Fehrenbacher. New York: Harper & Row, 1976.

Pred, Allan. *Urban Growth and City-Systems in the United States, 1840–1860.* Cambridge: Harvard University Press, 1980.

Quarles, Benjamin. *The Negro in the Civil War.* New York: Russell & Russell, 1953.

Ramsdell, Charles W. *Behind the Lines in the Southern Confederacy.* Baton Rouge: Louisiana State University Press, 1944.

Randall, James. *Constitutional Problems under Lincoln.* Urbana: University of Illinois Press, 1951.

Randall, J.G., and David Donald. *The Civil War and Reconstruction,* 2nd ed. Boston: Heath, 1961.

Reynolds, Donald E. *Editors Make War: Southern Newspapers in the Secession Crisis.* Nashville: Vanderbilt University Press, 1966.

Robinson, Charles M., III. *Shark of the Confederacy: The Story of the CSS Alabama.* Annapolis: Naval Institute Press, 1995.

Rowland, Thomas J. *George B. McClellan and Civil War History: In the Shadow of Grant and Sherman.* Kent, Ohio: Kent State University Press, 1998.

Sibley, Joel H. *A Respectable Minority: The Democratic Party in the Civil War Era, 1860–1868.* New York: Norton, 1977.

Smith, Edward Conrad. *The Borderland in the Civil War.* New York: Macmillan, 1927.

Stampp, Kenneth M. *And the War Came: The North and the Secession Crisis: 1860–1861.* Baton Rouge: Louisiana State University Press, 1950.

——. *The Causes of the Civil War.* Englewood Cliffs, N.J.: Prentice Hall, 1959.

Strong, George Templeton. *Diary of the Civil War, 1860–1865,* ed. Allan Nevins. New York: Macmillan, 1962.

Swanberg, W.A. *First Blood: The Story of Fort Sumter.* New York: Scribner's, 1957.

Tatum, Georgia Lee. *Disloyalty in the Confederacy.* Chapel Hill: University of North Carolina Press, 1934.

Thomas, Emory M. *The Confederate Nation, 1861–1865.* New York: Harper & Row, 1979.

Valley of the Shadow. http://www.iath.virginia.edu/vshadow2/

War of the Rebellion: A Compilation of the Official Records of the Union and Confederate Armies, Series I, Series IV. Washington, D.C.: Government Printing Office, 1891–1900.

Warren, Gordon H. *Fountain of Discontent: The* Trent *Affair and Freedom of the Seas.* Boston: Northeastern University Press, 1981.

Waugh, John C. *Reelecting Lincoln: The Battle for the 1864 Presidency.* New York: Crown, 1997.

Wiley, Bell Irvin. *Southern Negroes, 1861–1865.* New Haven, Conn: Yale University Press, 1938.

Williams, T. Harry. *Lincoln and His Generals.* New York: Knopf, 1952.

Wills, Gary. *Lincoln at Gettysburg: The Words that Remade America.* New York: Simon & Schuster, 1992.

Wilmer, Lambert. *Our Press Gang.* Philadelphia: J.T. Lloyd, 1860.

Winik, Jay. *April 1865: The Month that Saved America.* New York: HarperCollins: 2001.

Woodward, C. Vann, ed. *Mary Chesnut's Civil War.* New Haven, Conn.: Yale University Press, 1981.

Zornow, William Frank. *Lincoln and the Party Divided.* Norman: University of Oklahoma Press, 1954.

Index

About the Author

FORD RISLEY is associate professor of communications and head of the Department of Journalism at Penn State. He is the author of articles on the antebellum and Civil War press published in *American Journalism, Civil War History, Georgia Historical Quarterly*, and *Journalism History*.